Toys and Playthings

John and Elizabeth Newson met at University College London, where both read psychology in 1951. They have both been engaged in research and lecturing at Nottingham University since 1952, having chosen at an early stage in their careers to pursue the kind of research that demands a long-term commitment.

They have three children, and regard the experience of parenthood as an almost indispensable professional qualification, a necessary counterbalance to the study of child development as they encounter it in the learned journals. They founded and jointly direct the Child Development Research Unit at Nottingham. Their conviction that parents are the richest source of information about their own children is illustrated by their books on 'ordinary' children; but they are equally interested in parents' problems in coping with a child's handicap. They are actively researching ways of using parents' intimate knowledge to assess more adequately the individual needs of their handicapped children, and to put the tools for remediation into the hands of parents themselves. They are also exploring the earliest modes of communication between babies and their parents. Their books *Patterns of Infant Care in an Urban Community*, *Four Years Old in an Urban Community* and *Seven Years Old in the Home Environment* have also been published in Pelicans.

The Newsons' other research interest, the function of play in early child development, spills over into their main recreational pursuit, the design of toys. They are consultants to a well-known toy manufacturing company, and take an active interest in a family-run craft gallery and specialist toyshop in Enfield.

Toys and Playthings
in development and remediation

John and Elizabeth Newson

London
GEORGE ALLEN & UNWIN
Sydney

IMJ

First published in 1979

GEORGE ALLEN & UNWIN LTD
40 Museum Street, London WC1A 1LU

© John and Elizabeth Newson, 1979
First published by Penguin Books Ltd 1979

British Library Cataloguing in Publication Data

Newson, John
   Toys and playthings.
   1. Play   2. Toys   3. Child development
   I. Title   II. Newson, Elizabeth
   155.4'18   BF717

   ISBN 0–04–136020–6

Typeset in Monophoto Ehrhardt
and printed in Great Britain
by Biddles Ltd, Guildford, Surrey

Contents

Acknowledgements

There are many people to whom we should acknowledge our indebtedness, both for enabling us to do the work out of which this book was written, and for contributing insights.

The Nuffield Foundation and Action Research for the Crippled Child supported research on the design of remedial playthings and on the development of toy libraries as a resource for parents, and we are most grateful for their generosity.

Jim Sandhu and Roger Haydon, then of the Royal College of Art, collaborated with us in devising an exhibition of toys for handicapped children; Beryl Fosterjohn, mother of a blind child, first made us think about the need for toy libraries; Jill Norris, founder of the first toy library in the U.K., shared with us her expertise at a time when it was still unique: our debt to these four is especially longstanding.

Other colleagues who have contributed to our understanding of play include Peter Allen, Rosemary Evans, John and Pam Harris, Susan Lee, Susan Pawlby, Colin Prior, John Shotter, Derek Wilson and Olwen Wilson. We have also constantly learned from watching our trainees 'working' with children in our playroom. To all of these, our thanks.

Much of what we know about toys has come from observing children at play, whether on their own, with each other or with their parents. Much has also come from talking to parents about their children's play. We would like to thank the hundreds of parents and children who have shared their experience of play with us, including the three children we know best of all, our own – now no longer in childhood.

We have received help in preparing this book from a number of people too numerous to name: members of the toy trade, whether designers, producers, in marketing or at the retail level, and staff of museum collections. The *Nursing Times* and *Where?* allowed us to use material previously published by them. Dr Peter Barbor, consultant paediatrician, read and commented on the chapter on the sick child; Dr Geoffrey Matthews kindly allowed us to quote him in Chapter 4. Sam Grainger lent us his skill and sensitivity as a photographer, and provided much basic material from which the illustrations evolved. Beryl West typed chapter after chapter without getting flustered, despite the constant interruptions of a busy unit. We are grateful to all these helpful people.

For one of us, an earliest memory is of leafing through the catalogue of Paul and Marjorie Abbatt's pioneering toyshop. Many years later it was Marjorie Abbatt who persuaded us to write the first chapter of this book as a conference paper, and so inspired us to continue through the other ten. To her and to her late husband, Paul Abbatt, we dedicate this book.

1　Why Toys?

But First – Why This Book?

It is only during the last eighty years or so that the activities of children have been considered to be of any interest at all by more than a handful of eccentric individuals; but during that time a great many books on play have been written, mainly by psychologists who have, on the whole, been indifferent to the toys which focus and sustain play. Toys themselves only began to excite more general interest as a by-product of two trends: the nostalgia for domestic antiques which reached its full force in the seventies, when picture books on antique toys began to be found in every bookshop; and the playgroup movement, when community playgroups operating on tiny budgets created a demand for practical books on how to put together a stock of basic toys without spending too much money. A third movement, the demand by parents of handicapped children to learn how to use play remedially to help meet the child's developmental difficulties, led to the enormous growth of toy libraries and made people think again about what a toy was capable of doing for a child.

What we have tried to do in this book is to take a long look at toys, with the developing child as our starting point. This means that we are concerned not so much with 'the right toy for the right age', but rather to think about the logical basis for a child's movement from one stage to another, and to discuss how certain kinds of toys can complement and expand this growth. Right from the beginning, though, we want to emphasize that personality growth includes a sense of humour and a capacity to enjoy and to be fascinated, and we are just as much interested in why a child likes a particular toy and in the fun she* gets

---

* This book is mainly about children's toys, rather than about 'boys' toys' and 'girls' toys' separately. We have therefore adopted the (admittedly artificial) convention of using masculine or feminine forms in alternate chapters. Unless boys or girls are specifically referred to, 'he' or 'she' should be understood as 'he or she' in every case.

out of it, as in the toy's ability to stimulate learning. In any case, it will only stimulate learning if she *does* like it and finds it fun to play with.

Starting from the developing child, then, we must inevitably be concerned with the child who has problems in making progress because she is in some way handicapped. Here we have not been content to give a quick wave of the hand to the handicapped child in a tacked-on chapter, but have chosen to devote a considerable part of the book to thinking about her special needs. We might have written two separate books, one on normal children's playthings and one on toys for handicapped children; one reason why we have not done so is that most parents of handicapped children have normal children as well; most handicapped children do their growing-up in the context of a normal family. A more important reason, though, comes out of our own learning experience. It was only after fifteen years' work with 'ordinary' children that we became involved with handicapped children and their families, and when we did so we found that this detailed background of what growing-up was like for normal children was immensely important as a perspective against which to understand the difficulties for the child which arose as a result of handicap. Equally, though, another dozen years working with handicapped children and normal children in parallel has continually given us new insights into what is important in normal development. So we hope that those who are not themselves involved with a handicapped child will also find it worth while to think about what happens when normal development goes wrong, side by side with, and illuminating, the more usual patterns of growth.

Because child development has always existed, even before it was invented as a subject by psychologists and paediatricians, toys as a focus for play go back a very long way. Although this is not a book primarily about antique toys, we must certainly be interested in those toys which appear century after century in different disguises to suit the technology and the spirit of the time. Some of the material for this book has, therefore, quite relevantly we believe, been collected over the years from museums and libraries, from collaboration with the modern toy industry and toy designers, and not least from occupying that precarious vantage-point between industry and consumer, the specialist toyshop in which we are partners. We hope that people who simply like toys as objects will find something in this book to interest them; we suspect, indeed, that liking toys will be what all readers, whatever their reason for opening the book, have in common.

Why Toys?

Once upon a time, at a conference of psychologists, we happened to fall into conversation with a prominent government scientist and his wife, as we were strolling back from lunch. One of us happened to mention that our psychology department had just acquired its own small but nonetheless very expensive computer installation, and went on to remark that this would provide a beautiful new toy which a lot of people in our department would enjoy playing with. The scientist's wife was clearly shocked at the levity of this remark, and at the thought of the abuse of a very large sum of taxpayers' money, and she said as much. But her husband quickly stepped in with the reassurance that the word 'play' had obviously been used jokingly, and continued to the effect that academic psychologists were highly responsible people who only used such expressions as a modest cover for their earnest dedication to the pursuit of important scientific questions. Not being able to decide, on the spur of the moment, which of these attitudes misunderstood our meaning most thoroughly, we let the matter drop; but the incident brought home to us that not everyone automatically shares the developmental psychologist's view of the nature of play: which can be expressed in the paradoxical statement that play is perhaps the most serious and significant of all human activities.

To consider the role of toys at all, it is necessary to look briefly at this concept of play and its implications. Fundamentally, play seems to be a partly random and infinitely flexible activity which affords an opportunity for the extension and reorientation of both mind and spirit. The essence of play is that it has no rules. Here one must make a necessary distinction between 'play' as we understand it and the activity of taking part in games, which is also often described as 'playing'. The essential feature of a game is that it involves a formal confrontation between the player and his opponent (or one player in two opposing roles) in which all activity takes place within an agreed system of rules. These rules may be highly arbitrary, and the stakes may be as low as the mere prestige of winning or as high as life or death; but in either case the rules have to be obeyed, because basically it is the rule structure which defines the game. Once the rules are clearly being flouted or disobeyed, the participants know that the game is over.

Play, by contrast, may almost be defined by its absence of agreed rule structure; that is, if there are any rules in operation at all, they are private, internal and idiosyncratic. The child (or the grown-up) who is engaged in true play may allow her activity to be constrained by small rituals or established and familiar patterns of behaviour; but, because these are *her own* rituals, she has the right to jettison them at any moment and to move off in entirely new directions at will. It is this supreme flexibility which makes play the ideal setting or jumping-off point for creative thinking and imaginative invention.

This is not to say that children do not concentrate when they play: they do, and indeed their single-minded absorption and capacity to cut themselves off from ordinary distractions is often particularly striking. Possibly this ability to shut out the everyday world with its reality-bound constrictions is a very useful adjunct to exploring and stretching the boundaries of thought in play. Neither children nor adults are necessarily aware, when they embark on play, of just what goals they even hope to achieve; it is through playing, often almost aimlessly, with both thoughts and feelings – a kind of imaginative free-wheeling – that these begin to become clarified and crystallized and are seen to lead on in specific directions. Each new occasion for play contains in it some elements of past experience, and every child brings to her play the uniqueness of her own personality. Basically, then, play offers a stimulating environment for both intellectual and emotional creativity, and potentially each child's play is the perfect expression of herself as a developing individual.

Play comes first; toys merely follow. We do not play as a *result* of having toys; toys are no more than pegs on which to hang our play. In theory, toys are not needed; the child could happily wander through her fantasy world, her imagination supplying all that was wanted. Perhaps *because* the human imagination is so extensive and complex, however, children seem to look for solid and tangible reference points, as it were, from which to range the more freely. Just as language makes subtle and complicated thought possible, perhaps toys do the same for play. Children who have no toys as such learn to provide their own 'pegs for play': a circle drawn with a stick in the dust becomes a play house;

hanging creepers make a swing; a spoon, a sandal or a piece of wood, wrapped in rags, makes a perfectly lovable baby doll; a length of hollow bamboo is a toy canoe. Even privileged children who have many 'proper' toys will often improvise their own to meet the needs of their private imaginings. One of us, at the age of four, had a favourite 'doll' which was re-made every bath-time out of a wooden nailbrush and two damp flannels; it was called 'The Forsaken Merman' (after the narrative poem by Matthew Arnold), which reflected the child's mother's preference for reading her poems rather than nursery rhymes and the child's own delighted response, and it had a personality which is still real to the adult the child became. To quote an English toy designer, 'anything is a toy if I choose to describe what I am doing with it as play'.

Perhaps a baby's best toy is, potentially, her own mother. Watch the baby stare at her eyes, play with her fingers, become alert at her voice, finger her face, explore her mouth. Familiar yet changing, adaptable in some ways but in others unyielding, sometimes surprising, capable of

providing reassurance or active stimulus in response to the baby's need, both soft and hard, both sparkling and dull-textured, a machine for bouncing, rocking and lulling by turns, with a most intricate sound-mechanism over which the child has just enough control to find it fascinating but not enough for boredom to set in – here is an all-purpose toy whose versatility any toy-maker might be proud to produce. Through most of childhood the mother who will allow herself to be played with has an advantage over the most expensive toy. Mother is not always around, however, nor does she always wish to be played with; nor, of course, do we really want the child to fail to be weaned on to other toys, for to help a child towards the pleasure of independence is one of the toy's functions.

We do not believe, in fact, that there is any one toy or kind of toy which is 'best' for a child. Many different kinds of toys contribute to her many needs in different ways, for different moods and at different age-stages.

Babies and toddlers seem to get especial joy from toys which provide them with an experience that they can perceive as a completed event, or a 'happening'. Dropping a rattle from a pram and having it returned is a satisfying 'happening', and will be repeated as many times as someone can be persuaded to complete the baby's action. Pushing down a tower of bricks which someone else has built, dropping a shape through a posting-box hole, a penny into a money-box, a piece into a form-board – these are all 'happenings', which can be identified by the child's heightening of tension followed by a relaxation and smile of pleasure at the onlooker. The perfect 'happening' is perhaps some variation of peep-bo play in which the mother's face is hidden and re-appears: 'Where's Mummy?' – expectant tension – '*Here* she is!' As the baby becomes a little more sophisticated, she responds with delight to an element of surprise; for instance, where a ball pushed through a hole in the top of a closed box may re-appear randomly from any of four holes in the sides.

For the very small child it is enough that she is able to create this infinitesimal explosion in her world. She has made something happen, and she is satisfied – except that she would like to repeat it a few hundred times. The nursery-age child demands more; with her greater grasp of sequence and time, she wants things to develop and grow, including her own skill. This is where the toys which have *functional versatility* serve the child's specific need. By this we mean that, while some toys can only be used in rigidly defined ways (a bride-doll is a good example, but it is also true of a jack-in-the-box), others can be exploited by the child in all kinds of different roles to suit her moods, her personality and her ability. A plain wooden box can serve as a little table or stool, a doll's crib, the turret of a castle, a boat or a miniature doll's room according to need; a collection of planks, cushions and blankets can turn into tents, fortifications, or a hospital ward; a pile of bricks can be built into towers or roads, pushed in a long line as a train or arranged in ranks as a troop of soldiers. In general, toys which have a high degree of functional versatility also have a quality of being nondescript, and it is precisely because of this that they stand-in so successfully for whatever specific object the child has in mind. The very fact that a toy is ambiguous allows a child to use her imagination in filling out the details.

We would not want to pretend that there is no place in a child's play for thoroughly realistic toys, however, for it is obvious that children get a great amount of pleasure and satisfaction from realistic detail that mirrors the world they live in. Tiny windows in toy cars and a moulded metallic engine under a hinged bonnet, or dolls'-house furniture with drawers and cupboard doors that really open and shut: these give a special joy which cannot be ignored. Sometimes perhaps we overdo the 'plain polished wood' philosophy, and allow an adult aestheticism to over-ride an equally valid appreciation of the exact. We bought basic-shaped wooden animals for our university playroom because we thought they were beautiful; the children steadfastly ignore them, and play imaginatively and creatively with the mass-produced polythene animals, and the children may well be right, for they are a perfect example of the best that modern technology can produce. They are also cheap, and we need not worry if a tiny plastic lamb goes home in someone's obstinately clenched hand.

Children who are given a wide choice of toys will exploit the different qualities and properties of different kinds in a very eclectic and catholic manner. Replica cars and animals mix in happily with pipe-cleaner dolls, and all are made to inhabit a fantasy city in which wooden bricks, cotton reels, match-boxes and old cardboard tubes are eked out by the scale-model steel bridges borrowed from an older brother's electric railway. The truth is that a child absorbed in imaginative free play will make use of anything that comes to hand, and use it moreover to open out new avenues for her fantasy to explore.

In imaginative play a child tends to be limited more by the range of her fantasy than by her physical skill or lack of it; but children are essentially developing creatures who are in the active process of perfecting the bodily skills of manipulation, muscle co-ordination, balance, strength and endurance. Rural children improve their skills by pitting their bodies against the natural environment, and learn to make use of the flow of a stream or the slipperiness of snow; children in urban settings are more likely to be protected from taking physical risks in an environment that includes traffic hazards and high buildings, and for them the toy that stretches their physical prowess is a necessity. Such toys are especially valuable where they are progressive: that is, where they can almost infinitely extend the child's skill while allowing her plenty of satisfaction during the earliest stages. Swings, ropes and trapezes offer a good example: a baby of six months merely rocks in a supportive canvas chair, a three-year-old learns the complementary movements of back, arms and legs that get the swing going higher and higher; as time goes on she swings upside-down by her arms and somersaults between the ropes, and eventually, if she wishes, she can acquire the more hair-raising skills of the trapeze artiste. Similarly, scooters, tricycles and bicycles, roller skates, skateboards and stilts lend themselves to a remarkable range of skills, from what is no more than a hesitant moving around on something other than feet, to an acrobatic expertise which terrifies and impresses the adult onlooker. Toys of this sort have in common that they serve as extensions to the child's own body, allowing a physical range beyond what the body is capable of.

The swing, that classic and universally loved toy, has another property which leads us on to a further group of toys which seem to give something special to the child and which all share what we might call a hypnotic quality. The swing is hypnotic because it catches up the whole body in a rhythmic action which can be perpetuated with a minimum of active attention; but a bodily rhythm is not at all necessary for the hypnotic quality of a toy to be felt. Anything played with aimlessly in the hand – a stone egg, a string of so-called 'worry-beads' – can serve this function. Adults often make such a toy of a large finger-ring or a pipe. Such experiences in ordinary life are usually visual, however –

watching firelight, smoke, moving clouds or water. Three visual toys are particularly hypnotic. One is the small wooden top for spinning with the fingers. Another is the old-fashioned 'snowstorm', where a hollow glass ball containing a landscape or a flower is completely filled with water and a small quantity of white particles; when the toy is shaken, the 'snow' swirls round the ball, then peacefully floats down on to the landscape. The third toy, invented in our unit by Joan Head, has no name; it is simply a perspex tube, sealed at both ends, containing a ping-pong ball which exactly fits its width; held vertically, the ball *slowly* falls against the pressure of air to the bottom of the tube. Turn it over, and it does the same again. It is totally useless, and we cannot stop people playing with ours.

Perhaps the chief function of a hypnotic toy is that it allows the child to withdraw completely for a little while, and this is a very relaxing experience. It does something more, however: it seems to occupy just enough of the attention to free the rest of the child's awareness for creative and imaginative thought. Perhaps it fills up that part of the consciousness which would otherwise be distracted by more demanding stimuli. An ethologist might call it a displacement activity, in that it harmlessly discharges tension which might otherwise be expressed in more impeding ways. Be that as it may, children often do a lot of thinking as they swing gently to and fro, and research workers who stand talking in our playroom seem to use the toys in just the same thought-releasing way. It is essential that a toy should not demand too much activity of the user if it is to be hypnotic, and this means that a toy may have a varying significance at different stages of development. A wooden rattle may be action-provoking to a baby but hypnotic to an adult. Perspex shapes threaded on a steel spiral are a difficult problem to a two-year-old, but offer a very hypnotic occupation to a child of ten or eleven.

Somewhat akin to the hypnotic toys are toys which are mind-expanding in a rather different way. Far from occupying only a corner of the attention, they are both compelling and absorbing. Basically, these toys offer the child a new view of her world. The simplest of them is just a piece of coloured glass or perspex; hold it up, and the world is pinkly cheerful or blue and mysterious. A prism gives a different angle. Convex, magnifying and distorting mirrors allow the child a new and strangely revealing vision of herself. A gramophone or tape recorder

with the speed turned up or down gives her a novel perception of familiar sounds. Our own favourite is the kind of kaleidoscope *through* which one looks at one's surroundings; the most humdrum scene is multiplied and intensified to become a magical pattern of intricate symmetry. The essence of these toys' fascination is that they present the familiar in a radically unfamiliar fashion, which can only stimulate the child to look and listen with a heightened awareness. Although there are moments for most of us when our consciousness suddenly seems sharpened by some triggering sensation – a scent or a texture, perhaps – we know of no other way (short of certain drugs) by which this may be achieved, and these toys, few though they are in number, hold a vital place in the child's experience.

Toys which afford the child an opportunity for role-playing must be mentioned, for we could hardly manage without them. It is sometimes suggested that a baby brother or sister, or a pet animal, is a 'better', because more real, object for the child's mothering play. Obviously one should give a child every encouragement to act protectively to its younger siblings; but the relationship is too fraught with ambivalent feelings for this always to be either successful or really satisfying; moreover, there is a limit to the amount of mothering that a baby can accept from its brothers and sisters. We must also remember that a child plays with her doll not solely in the role of a protective figure, but also (like her own mother) as a power figure; little girls disciplining their doll families can be a disconcerting experience, especially for the mother who recognizes her own bossy voice. For the child to adopt a role of power is most valuable to the process of identifying with parents and internalizing their standards of behaviour; it is not much fun for younger siblings, however. So we still need dolls, and, of course, all the dolls' belongings that go with them and help to define the child-mother's role. And here we are, from cultural habit, talking about little girls in this context; but fathers are taking more and more of a share in caring for their babies and young children, and this newer view of Daddy will surely be reflected in how boys play. Having watched a little boy lovingly tucking up in a pram his soldier doll in full battle-dress, let's hope there are going to be a lot more baby boy dolls as well as girl dolls around, and more little boys who won't be ashamed to cuddle them.

One further important function which a toy fulfils, and which we must not forget, is as a focus for the pleasure of ownership. Every child has a need to cradle some small thing in her hands, be it only a tin soldier or a ragged peg-doll, and to say 'This is *mine*', without fear of contradiction. We do not want our children to be greedy or selfish; but at the same time the sense of belonging is intrinsic to the human condition (one might say essential for the survival of the family), and seems to be necessary to the child's perception of herself as a whole person. We begin to realize now, in caring for homeless children in institutions, how much it diminishes them as human individuals if they have no private belongings and no separate place to keep their own things, and what terrible destruction we do to their sense of identity if we deprive them of the experience of possession.

Where Next?

One of us was once asked to speak at a rather solemn European conference on what toys should be planned for the children of the future; and we must admit that the question caused us some difficulty. Were we supposed to be trying to create through a specific play experience a child who could cope with the future world? Or were we to plan a toy environment to complement the living environment of future generations? Such concepts are worth a moment's thought.

Children of the future need not be so very different from the child we look for today. They will have to be flexible, adventurous, quickly aware, capable of adjusting to change; for the one thing we can be sure of in an advanced technological society is that changes will happen at an ever-increasing rate, whatever they may be. A more closely-packed population will place greater strains upon social relationships, but is unlikely to destroy the family, which is an extraordinarily resilient institution; so the child of the future will need to be capable of making stable, loving, generous relationships with other people. All of these qualities seem to be what we hope for in our own children.

Clearly it is inevitable, whether we plan them or not, that toys will become more technically sophisticated. Already the traditional yo-yo has acquired a flashing light activated by its rise and fall; talking dolls and talking telephones work on randomly sequenced magnetic tape, and there is a doll's refrigerator which really feels cold inside. If we do not especially welcome these technological refinements for ordinary children, we must do so when it comes to the special needs of the handicapped: the deaf baby whose babbling has been made to trigger a display of coloured lights is in this way rewarded for producing the sounds she cannot hear, and thus continues to babble instead of lapsing into muteness; her speech when it comes may be immeasurably better because of the use of such a toy.

In contemplating toys for a future environment, it is easy to become nostalgic about the idyllic life of a child in the old-fashioned countryside, spending her days in tune with natural things, and finding her amusements in damming streams, climbing trees and watching the mice and beetles in the long grass. Because some of us grew up with these experiences and look back on them with love, we tend to count our children deprived if they do not have them too.

It seems that we have a number of choices in the more urban environment which we expect of the future. We may, for instance, deliberately try to create the rural surroundings of our childhood artificially, in the form of adventure parks with streams to dam, trees to climb and wild places to explore. What is difficult to re-create, of course, is the infinite *variety* of naturally wild country, the sense of privacy a child can have in country isolation, and the true adventure of exploring a secret place which she cannot be sure is known to anyone but herself. The secret places planned by a landscape designer are not quite the same.

Secondly, we may try directly to reproduce as artefacts the objects which our children found in nature. The most deliberate example of this that we have seen is the plastic conker. To play 'conkers', the fruit of the horse-chestnut tree is threaded on a string, with a stout knot on the end, and the opponents take turns to aim at each other's conker with their own, the loser being the child whose conker breaks first. The plastic conker is a red ball on a cord with four yellow inserted pieces which clip to its core; the impact of the two balls striking each other eventually dislodges the inserted pieces, and the loser is the child who loses all four pieces first. As a substitute it is very effective; but it is interesting that so accurate a substitute should have been produced at all.

Thirdly, we may try to analyse the *experience* given by the natural object and attempt to reproduce that, but in an entirely modern idiom. For instance, the designer Ron Dutton has produced an exciting climbing frame in a combination of steel and broad rubber bands. So far as we know, he had no direct intention of reproducing the essential physical experience of tree-climbing; but this is the result, in that the toy combines the important elements of rigid basic structure with a springiness which forces the child to make rapid physical responses and accommodations. The only thing that is missing, physically, is the occasional crack of a breaking branch – which might well be remedied by the use of a few press studs! Obviously, the *emotional* experience of the tree – variety, texture, the privacy of enclosing leaves – cannot be reproduced so easily.

The fourth alternative is to forget about trying to salvage our own experience for our children, and to assume that the new experiences which we cannot now envisage will make up for the loss, just as we ourselves do not seem to have suffered from losing the bear-baiting and public hangings which our forefathers thought amusing and instructive for children. Probably we cannot cheerfully accept this alternative, and indeed there is no reason why we should. The suggestions offered here are not really alternatives at all, but may all be followed in conjunction; children seem to thrive on a rich mixture of possibilities and opportunities, and we have no evidence that their capacity has yet been satisfied. Indeed, all the most recent evidence points the other way: that the majority of children, and especially babies, are so under-stimulated that their potential is never reached. And that seems a good enough reason (if we needed one) to go on inventing toys.

2 People as Playthings:
lap and cradle play

In talking about people and their role as playthings for a baby, we have in mind mainly the child's own family, since babies are usually brought up in families. Within the family group, it still tends to be the mother who is most in contact with a baby during its earliest months. We have no reason for supposing that, where a father is the main caregiver, his fathering (by which we mean his personal and individual attention to the baby) is radically different from the mother's mothering (by which we mean the same thing). Our shorthand use of the words 'mother' and 'mothering' in this chapter, then, should be taken to apply to whoever has major personal care of the baby.

Despite a certain feeling of reaction against Bowlby, few people nowadays doubt that babies need something more than simple physical care and protection. Warmth and love, conveyed to the baby by 'good mothering', are equally held to be necessary for the child's overall thriving. It is only comparatively recently, however, that the precise mechanisms of mothering have come under scientific scrutiny. Maternal warmth used to be thought of as a mysterious 'something' radiating from naturally successful mothers, giving their infants a protective ambience against potentially damaging experiences, but not really capable of being observed in scientific terms. While good maternal care has for many years been regarded as vital (particularly for the child's future emotional development), mothering as a practical skill has tended to be glossed over and neglected as if it were unanalysable: 'mothering is something which, if you're not maladjusted, you know you must have had'.

By contrast, infants themselves have been investigated directly and fairly thoroughly, especially at the newborn stage when they are accessible in hospital. The methods used by earlier researchers typically involved temporarily removing babies from their mothers and recording their reactions under elaborately contrived, carefully controlled, but highly impersonal conditions of observation. Ingenious gadgets were invented, such as the instrumented artificial nipple (to monitor the strength and duration of sucking bouts), and the 'scientific crib' which could automatically register the baby's every movement, sometimes relaying the information directly to a computer. The babies in these early studies tended to be enmeshed in a forbidding tangle of wires and electronic gadgetry, and perhaps this is why their mothers were often deliberately kept well away from the laboratory while investigations were proceeding.

Inevitably, however, research workers soon found themselves having to cope with problems which ordinary mothers could well have anticipated. They discovered that what babies can be persuaded to do is very much dependent upon their particular mood or state at the time of testing. In the early months, in particular, babies spend considerable time asleep; when they are awake they all too easily become distressed and untestable. In practice, therefore, the experimental babies frequently had to be removed from the apparatus in order to be comforted, walked about, talked to, cuddled and rocked. Only in this way was it possible to get them into that particular state of 'contented alertness' during which 'normal' behaviour can best be observed and documented.

Perhaps it was as a consequence of this that certain investigators began to turn their attention to the soothing techniques themselves as a focus for research. What kinds of stimulation, it was asked, would prove most effective in calming fractious babies? This line of research led to a number of reasonably clear, and at first sight potentially useful conclusions. It can be shown, for instance, that low-frequency sounds have a more soothing effect than those of high frequency; this led to investigations which not only confirmed that human vocalizations, of the kinds traditionally used by mothers to calm their infants, are well adapted to this purpose (as one might have guessed), but also suggested that very soon after birth the baby is capable of recognizing the voice of the particular person who regularly cares for him. Following a similar line of thought, the effects of repetitive and rhythmic stimulations were investigated; it was demonstrated that for newborn infants there is an optimal rate at which the cradle should be rocked in order to inhibit crying, and, what was more, that this rate was 100 per cent effective! This research used a mechanical device rhythmically to rock the crib at different rates of oscillation and the most effective rate was a surprisingly rapid sixty complete up-and-down cycles per minute.[1] It has also been claimed that rather similar sound rhythms have a quietening effect on fractious babies, and this has led to speculation that the throb of the human heartbeat, which every infant presumably becomes very familiar with during the months before birth, might have a particularly soothing effect. It is now possible to buy a cassette tape recording of a genuine maternal heartbeat, together with other intra-uterine noises, for mothers to play to babies when they are restless or otherwise difficult to calm down before sleep.* In Japan a simulated vinyl breast, with rise-and-fall action comparable to adult breathing rate, has similar claims made for it.

Obviously, however, there are limitations when we come to apply research evidence of this kind. It is one thing to demonstrate that a group of newborn babies will be pacified, to some measurable degree, by a particular alteration in their environment; it is quite another to suppose that all babies will automatically be soothed, on a series of occasions, and as they grow older, by repeating the same form of mechanical stimulation day after day. In fact, if we did discover some truly mesmeric stimulation which worked every time without fail, research would probably be needed – as in the case of soporific drugs – to ensure that there were no unfortunate long-term side effects. Probably, too, mothers themselves would find distasteful a technique so effective that it labelled their babies as automata; we tend to like our babies to have some degree of unpredictability and cussedness about them, and responding to this is perhaps what mothering is all about.

More recently the whole idea of experimenting with newborn babies in laboratories is being questioned. One reason is that the artificial conditions which experimentalists have regarded as scientific may actually prevent babies from displaying the sort of behaviour they typically show in familiar everyday situations with people who understand their idiosyncratic foibles. Evidence has also been accumulating that babies are likely to be kept alert and happy if they are given *changing* patterns of stimulation, rather than by repeating the

---

* The one we found was a Dutch version (not that that made any difference to the English baby we gave it to): 'Mama's Muziek', EMI–Bovema, Holland. Chicco, an Italian toy firm, also market a soothing device which is supposed to be set to the mother's heart-rate and thus beats out a rhythm specifically tailored to the individual baby.

same stimulation many times in succession as is often demanded in conventional experiments. This makes sense in terms of real life; mothers typically learn to hold a baby's attention by varying the things they do to comfort and distract him, deciding what to do from one moment to another mainly on the basis of how the baby seems to be reacting.

Systematic observations have confirmed that, while babies are especially sensitive to new forms of stimulation when these are first presented, their interest does quickly wane with repetition. In particular, if it is made possible for a baby to exert some direct control over what he sees, he will tend to give a rapid initial burst of activity which is followed by an equally rapid decline in interest as the effect he produces becomes routine and predictable. This has been demonstrated, for instance, by sitting a newborn infant comfortably upright and arranging matters so that a slight head-turn in one direction activates a display of coloured lights. Under ideal conditions, a baby as young as one week will very soon learn to turn his head just the right amount to switch on the light display; but babies also seem to get bored with the effect rather quickly. This is not due to fatigue, however; if now it is arranged that the baby can only switch on the light by turning his head in the *opposite* direction, he first 'experiments' by trying to turn on the light using the old movement pattern, as if to prove that it no longer works; and when, by accident, he discovers that a movement in the opposite direction is needed, he again shows a renewed burst of light-switching, as if to reassure himself that he can control the effect as he did previously. Once again, however, he will soon lose interest as the new movement becomes fully predictable. The lesson of such observations is that human infants can show extremely rapid learning ability, providing that we give them the opportunity to demonstrate this; but mechanical and repetitious forms of stimulation are more likely to send a baby to sleep than to keep him alert and attentive. As many parents discover, young babies often sleep especially well during car journeys.

In demonstrating how 'clever' normal infants actually can be, it is now recognized that the position in which the baby is seated is fairly critical. It is only when he is held in a reasonably upright position with comfortable bodily support that a newborn baby is likely to remain attentive for any length of time. At birth, the baby has a brain which is relatively larger, compared with the rest of his body, than it will be later on. Partly because of this, to begin with he will find it an effort to hold up his head for very long at any one time in order to look about. If, however, the baby is properly awake, and is held in an upright position with a little head support from a responsive hand or shoulder, he will soon begin to show curiosity by searching about with his eyes. It is an interesting point that it is extraordinarily difficult for an experimentalist to devise a supporting structure which is as effective in propping up a baby as a human caregiver, who can constantly adjust to the baby's movements so as to avoid any approaching discomfort and ward off distress.

It may be that some of the bemused expressions that appear on the faces of young babies are the result of not being able to see more distant objects very clearly: ophthalmic evidence seems to suggest that they can only focus sharply upon objects quite close to them. Things and people must thus swing in and out of their field of view in a rather surprising and confusing way. Other detailed studies have shown, however, that the visual apparatus as a whole is remarkably well organized in the sense that, given optimal conditions, the two eyes can converge and fixate in near-perfect co-ordination, although they may have difficulty in maintaining this focus. And babies can use appropriate head-movements in tune with precise 'eye-pointing', so as to home in very accurately on quite small moving targets, provided that there is enough visual contrast for these to stand out from their background – a small torch beam, for instance.

In general, then, it is now recognized that, as early as the first few days after birth, the baby is capable of reaching out with his eyes to investigate his surroundings, even though his hands are still very inefficient; and that this naturally inquisitive activity is really an early form of exploratory play. It is difficult to be sure how much babies can learn from looking around them at this age, but many are clearly more contented when they are comfortably propped up for part of the time and have interesting things in sight. Obviously this kind of research throws a new light on the old arguments about how much babies need to be picked up and carried about. Cross-cultural studies have long observed that babies cry least when they are brought up among people who regard it as normal to carry the baby in a sling against his mother's body, rather than making it a moral duty to 'put him down' in a kind of cage, or a box on wheels, as soon as he stops making active demands,

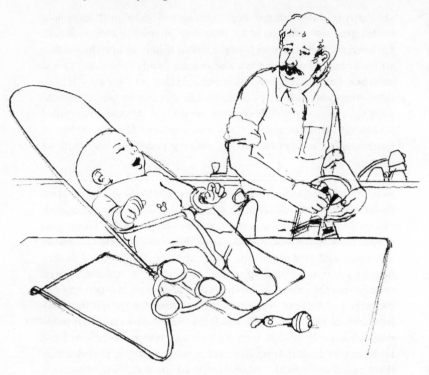

which seems to be our own rather odd tribal habit. It seems fairly clear that babies well under six months can be expected to become bored and discontented if they are left on their backs with sideways vision obscured and nothing but a ceiling to stare at.

Some researches have suggested that not only a baby's immediate performance but his developmental progress is in fact accelerated by the upright position.* Certainly his opportunities to look about him and take in information are improved by being carried upright; in the same way a reclining baby-seat, while providing full support for his head and back, allows a wakeful baby to explore his visual world. A ride in the pram offers both a sense of movement and a change of scenery, and prams nowadays are more likely to be designed so that babies can

* For instance, both Ugandan and Moroccan babies are said to be developmentally forward during the period they are carried around upright in slings.

easily see out of them. Slings and baby-seats, or a pram brought into the living area, also give the baby a better vantage-point for wordless conversations with the people around him. Jim Sandhu, a designer of environments for handicapped children, found that, when he raised immobile children in a nursery to a level closer to their nurses' faces, they were in fact talked to far more often.[2]

Looking at Objects and Faces: gazing play

A great deal of work has been done on the kinds of things which babies prefer to look at, and it is clear that, from the beginning, they have an astonishing capacity to distinguish between different visual patterns and even to discriminate patterns which have been seen (or heard) before from those which are new to their experience. The fact that very young babies can 'alert' to a novel stimulus is especially interesting, because it implies that they must have a much more sophisticated memory capacity than was previously supposed. Should we, then, deliberately try to provide stimulation for babies, other than what they naturally get from the hubbub of family life?

When the research findings on pattern recognition first became known, some people were tempted to conclude that babies could be given extra learning experience, and possibly be made more intelligent, by providing them with special equipment such as automatic film projectors which they could control by their own movements so as to project changing pictures at close range, perhaps on the side of the crib. Taken to its limits, we might imagine a new generation of super-babies programmed by computers from birth to play and learn at maximum potential. On the whole, however, even a very sophisticated computer would provide at best a mediocre substitute for an attentive human caregiver who reacts to a baby sensitively and with anticipation in the light of what he has been able to do in the past or seems about to do in the next few moments. Human beings, particularly the 'ordinary devoted' mother or father (to use Winnicott's phrase),[3] are likely to go on being rather more effective than even elaborate computer-controlled devices when it comes to keeping babies contented, and interested in what goes on in the world.

One reason for this is that, in practice, the child's interest in static objects is extremely limited during the first three or four months: so much so, that one can usually only get a response to ordinary objects at all by picking them up and jiggling them about, or actually placing them in the infant's hands. Even then, the baby may seem unaware of what he is grasping, and once the object is dropped there is no attempt to search for it.

In contrast, even the youngest babies will regularly watch other living creatures, including (especially) other human beings. Three things seem to be of fundamental importance to this preference. One is that it is mainly living creatures which have the quality of spontaneous movements of 'self-deformation' or internal change; it is interesting that most of the other common objects which share this property (like glove puppets, or a balloon being blown up) share it through being under living control: the exceptions, like mobiles and leaves moving in the breeze, also attract and hold the attention of babies. The second factor is that animals and humans share certain qualitative features in the way they move. They show a characteristic rhythmic pattern in that their actions repeatedly build up to a crescendo of movement before subsiding again. This seems to create a series of 'happenings' for the baby which are intrinsically interesting; we shall return to the idea of happenings later.

In the third place, it is important to realize that, when adults and older children react to babies, their responses will be influenced both in timing and in content by what the baby is doing, has done or is about to do. Thus, from the baby's standpoint, other people will be recognized as having the very special quality of being responsive to his own actions on a moment-by-moment basis. As we have seen, babies seem to be particularly alert to forms of stimulation which are responsive in the sense that the baby can attempt to bring them under his own mastery or control; in everyday terms, babies are like the rest of us in wanting to know that when they do something *to* someone (even if it's just focusing on that person and tilting their head slightly), she will do something *in reply*. The difference is that, while we can make objects respond to our actions, babies can't as yet; their power is solely over people.

Now when we film mothers and babies in 'conversational' interaction with each other,[4] and analyse the film frame by frame, what do we see? We find that what adults quite spontaneously and unselfconsciously do to amuse babies is geared in the most sophisticated and delicate ways to actions which the baby itself is making in responding to the adult. Furthermore, the mother intuitively varies her modes of responding as she goes along, so that what is coming next never seems boringly repetitive or predictable. The situation may be summed up by saying that ordinarily responsive human caregivers have all the characteristics which make them uniquely suited to attract and hold the attention of babies.[5] It is the moment-by-moment *responsiveness* of the mother, not the fact that the mother is so familiar to the baby, that is important; at Edinburgh University, John Tatam has shown this by comparing babies' reactions to their mothers talking through a glass screen, first when the mothers could see their babies and secondly when they could not; in the second case, the babies quickly seemed first confused and then disturbed.[6] Given the fact that (as we have seen) when babies are picked up they tend to be held in the positions which make active looking and sustained attention most possible, we reach the conclusion that young babies are most likely to be able to attend and learn if they are helped to do so by a sympathetic caregiver, who, by knowing the baby and responding to him as an individual, will also be providing him with stimulation of the most appropriate and compelling kind.

We began this chapter with the suggestion that 'mothering' – or sensitive baby caregiving – deserves much more detailed analysis if we are to understand why it is so important. This is not to say, however, that as parents we are likely to be better caregivers if we become selfconscious about the complexity of what happens when we act naturally. The evidence simply suggests that there are good reasons why parents should not be afraid to take their cue from the insistent demands which ordinary babies make, and should not stifle their natural inclination to treat babies as sensitive and responsive individuals with needs and feelings similar to their own. In practice most parents are highly responsive towards the things infants do and – as they come to know their own babies – towards the things they are about to do before they have actually done them. In short, we 'instinctively' respond to babies in the most complicated and precise ways, using actions and reactions which we do not need to be conscious of; though the fact that we are using split-second timing can easily be demonstrated in slow-motion recordings.

This is why, to begin with, face-to-face play without toys of any kind will completely satisfy the baby. In the first chapter we suggested that the human face is the first toy, and a very special one indeed. Let us consider this idea again. The eyes are very shiny and bright, and make continual quick little movements which are different from the slower movements of the head. They have eyelids to act as shutters which sometimes flick closed and open again, and often partly hide the eyes themselves. The rest of the face, and particularly the mouth, is highly mobile, and when the lips part, flashes of white teeth and the tip of a moving, glistening tongue can be seen. Along with all these movements go *linked* patterns of interesting sounds. It is surely this uniquely dynamic combination of sights and sounds, *geared to the baby's own rhythms but also reflecting fundamental biological rhythms,* which makes the human face such a powerful stimulus throughout our whole lives.

Less obviously compelling, the adult's hand becomes the second potent toy. We have already mentioned that, well before the child is interested in an object-toy, his attention can be drawn to the object by having it jiggled in the hand; then, if the hand puts the object down, the child will continue to gaze at the hand rather than the object. It is not that the hand is moving and the object is not: mechanically jiggled toys are of not much interest early on. Here again, the power of the

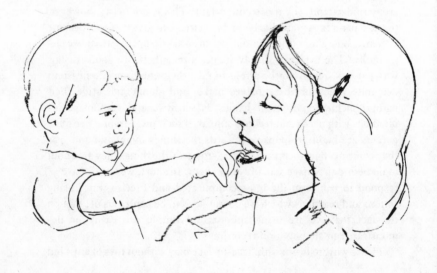

hand is that it moves *responsively* to the infant, goes out of its way to 'hook' his attention, as a mechanical object cannot. Parents quickly learn to use their hands for lap and cradle play: to walk their fingers slowly forward and pounce on a tickly place; to trace the baby's features delicately with a forefinger; to click thumb and fingers and drum out a rhythm; and eventually to formalize these finger-plays in 'round and round the garden' and 'this little piggy' incantations.

Conversations and Turn-taking

Although parents do naturally include words when playing and communicating with their babies, speech itself must at this stage be a one-sided affair; but what is remarkable is that, from birth onward, a baby who is happy and alert is already able to join in what can only be described as intimate conversations that do not need words. When mothers talk to their babies face to face, the babies seem to know exactly how to enter into such conversations; they first listen and then try to 'say' something themselves, taking turns in the most conversational way, even though they must express themselves through mouth, nose and eye movements, and have only grunts, coos, coughs and gurgles to offer in place of real words. This natural readiness on the part of very young infants to engage in two-way social exchanges involving looks, gestures and occasional vocalizations has only recently been systematically investigated and described;[7] but its importance can hardly be over-rated. The implication is that babies are *innately* social and are already fully equipped to play an active role in guiding other people into close interactions with them. They can already make use of a language-without-words, within which smiles and frowns soon begin to be used to express pleasure and displeasure, and different kinds of vocalization start to take on meaning as signals of delight or distress. From a very early age, babies are also capable of registering expectation and surprise, and expressing through intake of breath, pursing of lips and widening of eyes, followed by exhalation and laughter, the build-up and release of emotional tension. Soon they begin to show interest and anticipation in response to events that recur when they are being picked up, comforted, fed, changed or bathed. In this way, babies and their parents are bound to build up a whole repertoire of social rituals, in which each knows how to take part by repeated response to the invitations of the other.

It is the gamelike and playful quality of these early rituals which is particularly interesting, because it seems clear that the baby early on reaches his most sophisticated level of play in relation to person-playthings rather than object-playthings. Partly this seems to be because adults tend to assume that the child's actions are meaningful even if they are not yet so; and through this assumption they *create* meaning for the baby. The baby's actions are treated as purposeful and therefore they quickly *become* purposeful. To put this another way, the natural history of the child's understandings can, as it were, be re-written by his adult companion to make them more consistent and more significant to him than they could have been if they had not been expressed in the presence of a responsive caregiving person; and to some degree this will be true not only when the responses he receives are kind and sympathetic, but even when they are hostile and angry. We will come back to this in chapter 5.

'Happenings'

A baby's stream of experience is not smooth and continuous: it is punctuated by an endless succession of 'happenings'. But the baby is not merely a passive receiver of experience; his own active seeking of experience is of paramount importance and he seems to be determined either to discover or to create happenings. Like Kipling's Elephant's Child, he has an insatiable curiosity in the form of an inbuilt happening-hunger; and, from the point of view of developmental progress, it may well be that a hunger for happenings is as necessary as the biological hunger for food and drink.

We described some 'happenings' in our first chapter, and what we mean is a short sequence of events which is bound together as a coherent unit in the child's experience because it usually leads to an exciting or satisfying outcome. Because it has a dramatic end result, a happening comes to command the child's attention; but it is a mistake to assume that happenings normally exist as events external to the child and independent of his own activities, expectations and intentions. It is true that some external event (such as a sudden noise) may halt the child in his tracks and temporarily disrupt the pattern of his play; but this is so only because the child has long since learned that such signals might well be happening-indicators.

What counts as a happening seems to depend upon the baby's previous experience and expectations. Unless we know the child and the situation extremely well, we cannot predict what sequence of events will have this quality of a 'happening' for him. On the other hand, we can learn this through observation, because retrospectively we can see that certain sequences definitely do have this significance.

Perhaps the most interesting group of happenings are those which the child invents or creates for himself, out of his own spontaneous activity. If a pleasurable event is experienced as normally following some chain of activity on the child's part, he will have a built-in tendency to repeat that chain – to re-create the happening. We can then see a characteristic pattern of sustained attention which builds up to a climax, and is often followed by a clear release of tension: a sigh of satisfaction, a smile and glance at an adult, or, later on, a voiced 'Dah!' or 'Dere!' Particularly exciting patterns of activity are rapidly developed into happening-games, in which the baby exults in his power to create a rather dramatic effect and to repeat it over and over again. The social games that children most enjoy at this stage are 'anticipation games', in which the child can partly control and manipulate some other person to create happenings for him: peep-bo games especially (Where's that baby? – *there* he is!); but also games of throwing down for someone else to pick up; games that end in a hug or a tickle or a mock-fall, such as pat-a-cake, 'round and round the garden' and 'this is the way the farmer rides';[8] and conversation games of ritual imitation and counter-imitation, in which familiar noises such as mock-coughs and sneezes, blowing or explosive sounds are delayed just long enough for both partners to savour their mutual anticipation – aaaa ... tchoo! These forms of play are exciting yet not frightening to the baby, because they have a 'surprise' ending which he is expecting and can therefore feel comfortable with.

Long before verbal communication is possible (in the sense of the child understanding the actual meaning of words), mothers seem to communicate with their babies by engineering happenings which are in some way geared to what they want the baby to do. Susan Gregory, a developmental psychologist who was studying how babies begin to learn to discriminate different shapes, asked mothers to teach their babies to complete simple form-boards, and filmed them doing it; the communication patterns that she observed turned out to be more interesting than the learning patterns that she had set out to study.[9]

Dr Gregory found that mothers were creating interest for the baby in the board and its pieces by embedding both in a happening-rich context. As the baby held the pieces and waved them or banged them somewhat randomly, the mother would build up expectancy and excitement in tone of voice, gesture, set of her body as she held the child, and facial expression, all leading towards a tension release as either she or the baby placed the pieces with a satisfying 'clonk'. Each mother had her own characteristic pattern of intonation and gesture to signal the approach of a happening, and finally to confirm that it had happened – an *impression* of 'hurrah', if not an actual verbal 'hurrah'. In each case, what somehow got communicated to the baby was a tension build-up followed by a tension release *which paralleled the*

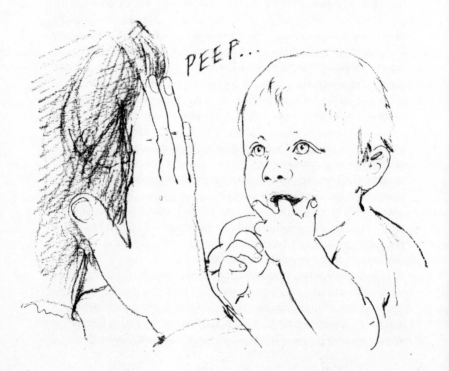

PEEP...

actions of the two of them. Sometimes the mother would arrange happenings for the baby to observe; sometimes she would put the baby through the movements required to produce a happening; sometimes she would set up a situation in which the child's spontaneous movements would very probably trigger off a happening. In short, the mother was shaping the baby's whole activity by selecting and emphasizing happenings which were relevant to the task, at the expense of those which were not. In this sense, mothers and fathers playing with their children, with or without a toy, structure the child's experience in ways which the child himself would not do if left to his own devices.

Out of all this mutual play, the adult and baby develop a shared frame of reference. Each knows the happenings to which the other is responsive, and they are thus in a position to communicate their intentions effectively to one another. Babies whose parents both play with them, or who have older brothers and sisters who give them a lot of attention, often develop different styles of invitation and response for different people: they have learned one frame of reference for one person, and a slightly different one for another, according to the style of play they experience from each.

People often talk as if the tendency of parents to treat tiny babies as if they already had a considerable degree of understanding was a rather sentimental aberration of parenthood: natural, perhaps, but nonsensical. The kind of research we have mentioned in this chapter shows quite clearly, however, that these early exchanges of looks and murmurs are a form of social play which has a central role in the child's progression through the early stages of intellectual and emotional development. It seems right to call it play, both because it is enjoyable to parent and child for its own sake, and because from the beginning the baby is able to take part in a relatively autonomous way. Dialogue-games are the first games parents and infants play together, and active involvement on the part of the adult goes on being important throughout babyhood if play is to be a rewarding and satisfying experience. The baby's first signs of genuine amusement, his first imitations and his first person-directed protests will all develop in this context. It may well turn out, as these early conversational patterns are more fully investigated, that the kind of person-to-person rapport that they generate between adult and child is essential to the proper development of linguistic communication at a later stage.

Trialogues

The child's earliest toy is the parent; it is also the parent who introduces, and in a sense commends to the child, the first object-toy, moving it in the hand to catch the child's attention. In talking earlier about the hand as a toy, we used the phrase '*hook* the child's attention'; watching mothers trying to use a toy in play with their babies at the stage when the baby prefers his mother's face to any toy, there is very much the feeling of an angler 'playing' a fish. Sometimes the mother will lift up the toy to intercept the baby's focus on her own face and will then gently draw the child's gaze sideways by moving and rattling the toy; or she will anticipate the baby's head-turning or loss of interest, and shift the toy back into focus or make it move in a different way.

What the mother is doing here is to create a mother-baby-toy triangle which still has the same quality of responsiveness that we saw in the dialogue. The turn-taking pattern of conversation is enlarged to include the toy; and, although the mother is in physical control of the toy, she does not use it to emphasize her own part but to *alternate* with her part: that is, her voice and gestures and the toy-rattling will rarely clash, but will each take their turn, both with each other and with the baby. Typically we have a pattern of mother speaking, then shaking the rattle, then leaving a space for the baby to gurgle a reply, which mother then takes up as a meaningful message: 'Look at this, then!' ... rattles in baby's focus, smiles and waits a moment ... baby coos and waves ... 'Yes, it *is* a lovely rattle, isn't it!' Because the mother is alert to take up and build on the baby's signals, whether they show increasing or waning interest in the toy, she is able to sustain his attention to it in a way that the toy at this stage, however delightful, could not do for itself; and gradually by this means the baby's span of concentration for objects will be extended.[10]

To sum up, the mother (or father) *is* the baby's first toy and *mediates* the first object-toy: thus the mother-baby dialogue develops into the mother-baby-toy trialogue; from this trialogue the mother withdraws progressively as the baby is enabled to attend more closely to the toy and appreciate some of its possibilities without her help. There does indeed come a time when the baby begins to be so absorbed in object-toys that the mother feels almost neglected; we have observed in our own unit how at this stage the mother will often bring her own face close to the toy in order to hook the child's attention back again! But this is just one more example of the changing balance between plaything and play-companion which adjusts with the child's age and stage, and will continue to do so throughout childhood.

3 Toys For the First Two Years: a developmental progression

Babies start by being interested mainly in people; they go on to develop a selective awareness of objects which are manipulated for them *by* people, and which therefore move in time with, and in response to, their own movements; eventually they come to show an interest in an object for its own sake, so that the toy begins to come into its own. This progression runs parallel to the baby's increasing activity, and her greater ability to control her movements so that they work more efficiently for her. By the time she is three or four months old, her eyes are becoming better at focusing, and the two eyes are working in conjunction more successfully: this means that they will be better able to find and stay with something which she enjoys looking at, and that they will be capable of following a moving object without drifting off or overshooting. Along with the ability to fixate and hold with the eyes go reaching and grasping movements: these were already, in a very primitive form, beginning to accompany the baby's eye movements when she was little more than one week old; but by five–six months the reaching has become more purposeful, therefore more effective, and hence far more rewarding. The baby's hands themselves become more actively receptive to things that she might hold and look at. Before the age of two months, her hands remain closed for the greater part of her waking time, and the grasp reflex that she was born with tends to keep them closed, in that the touch of her own fingers on her palm reactivates her gripping; as her neurological structures mature and the grasp reflex weakens, her hands open out for more of the time, ready to take hold of the toys she is beginning to reach for.

During the period when she is still reaching for things without a very strong expectation of getting them, the baby spends much time in very active looking: her attention may be held for minutes at a time. And the things that fascinate her, as we saw in the last chapter, usually have certain qualities in common with human faces, in that they tend to

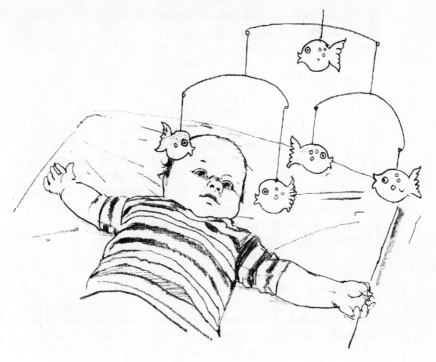

move gently, not too predictably, but not suddenly enough to alarm her. If we put a baby's pram under a tree, she will be entranced by the stir and ripple of branches and leaves; close to the window on a wet day, she will enjoy the quick flurry of rain on the glass and will stare at the drops running glistening down the pane as the sun comes out again. Mobiles and wind-chimes which sway or tinkle in a draught, plastic or metallic-paper 'windmills' for the pram, bouncing toys hung on long loose springs, a carousel balanced finely on a pivot: all these have a feeling of randomness in their movement (as do moving reflections or shadows on a wall, flames in a fireplace, or falling snow) which is extraordinarily attractive to babies and continues to exert a fascination. It is an odd observation that small babies also seem bemused by the drunken rolling of off-centred 'wobbly balls'. Bouncing toys and carousels are limited in that they must, of course, be set moving for the baby by an adult; mobiles and wind-chimes not only use natural air currents but have the additional advantage that they can be most successfully home-made out of scrap materials.

As soon as a baby can be propped up a little, she will also begin to show interest in the rest of the household. Parents often notice that the amusement provided for the baby by an older toddler wandering around can make a second baby less demanding and more contented than their eldest was at the same age. A cat, a dog, or even a budgerigar can serve much the same purpose. However, adults and rather older children are likely to be more sensitively responsive to her, and to time their conversations with her in a way that she will find more satisfying. Even when the baby starts to enjoy toys, then, we should not expect them to become in any sense a substitute for the person-to-person play and interchange which we described in the last chapter. Moving objects will attract her and teach her to look searchingly into her world, but it is still people who matter most.

Fingers and Toes as Toys: body games

If a baby cannot see much from her pram or carrycot, she may still be fascinated by the movements of her own body. It takes time for the two hands to come together in finger-touching play (about four months, and longer still for her to reach a hand across the mid-line of her body); but once this does happen, perhaps accidentally at first, her hands are in such a position that she can see them better, and she will soon learn to 'finger her fingers' on purpose, often gazing at them with great intentness. The baby acts as if finger-fingering was a sensorily rich experience: and so it is, for she is receiving tactile sensation from both hands, kinaesthetic sensation from the movement of her wrists and visual sensation from the gently twining hand/toy (which is which?) right in front of her eyes.

To start with, however, babies seem to watch their own movements as if their fingers and toes did not quite belong to them. At first, hands and feet are not used on their own, but as part of a movement of the whole body. When feeding, for example, the baby may pummel the breast or bottle with her hands and tread with her feet at the same time. Soon she will begin to use arms and legs together to push and shove; to thrust up her head and shoulders whenever she is placed face downwards on her tummy, and to swivel sideways; to kick out backwards and, if her feet meet a solid surface, to thrust herself forward bodily while grabbing with her hands. Placed on her back on the floor, she will flail arms and legs together, but will eventually learn to *use* them together (which also means using one more strongly than the other) in order to roll over.

Most babies enjoy being taken into deep water with their parents, so long as it is not too cold, and at an early age show the natural swimming movements which will later on have to be re-learned. The more everyday experience for western children, bath-time, still gives the baby a new dimension for her play. Even before she is ready for bath toys, the sensations of splashing and being splashed, of being moved about in the water, of being smooth-soaped and rough-handled in a warm towel, provide ways of knowing her own body better. It is worth taking thought over making bath-time totally enjoyable. For instance, both the baby and the adult bathing her will feel more secure and free to play if she lies in the big bath on a nappy (to stop her slipping) in just an inch or so of water: she still can't be left, of course, but both the adult's hands will be free, and the baby can wriggle about and learn to take a splash or two without being frightened.

Once she's old enough to sit up firmly without support, she will enjoy sharing a bath with an older toddler so long as she feels secure; but it can be a problem to provide two different degrees of security for children of different ages in the same bath. A strategy that often works well is to put a plastic clothes-basket into the bath for the baby to sit in; this gives her her own enclosed pool (which also keeps bath toys within her reach), something to hang on to if things get exciting, and the stimulating company of an older child. Again, of course, it is not safe to leave them on their own.

Bath-time, even without a brother or sister, offers babies a special opportunity for social play: partly because the touch of water, a chilly draught or the parent's hands on their bare skin leaves them breathless and giggly, but also because the things that happen at bath-time tend to be the same every night, so that babies quickly come to look forward to the next part of the ritual. Soon they are thrown into fits of laughter by the approach of a hand which might tickle, or by the threat of a raspberry-kiss on the tummy. These private games which develop between parents and babies, like the lap and cradle play that we have already discussed, give the child practice in the sequencing and anticipation of events; they are also probably very important in making her feel special and wanted, and generally developing her concept of herself as a person.

Touching and Feeling

At first babies seem to touch and feel just because they enjoy it, not in order to find out about what they are touching: that is, they will scratch at surfaces or finger their own clothes without turning their whole attention to them. Because babies have an inbuilt urge to suck, they soon learn to bring their hands to their mouths and, if they are not given a comforter, to suck fingers or thumb. Even when the sucking reflex weakens a little, anything the baby manages to grasp will be brought to her lips for mouthing. Hand-to-mouth movements are not very skilled to begin with, and babies can easily startle themselves by hitting their own faces when playing in this way. It takes several months for a baby to forget the urge to suck, taste and bite long enough to stop mouthing a toy and look carefully at it. This is one example of how developmental progress does not just depend on the baby learning to perform new actions: it equally depends on her learning to *inhibit* actions which are deeply rooted and which impede more flexible and intelligent behaviour.

Rattles

During this stage of coming to grips with the world of objects, a baby needs to be provided with a variety of different things to grapple with. Obviously these should not be breakable, sharp or toxic; and they are likely to end up in her mouth, so it is a good thing if they are washable. Hand-to-mouth toys should be easy to grip and safe to bite, so one needs to look for things that will first fit the baby's grasp and not scratch her gums, secondly give her something to look at and listen to, and thirdly offer possibilities of finger exploration. Not all these design criteria need to be met in the same toy, but it is surprising how many rattles, both ancient and modern, do manage to combine them.

Some of our own collection of rattles are shown on page 46. The first is a large, hard seed pod with a shiny, bumpy outer surface and rattly seeds inside. We found this particular one in a flower arranging shop, and it may well be toxic to bite, so we should have to know much more about it before actually giving it to a baby; we have included it here because the first rattles must surely have been found objects of this kind. The second stage would have been to embellish or assemble found objects: a gourd carved and stained, or pebbles with beach-worn holes strung together on a thong.

The Victorian rattle of silver and mother-of-pearl, with a whistle at the end, would not be very durable in a baby's hands, and the bells are scratchy to the gums. Arnold Haskell, who has a collection of Georgian and Victorian rattles in silver, coral, ivory and mother-of-pearl, surmises that these beautiful and delicate toys were 'given to flatter the parent as much as to amuse the infant . . . the fact that when found they are usually in excellent condition suggests that they were never hurled out of a cradle in play or petulance but were used to amuse the baby by the mother or nurse and they often hung from a chatelaine'.[1] Often, as in ours, one or two of the original bells are missing – no doubt an occasion of long-past panic. Other examples of rattles that would need adult supervision are the Roman terracotta ones in bird or animal shapes which can be seen in the British Museum: limited for babies' independent use, carved pottery rattles are fun to make (as a commemorative toy perhaps?) if you have access to clay and a kiln.

The wooden rattles shown here come from Scandinavia, England, Germany and Japan; they are polished, or finished in polyurethane, and are a delight to the adult eye. One has to admit that babies are less immediately attracted visually: the natural grain of the wood is not something that a baby sets much store by. They are very pleasant to hold, however, bite and pass from hand to hand, and most of these have interesting holes or recesses for poking fingers into. The noise is usually a gentle rattle made by wooden balls inside: good for a small baby, who often doesn't like the high jarring note of some plastic rattles. Some have a caged ball, bell or glass marble for the child to poke at; others have balls that roll past the holes into darkness again for a 'now you see it, now you don't' experience. Or the noise may be a clackety one made by sliding pieces along a dowel, or dowels through slots; or the wood is shaped and slotted like a bell, to give an especially musical tone. A few

wood

plastic

silver and mother-of-pearl

pottery

cane

wood

wood

plastic

wood

TRINGLES plastic

seedpod

plastic

RUMBA

RING-A-LING plastic

wood

Socialisation

Gender

Language R-scheme
idents.

TV   toys   Language

catalogues   parents' choice
of C' mas presents

Conclusion

City College, St. Albans
Hatfield Road, St. Albans, Hertfordshire AL1 3RJ
Telephone (0727) 47070. Facsimile (0727) 47071

Principal: John W Loveridge BCom Cert Ed FCollP MBIM
Vice Principal: R Barrie Mort MA (Oxon) ACIS
Vice Principal: Martin Lemarie MA BSc(Hons) DMS FCIOB MBIM

DEPARTMENT OF GENERAL STUDIES

A C C E S S   C O U R S E

1. The aim of the course is to develop
   and to help them acquire knowledge
   completion of the course, to enter
   comparable to that of students who

2 The course is a one year multi-exit
   return to study and to take a degre
   route is impracticable or inappropr

3. Our major target group is of adults
   who have been educationally disadvar
   enabling people from a wide variety
   educational system.

4. Structure and Content   The course i
   per week of classroom-based activity
   spend additional time in discussion,
   research etc. One-to-one tutorials
   class-contact time.

wooden rattles are painted or (better) polyurethane-stained in recognition of the baby's liking for bright colours; one very successfully
uses bright-coloured plastic balls inside a natural wood slotted
cylinder. Of other natural materials, cane rattles have a pleasant and
bitable texture, but tend to be unadventurous in shape, though there
seems no reason why this should be so.

There are a great many cheap and nasty plastic rattles on the market,
some made of thin, brittle plastic that easily cracks into sharp
dangerous slivers, many in coy animal shapes that the baby can neither
recognize nor manipulate. However, things have moved on a little in
design since Arnold Haskell wrote, ' I have yet to see a plastic one that
could be described as anything else than "cute and hygienic".' Our
own favourites are illustrated. The oldest of these (which perhaps
Haskell did not count as a rattle) is Kiddicraft's Tringles, a collection of
curvilinear triangles (if they can be thus described) which were, until
1977, threaded on a silver chain, now alas replaced by nylon cord. In
heavy ABS plastic in clear bright colours, it used to be claimed that the
shapes had been designed so as not to stretch the mouth. In our
experience, babies try to shove two 'corners' in at once, thus stretching
their mouths like mad; but why anyone should mind them doing so is
beyond us. This rattle has been going strong since the 1940s, and well
deserves its long life; the toy itself, as well as the design, is virtually
indestructable, and in the early stages the cord can be used with only
two or three shapes to make it light enough for a very first rattle.
Kiddicraft also make other particularly well-designed ABS rattles,
notably the Bangle Rattle with shapes sliding round the 'bangle' and
Flip Fingers. The Mothercare dumb-bell (Rumba) and the Pedigree
Ring-a-ling are designed to be easily grasped, but the latter is
particularly intended to encourage hand-to-hand play, with gripping
places all round it; both use clear reds and yellows with transparent or
white, both have a muted unstrident sound, and the Ring-a-ling
includes finger-tip-sized holes for probing into. The transparent
polycarbonate sphere used to come with or without a frame handle,
though we haven't seen one on sale for some time: half-filled with
water, with a little yellow duck floating inside, both babies and older
children find this a fascinator, especially as the duck swims on happily
whichever way up it is held.

The best of the plastic rattles seem to be made in really good quality heavy gauge plastic such as polycarbonate or ABS plastic, which takes good clear colours; polythene and vinyl, being soft, rattle less effectively and collect more dirt, though there are some rather nice hedgehog-textured shapes with bells inside. A particularly successful polythene rattle which parents can make themselves consists of a 'gamester' ball which is sold in several sizes as a practice ball, with holes all over it; a bell should be chosen (from a handicraft or pet shop) of a size which needs to be *pressed* through the biggest hole, so that it will not fall out again. The baby will find she can grip the ball easily by hooking her fingers in the holes, and the shiny bell can be peered at as it rattles about inside; different sizes of ball suit different sizes of baby. What we should *like* to see produced, using these holey balls, is a ball-in-a-ball-in-a-ball, with a bell in the middle. This is not a new idea – these fascinating objects can be seen in museums, carved out of a single sphere of ivory or ebony, and we have a five-ball one in lignum vitae – but it is a nice example of a puzzle-toy that is engrossing for a finger-poking baby long before she can appreciate the concentricity which makes it such a satisfying object for children and adults (even though modern technology would be cheating in its making).

In talking about finger-poking babies, we are already beginning to move on to the next stage: from hand-to-mouth to something altogether more exploratory. Perhaps, indeed, what is important about a good rattle is that it should bridge that progression: that it should at first be satisfying just to feel, mouth and listen to, but that it should have potential for more visual and manipulative play. One of the reasons why, during the hand-to-mouth stage, babies seem more interested in the *feel* of objects than in the objects themselves is that while the baby is still lying down, anything she drops will probably roll out of sight; and at this stage objects out of sight are also out of mind. Once the child can be comfortable sitting up, she is more likely to see where things have gone if she drops them; and as soon as she no longer needs her hands to support herself, she is in a much better position to investigate things on their way to and from her mouth.

Curiosity Play

Even after they can sit up properly, most babies still bring things to their mouths for a long while; at the same time they are gradually thinking more about what their hands are doing and becoming interested in how objects look from different angles. The hands' increasing co-ordination makes it possible, indeed, for the baby to realize that an object *has* more than one angle; this realization leads her to wish to look all over the object, and this in turn demands more and more delicate skills from her hands. As the toy is moved down from her mouth, the baby literally seems to uncurl and to look outward in a more adventurous way. Things in general, and playthings in particular, now seize her attention.

This stupendous partnership between hand and eye opens up great vistas of activity and understanding. Food, for instance, suddenly becomes interesting in an entirely new way: as a medium for play. Now it is something which sticks to the fingers, which can be moulded, squashed, crumbled into tiny pieces or smeared on other things to make coloured marks. Drinks can be bubbled and sprayed, or they can be spilled to make puddles for dabbling the fingers in. Bowls can be emptied out, or the contents can be removed in handfuls. As they wipe up the fifteenth congealing glob of puree from the floor and pursue soggy lumps of toast up the baby's sleeve, parents can be forgiven if words like 'discovery' and 'creativity' are not uppermost in their minds.

Nonetheless, this is what it's all about. From about six months onward, children begin to make a most determined onslaught on their environment, and the curiosity play of this period is both a stimulus to, and evidence of, their developing understanding. Now the baby *wants* to find out what happens when you squeeze, punch, pound and bite objects: that some things tear or break, others stretch and bend, still others clatter or bounce. Through endless experimentation, children begin to discover the nature and properties of all the different materials which they encounter in the world. It is undoubtedly a period of extremely rapid learning, and during this time babies sometimes seem to withdraw their attention from adults a little in order to concentrate on a toy – a change that mothers can find a little disconcerting, as we mentioned earlier on.

Sometimes a baby will seem destructive at this age; certainly if she comes upon a heavy book or magazine, she is likely to pick it up by one page (relative weight and tensile strength are not things she knows about yet, though she is finding out fast), and once the page has come out in her hand, she will screw it up, bite it, wave it and throw it down, and come back to it for another try at tearing. She is interested in testing the limits of the materials she comes in contact with, and this is a necessary part of curiosity play; in fact, 'exploiting' a piece of airmail paper is one of the items at seven months in a developmental test, and to pass it the baby has to 'actively wave, exploit or otherwise play with the paper in a purposeful manner'.[2] Meeting her needs at this stage becomes a matter of giving her plenty of different things to explore which are either expendable or indestructible.

The things she plays with now do not have to be expensive toys. In this era of lavish packaging, some of the best play material comes wrapped round other things: lengths of clean string, the crackly moulded linings from chocolate boxes, shredded paper packing, the card outer boxes of cosmetic preparations – all of these can be happily 'exploited' by the baby, provided someone is around to make sure she doesn't choke on the bits she pulls off. Other toys can be made for her

with little or no expenditure. Tins, small strong jars and plastic bottles and canisters can be quarter-filled with lentils, water, ping-pong balls (experiment for different noises) and their lids tightly sticky-taped on, for rolling and shaking; bright buttons and bells can be securely sewn to an odd piece of velvet or fur fabric; a collection of interesting ironmongery can be screwed down to a piece of wood (one of our children had a bolt, a chain, a switch, a hinge and a turn-button). Most households have an accumulation of bits and pieces which will make an instant toy if strung together on a bootlace: testing this statement at the moment of writing, we found in five minutes a key, cotton reels,* an empty cassette, the red pouring top from a squeezy bottle, a brass handle, the ring from a light fitting, an old purse-diary, a rubber pad covered with tiny suckers for keeping soap dry, and lots of lids, corks and buttons.

*US usage: thread spools.

Bought toys for this stage either need to be interesting just to look at, to finger and to mouth, or whatever they 'do' has to happen as a result of fairly accidental pushing and swiping. Transparent balls with a spinning butterfly or other device inside are a visual delight; tumbler dolls that bounce back are less frustrating for the non-crawling child than something that keeps rolling away; an enormous ball is satisfying to push at, and can usually be kept within bounds by an arrangement of the furniture. Push-and-bounce-back toys may be anchorable by a rubber stem and suction pad; one needs to test the strength of the action before anchoring them close to a small baby, as some hit back rather than bounce. Toys that rock, swing or spin will be enjoyed, but if they are easily overturned the baby will have difficulty in getting them back into position. Of the toys illustrated here (Fisher Price chime ball, Escor wooden swingboats, Escor wooden maypole, Escor car merry-go-round), only the first cannot be upset; nonetheless, the others can quite appropriately be bought for a baby of this age, since they have a continuing potential for her to grow into. A good toy outpaces development.

In fact it is important not to forget, when buying a toy, that a child may get a great deal of pleasure from a toy which she cannot yet use 'properly', either by playing with it at a lower level or by persuading adults to contribute the difficult bits. For instance, a baby who is only beginning to shunt around on her bottom and is still at the push-and-swipe stage may well enjoy a wheeled musical toy designed for toddlers, even though she can only push it to and fro from a sitting position. Or a child who has no idea of building up graded pile-ups will be delighted to have an adult do the piling up while she does the knocking down. Toys which have a build-up to an exciting climax, like the pop-up cone-tree or trigger-jigger (see page 178) can initially be wholly demonstrated by the adult, with the child contributing at first just the tension of anticipation, later the pressing of the release knob, and only eventually taking over the full sequence. Similarly, musical boxes can at an early stage be just a matter of listening to what the adult has set going; then the child explores the box and finds she can produce occasional notes by a random push of the handle or key, and in time learns to start the mechanism more competently or even to cope with a whole sequence of settings such as the Fisher Price 'record-player' musical box demands.

The Development of Concepts

Hide and seek

We can guess that objects have begun to be important *in themselves* to the baby when she begins to miss them: when, for example, a toy falls out of sight and she actively searches to find it again. Looking for something she can't actually see must mean that she has an *idea* of what it is and an *understanding* that it must still be around somewhere.

We can test how firm this understanding is quite easily. Waiting until the baby is clearly attracted to some small toy and is about to reach for it, we quickly drop a small handkerchief over it. Early on (before eleven months or so), the baby immediately forgets the toy, although she may transfer her interest to the handkerchief and pick it up. It will be fairly obvious if she has picked up the handkerchief for its own sake, because, if she then notices the toy that she has uncovered, she will look slightly surprised. As her understanding develops, however, the baby will not be fooled by something being hidden under a cover in this way; if she wants the toy, she will immediately snatch off the cover and get what she is after. In fact she will then only show surprise if, when the cover is removed, she finds that the object has actually gone away.

Toys that allow the child to play with this concept of 'object permanence' include anything with a hide-and-seek characteristic. The simplest are just sets of boxes with lids, into which the child can put small toys and enjoy 'finding' them again; these can, of course, be collected for nothing, but Galt and Chicco both do a beautiful set of size-graded lidded polythene cylinders in a variety of clear colours, and this serves as a fitting and pile-up toy as well. Remember that the child will be able to fit the lid on a round box before she can manage a square one. More complicated are some of the pop-up toys, where people or animals pop out of holes, or from behind another part of the toy, when a lever is pressed or a string is pulled. A traditional pop-up toy which is still around is the puppet-on-a-stick, where the puppet is pulled down into a cone to hide and then made to jump into view. A Jack-in-the-box is another traditional toy of this kind, but the action tends to be rather startling for a baby of this age, and perhaps too fast for her to learn much from it; putting Jack back in the box is also much too difficult a task, whereas the baby can begin to experiment at once with pulling the stick puppet back into its cone. A toy that used to be sold by street vendors consisted of a rubber bulb which, when squeezed, allowed a comic figure in thinner rubber to inflate and leap up out of the end of the bulb, to be sucked back inside when the pressure was released.

There are a number of other toys which allow objects to disappear and reappear. A simple cloth bag full of cotton reels, its mouth drawn together with elastic leaving a hole big enough to invite the hand's exploration, is an exciting toy at this age. A wooden tunnel into which the child pushes bricks until they emerge the other end is much more interesting at this stage of development than it looks to the adult. More complicated versions of the tunnel principle are the 'sausage machine' toy, in which wooden pegs are hammered into a narrow tunnel to pop out explosively one by one at the other end, and ball-rolling toys where the ball is either dropped into the toy or hammered into it through a tight opening, rolling out via a sloping tunnel or a shuttered exit; Brio make good versions of these.

Relationships

Another way in which the baby demonstrates her increased under-standing is in give-and-take play. Try offering her a small object – perhaps a wooden cube or a teaspoon – and, once she is holding it, offer her another. To begin with, the one being held will be dropped every time another is offered: the old is completely forgotten the moment she begins to concentrate on the new. It takes time to learn to think about two things at once. She will probably be well over six months old before she manages *not* to drop the first in attending to the second: realizing she might need both, she now goes on holding it firmly while reaching out for the new one. Once she can hold two at the same time, try offering her a third. This presents her with a more complicated problem, but in time (though probably not until she's well past her first birthday) she will solve it. Before reaching for the third, she will find a place to put one of the first two – perhaps wedged in the top of her dungarees, or in a crook of the elbow. Here is clear proof that she is learning to think ahead and to work out solutions to problems.

Being able to think about two things at once is important for all sorts of activities. To give a very simple example: when a baby is being spoon-fed, she will soon want to hold the spoon and feed herself; but, to begin with, her most likely mistake will be to turn the spoon over and so lose the food before it actually reaches her mouth. She needs not only more *skill*, but more *understanding* to put this right; she has to attend to both the food and the spoon at once, and consider the best way of keeping one in the other until it is safely in her mouth. Once she can think of two things *in relation to each other*, she will be able to put tools to work, which is probably the most significant human ability apart from speech. Banging often becomes a favourite occupation at this point. A spoon can be used to bang something else, such as a plate, and she finds that this produces a noise which is different from banging the spoon on her bib or on the table-top, or rattling it in her cup. Once again she is learning about *relationships between things*. Towards the end of the first year, simple banging toys give the child great pleasure; a wooden xylophone or rubber-skinned drum make a reasonably bearable noise, and a hammer-peg toy will keep her interest for a long time, since she will not learn to sort and fit the pegs until later on.

Playing hide-and-seek with objects, in the ways we have already considered, focuses upon the object hidden; from around the first birthday the hollow objects *in which other objects might be put* exert their own fascination. Holes attract the baby's attention, and are investigated by poking fingers; quickly she discovers that putting one thing in another makes something interesting happen – the combination rattles, the inside thing disappears, maybe the hole itself disappears. Then she finds that only some objects have this interesting property of being able to contain other objects: for instance, that a small ball will fit into a large cup, but a small cup will not fit into a ball however large it is. In fact, *only some objects have both outsides and insides:* and when a child first makes that discovery, she may spend a long while exploring this remarkable notion of the container and the way in which things can be contained inside it. She is likely to become so engrossed by this that just filling and emptying hollow containers becomes a game in its own right.

Here again the baby will demonstrate to the observer how her ideas are developing. When it first begins to occur to her that she can put one thing in another, she will often show that she understands this by holding the smaller object over the container, ready to drop it in, but find it difficult actually to let go. Then when she does start putting things in and letting go, she quickly finds that it's just as much fun emptying them out again. If she is then given a dozen wooden cubes, and you try to get her to put them *all* into a tin or a saucepan, she'll start enthusiastically enough, but she'll probably empty the first few out before she's got them all in. Completing a task of this sort needs a sense of order and system, which she hasn't yet got. It takes time to learn, not just to go on putting things in, but to stop herself emptying them out until she's finished the first job, and she is not likely to reach this stage before about eighteen months. In the same way, once she can place blocks carefully enough to make a tower (around twenty months), she'll still find it difficult at first to resist the temptation to knock it down before all the blocks are on.

Getting Mobile

Earlier on we mentioned the frustration that a roll-away toy can cause to a non-crawling baby; but in the end, of course, this kind of frustration motivates the child to start moving. The child who cannot see the interesting things that are just out of reach is heavily handicapped, and needs special help to penetrate her apathy, as we shall see later on.

Once the child can get around in however makeshift a fashion, whether by shunting or bottom shuffling, creeping or crawling, the rolling toy really comes into its own as something that can be fully exploited by the child. Balls and balloons, rattles in cylindrical shapes, rollalongs with a weighted figure in the middle that stays upright (a version of the bounce-back Kelly doll), wobbly balls with an eccentric rolling action: all these stimulate the child to push, follow, and push again. Simple wooden toys with wheels have the same function at first, later to be used for imaginative play as well; but for the moment it does not matter to the child that the object is said to be a lorry or an engine, it is just a good roly toy (although its status as 'lorry' may encourage adults and bigger children to make interesting noises as they play with it). The advantage of wooden vehicles with wooden axles is that the slower action suits the baby's own speed at this stage.

Scooters and Walkers

Big wheeled toys will be appreciated by a baby still at the crawling stage, if they are stable enough for her to heave herself up on. Thus, if they are on castors or ball-bearing wheels, they must also be very low, so that if they shoot from under her only a gentle tumble will result; a tyre on castors can be bought (expensively), a board on castors, edged with hose-pipe for the furniture's sake, is almost as good, and a number of firms (such as Chicco) market plastic-bodied scooting toys of this kind for babies. Where the toy is larger still, the baby will eventually use it to pull to standing, and it is important that it should be firm enough and slow enough not to tip or run away with her. One craftsman in wood (W. G. Green of Crowdys Wood Products) has designed an untippable pushalong truck on rollers rather than wheels, which makes it exceptionally stable. Many firms market 'baby walker' trucks with a very upright handle set well forward to prevent tipping, and these are especially useful both as walking aids and as containers which can be loaded and unloaded with the child's bits and pieces. The beautifully solid wooden pram with wooden wheels and axles, made by Woodpecker Toys, serves the same purpose and starts a second life once the child begins to enjoy cossetting dolls and stuffed toys.

The term 'baby walker' is also used for a quite different piece of equipment: a frame on small wheels or castors, usually with a canvas sling-seat in the middle, into which the child is put to aid her walking. Such frames have been used for many years. There is a very fine wooden one with multi-directional iron castors, probably dating from the early eighteenth century, in the nursery at Christchurch Mansion, Ipswich; it has no seat, but a well-padded leather confining ring to encircle the baby's waist and support her under the armpits. There is a rather similar doll-size version in the Nuremburg Doll's House at Bethnal Green Museum, which is dated 1673. In the National Gallery is a picture by Coques, a painter of the Antwerp School in the mid-seventeenth century, showing a little girl in a baby-walker entirely of wood, the support at the top being a square surface with a hole cut in it: perhaps it hinged open at the back (as does a wooden walker of similar date in the London Museum), otherwise it is difficult to see how the voluminous skirt could have been pushed through. Gamages' (London) catalogue for 1913 shows a 'baby walker and supporter' which they claimed to be 'the most sensible and practical baby walker yet invented',[3] in which the baby is strapped into a kind of corset; one suspects that the set of the wheels (as in the Antwerp example) would make it impossible for the baby to change direction, and that she would be confined to a forward or backward movement. In fact it is rather typical of baby-walker frames generally that, although they may allow the baby to walk around a little earlier than she might otherwise have done, they do tend to constrain her in other ways, by limiting her flexibility of direction and her access to nooks and corners, and by distancing her from the toys she might like to play with.* Unless the child is handicapped, she is likely to be more stimulated by being allowed to pull herself up on the sofa and teeter from one piece of furniture to the next until she is ready to let go in her own good time.

If we are going to spend money on mobility equipment, at this stage between sitting and walking, we might think about increasing the baby's opportunities for either scooting or rocking. A simple wooden seat with arms and a tray fixed in front with a rim to it, set on castors, will allow her to scoot around from a sitting position and give her a surface at a convenient height to use toys on. Some high chairs dismantle to make this kind of scooting chair, but these are often in fact too heavy for the child to move easily. A great variety of rocking chairs is available, often with a horse's head and neck set between the child's legs, which serves the double purpose of keeping her safely in with something to hold on to, and leading her towards notions of symbolic and representational play. An indoor enclosing swing offers yet another kind of motion (up and down as well as to and fro if the cords are elasticated) and, hung in the doorway of the room most likely to contain an adult, gives a good vantage-point for conversation. All of these toys, however, have the inbuilt danger that they can become dumping-places for the child: they are good places for her to be only so long as she is alert, comfortable and active. Once she begins to slump into an uneasy

---

* Some baby-walkers were still more restricting, and seemed more designed to keep the baby in a confined space than as an aid to mobility. The Cambridge Folk Museum has two 'baby runners' from the eighteenth century; in the first the baby is put through a hole in a square tray which slides along the grooves in the sides of an oblong frame; in the second, a wooden waist-ring is attached by a fixed arm to a heavy pole from floor to ceiling, the pole itself rotating as the baby walks in a circle.

doze, or to squirm in an effort to escape, she needs to be taken out to give her more freedom to change her position.

Pushalongs and pullalongs

Shunting, crawling, and eventually walking with or without support all give the child a new perspective on her surroundings. She may become so exhilarated by her new-found mobility that other developments seem to mark time for a while as she tries out all her physical skills. She will probably now be abandoning her pram for a push-chair, and all sorts of toys with wheels become objects of interest, whether pushed, pulled or sat upon. Once she can walk without support, the pullalongs and pushalongs that do not themselves offer support seize the child's interest, and an individual toy may become so loved that it seems an inseparable extension of the child. These toys have a particularly long history; Gwen White[4] illustrates an indeterminate animal on four wheels, found at Ur and dating from two and a half thousand years BC, and a most beautiful pottery Indian bird rocking between two large wheels from Mohenjodaro, of a similar antiquity, which might have come from the drawingboard of a modern designer such as Patrick Rylands; Mothercare has a not dissimilar duck in plastic! The Mayan civilization had wheeled toys although they did not use wheeled transport.

Children vary a great deal as to when they first walk alone, but most will do so some time during the second year. As we've already suggested in relation to rolling toys, we will not expect early-walking children at first to be aware of whether or not the push-or-pull duck or puppy is in fact duck-like or puppyish; the main thing to start with is that the toy should accompany its owner without upsetting, preferably looking and sounding interesting in the process.

On the whole, pushalong toys on sticks immediately precede pullalongs on strings in the developmental scale, because they give the child a slightly steadying balance-point, whereas the string-toy tends to draw her off balance if anything. There are a great many pushalong toys: the best have solid wooden handles with a knob to hold, securely anchored at the base; some of the worst have fit-together tubular plastic handles which both bend and come to pieces in the hand. Escor produce a beautifully simple one in painted wood: two big wheels with bells between them. Fisher Price make a transparent plastic cylinder with beads inside, and used (alas) to produce an even better Corn-popper, a transparent half-sphere on wheels in which the beads by ingenious use of a shaped axle were impelled violently against the walls of the container, making a most satisfying popping noise. A more complicated pushalong from the same firm has little men popping up in turn. There are some excellent cheaper ones in strong tin, with wooden handles: usually either a cylinder containing chimes or bells, or two wheels flanking open bells fastened to the axle, each with a wooden clapper bead on a thick rubber stem. One of the most charming (from Willis) is a wooden duck between two smallish wooden wheels into each of which is attached a flapping rubber 'foot' at opposite sides of the axle; as the axle rotates, the feet in turn flop down with a gentle slap, and the child's own uncertain gait gives the duck an engaging waddle. A wooden pushing toy from Portugal has a manikin fixed to the handle who appears to drive the wheel by pedalling with his hinged legs; we recently acquired a street-toy, home-made in wire by a Rhodesian child, where a man pedalled a tricycle with a similar action.

Pullalong toys can, of course, be more flexible since they do not have to take a stick handle. Nor do they necessarily need wheels, so long as the underside can withstand wear and tear. A flat-bottomed wooden boat or a long snake of cotton reels strung together make satisfactory pullalongs. A round tin with a tight-fitting lid, a couple of pebbles inside and a hole punched at each end, can be pulled on a loop of string and is even better if a dowel rod is pushed through for an axle. Crowdy's wooden tractor with detachable rollers made us think that it would be interesting to have a series of detachable trailers for a pullalong vehicle, each making a different kind of noise. Mothercare market a plastic pullalong of threaded finned bobbins which turn and click: they only work on carpeting, however, and this is something to check when buying a pullalong – that it will function at its best on the surface where it is likely to be most used.

Although many of the pullalong vehicles and animals have a function as representational or symbolic objects, we shall merely consider them here for their qualities as pullalongs. Basically, they need to have enough weight slightly to resist the pull, if they are not to come flying

loose ball

into the heels of their owner. For this reason, hardwood is a better material than plastic for this purpose. They also need to be designed to be fairly broad-based with a low centre of gravity so that when pulled at the angle determined by the child's height they will not tip over: one suspects that some of the charming wooden horses on narrow platforms with wheels shown in Kate Greenaway's illustrations would quickly have fallen on their dappled sides. Sometimes, however, the string only needs to be lengthened for poor balance to be put right. There also ought to be a toggle or loop at the end of the string, suitable for the child to grasp, and this again can easily be provided if the toy itself is satisfactory.*

Solid wooden vehicles which are particularly suitable as pullalongs are best represented in the UK by Woodpecker Toys (John Spence), Beck Toys and Escor Toys. The first two use a natural finish: the last the bright painted finish for which they are deservedly well-known. The Escor pullalong vehicles have the additional advantage that the toys can also be used for other purposes: they carry large or small numbers of peg-men, who can be fitted into either vertical or sloping holes, or on to pegs. All three purposes of pullalong, fitting toy and representational toy are equally well served in these designs, and because the different functions are paramount for the child at slightly different stages, the toy is likely to have a long play-life. In heavy plastic, Matchbox and Fisher Price both make vehicles with peg families to fit in them, with the same advantages.

The best of the pullalong animals seem to be in painted or varnished wood, and many have some kind of built-in wriggle or dip to their movement in order to increase the vivacity of the creature: a tight-coiled spring for the tail, with a bobble on the end, is a favourite addition. Brio makes several small dogs; Matchbox and Fisher Price have larger sized, rather cartoon-like dogs, and the latter's Snoopy Sniffer is the oldest toy in their range, dating from 1938. The Greek firm, Kouvalias, markets a little dog of particularly ingenious design:

---

* There are regulations forbidding the use of a grasping-bead on the end of a string, on the somewhat unlikely grounds that this might become entangled with the wheels and form a loop in which the child might hang herself. Parents must use their own judgement here, and may wish to try out the tangle-ability of a particular toy's wheels and toggle, together with their own child's skill and patience in disentangling. A soft roll of felt, stitched into a toggle, might be the answer if the child finds loops difficult to manage.

his feet are near-hemispheres, and when pulled along they rotate, giving the dog an irresistibly comic gait. The same firm produces a swan carrying an egg in the hollow of its back which turns over and over as it glides. Jas, the Czechoslovakian toymakers, have solidly charming ducks and hens which waggle their wings. Probably the most successful plastic pullalong creature is Kiddicraft's delectably undulating Clatterpillar, first produced in 1978 and clearly a superstar.

In a class of their own are the action pullalongs. We have already mentioned mobile features of some of the animals, and this also applies to certain vehicles: the Matchbox family 'camping car' has a slight bobbing movement, for instance; but for some pullalongs, action is paramount. A comparatively simple one which has been about for years is a platform on six wheels, carrying six vertical pegs on each of which is threaded a coloured brick: the friction of the wheels turns each brick, to great visual effect. Russian wooden toys have a long tradition of 'doing things', and their pullalongs have men and animals banging drums and xylophones, pedalling, twirling and tumbling, and so on. Others have carousel features. Perhaps the most galvanizingly active pullalong we know is again from Kouvalias, and we are not sure what to call it: it has an insect's body in painted wood, with antennae of tight-coiled springs, each with a wooden bobble on the end. On its back it carries an array of similar springs, each with a different-coloured wooden bobble, and this contraption twirls as the creature is pulled along, the springs waving randomly and the bobbles striking each other to make a clicking noise.*

Eventually, of course, the pullalongs develop into trucks while the pushalongs give place to barrows. There is a basic difference, however. Because these later developments are essentially *containers*, they cannot afford to tip over, and therefore need considerably more skill for their manipulation. This is particularly true of wheelbarrows, which need to be lifted and balanced as well as pushed and steered, and both children and parents are often disappointed by the too-early introduction of a wheelbarrow, even in the excellent design (Mothercare and others) where balance has been made easier by the replacement of the wheel by a ball. The child needs to be completely steady and certain in her standing and walking before she can manage a barrow. We shall be returning to vehicles of various sorts in chapter 4.

* It turns out to be called a Flying Octopus!

Thinking and Experimenting

During the second and third years of life, and on through childhood, language will develop as a major source of shared understandings with other people about what the world is like, but language alone is not enough: learning comes by doing as well as by listening. Words take on meaning for the child because they provide a running commentary on her own *actions* or those of other people. And here the urge to imitate is important, both as a major factor in the pre-verbal and verbal dialogues between parents and child (Susan Pawlby[5] has commented on how these dialogues seem to 'come alive' at the moment when one of the participants imitates the other), and as a stimulus to further exploration and experimentation by the child on her own.

But the child can't necessarily do something successfully just because she has seen it done – if this were so, we should all become expert in sport just by watching the Olympics on television. Practice is necessary to develop any kind of skill. Much has to be learned by trial and error which cannot be learned in any other way – as the child herself will demonstrate when she first tries to use scissors, prise open a cocoa-tin or unzip a banana. Apart from working out the most economical and effective movements, a child also has to learn to grasp the *logic* of how things work if she is to succeed in imitating all the interesting things that she sees other people do. There is, for example, a great deal that she needs to discover about bigness, heaviness, squashiness, balance and a hundred other deceptively simple ideas which as adults we take for granted when we try to copy someone else's actions. In many cases, understanding only comes by a combination of thinking and doing. How does a child learn that some forms of cloth, like her father's trousers, are firmly anchored so that she can haul herself up on them, whereas others, like a tablecloth, give way?

Actions without words must precede words without actions: concrete manipulation of objects makes a good foundation for abstract manipulation of ideas. A child needs to see numbers in terms of her fingers, or beads or blocks, before she can conceptualize *5 take away 2 leaves 3* as meaningful. The concept of size must be played with and tried out in many different yet related ways before the child is thoroughly at home with it, and her notions are rehearsed through play experiences: Daddy is tall enough to touch the ceiling, but I can only reach it if he lifts me up ... some containers are so tiny that even a little finger won't go in, but some boxes are so big that I can get inside and be hidden. There are puzzles to be solved. How is it that most of me gets inside a flat pullover, but that this square peg won't fit into that round hole however hard I push? How does all that bathwater get out through one tiny plug-hole? ... and (dreadful thought) can I be sure that I won't slip down the hole myself? – especially as I'm littler than the bathwater! Small babies are seldom afraid of plug-holes: to be afraid, the child has to be clever enough to understand 'things go through holes' but *not* clever enough to know that 'water can trickle through a hole, but solid things like my body can't'.

Fitting Toys

The most successful 'concept' toys from about eighteen months on are those which present the child with a puzzle to be solved at a level of understanding only just within her mental grasp: to reiterate, a good toy outpaces the child's development. The actual physical skills needed should not be too difficult, and the result should be immediately satisfying because the child can *see* that her action has paid off. Fitting and slotting toys make demands both on her eye-hand co-ordination and on her logical thinking. Toys with pop-in peg-people are the simplest in terms of shape discrimination, as they are usually all circular in section, but the Escor toys already mentioned provide a good variety of manipulative problems: the interchangeable peg-people have a hole in the base, so that some have to be fitted on to short pegs (soldiers, maypole) while others have to be slotted *into* holes which is easier (most of the smaller vehicles, boat). Some of the larger toys provide both these problems in one toy (large merry-go-round), while some have built-in instability (carousel, maypole, swings) to make the task more difficult and indeed two-handed. The car merry-go-round is still more complicated: the peg-men fit simply into the cars, but each car has two holes to be fitted simultaneously on the roundabout base, which itself then has to be fitted onto its pivot. Lego's Nursery Bricks range has wheeled bases on which to build large-module trucks and vans, and peg-people to ride them: this is a beautifully designed first construction toy, which can also be extended as the child grows.

Shape-posting boxes combine the idea of containers with the notion of matching a shaped *piece* to the same-shaped *hole*: a complicated thought if one is thinking it for the first time! They vary a great deal in how much thought has been given to their design; too often, for instance, it is possible to push a shape through an alternative hole by twisting it around a little, thus defeating the intention of the toy to be self-correcting in teaching shape discrimination, and this needs to be checked when choosing. Other criticisms may be more open to question: for instance, it has been suggested that the Tupperware posting sphere (highly interesting to most children) is unsatisfactory because the child cannot survey and compare all the shapes together; and that shapes should be as near two-dimensional as possible so that the child is not distracted by the side-shapes of the pieces. While not meeting these criteria certainly makes the task more difficult, children do eventually devise strategies for coping; we ourselves become less purist about such matters as we watch children play.

Simple inset puzzles with lift-out pieces in the shape of real objects to complete a picture are the earliest fore-runners of the jigsaw puzzle; some have other pictures behind the lift-out pieces, as in Galt's See-inside inset puzzles, which show the contents of a shop behind its shopfront, and so on. In the case of all these shape-fitting toys it has to be remembered that once the child has mastered the problem – once it holds no mystery or surprise for her, that is – she is likely to lose interest in it. In buying such toys, one therefore needs to ask oneself two questions: how much other play potential has the toy got? or how many children will have access to it? There are many toys (such as inset puzzles) which have a short interest life for the individual child but which will be excellent value for a large family or a playgroup; the posting-box has an extended life because it is interesting as a box to hide things in, as well as for its intended task; and peg-people fitting toys retain still longer interest for symbolic play, just because the pegs *are* people.

Earlier on, we suggested that babies are not very good at finishing games of putting a lot of objects in a tin or piling up towers of bricks because they have no sense of order or system, and therefore keep on interrupting themselves to empty out or knock down. Order becomes more and more interesting and meaningful to a child as time goes on,

and once she's past her second birthday she will begin to want not only to finish what she has started but to make logical sequences and patterns. Nesting cups (or saucepans of different sizes) give her her first concepts of 'big, bigger, biggest', because they will only nest properly in one order; pile-ups give her further experience of size order and sequence. Most nesting toys do in fact also work as pile-ups when turned upside down, and there are many different makes, mostly in polythene, a few in tin (Chad Valley especially well made), and occasional square ones in wood: square nesting boxes are, of course, more difficult for the child than round ones. The set of lidded boxes already mentioned will nest and pile effectively, with the interesting complication of the lids as well. Other nesters are the traditional eggs and dolls in wood from Russia, usually in sets of three or five, although Mr Krushchev gave Queen Elizabeth a set of thirteen; nesting eggs and barrels are also available in plastic from various makers. Nesting toys that pile up as well are usually self-correcting in the sense that they will not pile in the wrong order; but there are many versions of a toy consisting of size-graded rings stacked on a central vertical peg, for which an adult's help is needed at this stage to grasp the principle required. Some of these, mainly the wooden ones, stack into a human or upright animal figure when correctly ordered and topped with head or hat. A similar toy which demands sorting by both number and colour is the Escor graded abacus, in which a row of vertical pegs of graded lengths have to have large wooden balls threaded on them so that the five balls in one colour are stacked on the longest, the four of another on the next longest, and so on down to one.

This toy is much loved by children who are still too young to understand its full implications, but who just like stacking the balls as they come, and that is no disadvantage; the useful life of a toy is much prolonged if it can be played with at a number of different conceptual levels. We should not insist that a child plays with a toy 'correctly', for in working through its different possibilities she will be making her own scientific discoveries. Eventually she is going to need the concepts of categorizing, grading and sorting, into shapes, sizes and so on, in order to acquire the basic skills of reading and writing; but she will need even more the repeated experience that by exploration, maybe in the company of a helpful but not too interfering adult, she has the power to find out things for herself.

4 Some Timeless Toys and Play Equipment

In this chapter we shall consider three groups of toys which are 'timeless' in two senses. They are toys which meet the needs that children have always had: to explore, to invent, to create, to test out their skills, to show off, to stretch their physical limits, to fantasize, to role-play and to act protectively to something less powerful than themselves. They are also toys which grow through time with the child in that, although some may (like his clothes) need to be exchanged as he physically outgrows them, the function of the toy remains valid for him over a very long period of childhood, so that it can be used by him in ways that reflect the stage he has reached in growing up. The three groups we have chosen to look at more closely are firstly the so-called 'big-muscle' toys for 'physical' play; secondly, bricks; and thirdly, dolls.

'Big Muscle' Toys

The nursery education equipment catalogues place heavy emphasis on the need to provide children with toys that exercise their muscles and promote whole-body co-ordination; but if civilized society did not increasingly restrict young children's everyday environment, there would of course be no necessity to organize children's exercise for them. Country children are still able to develop big-muscle co-ordination jumping streams or negotiating stepping-stones, riding a recalcitrant horse (or cow), climbing trees, leaping through heather, slithering down screes or sandhills, scaling tussocky hillsides or rolling down grass slopes. For urban children, trees are likely to be either too small or inaccessible, riding animals hardly exist except for the privileged few, and even lamp posts grow higher and less usable; and the precarious traverse of the urban landscape of walls, roofs, fire-escapes and railway sidings, which might be thought to make up for the loss of more 'natural' adventure space, tends to lead children into unmanageable dangers and therefore to be forbidden. Probably the majority of urban children have seldom or never known the experience of simply running in a space big enough to outlast their own energy; for many pre-school children, freedom to play means a small garden or yard with the gate necessarily closed for their protection; for others, play takes place in a high-rise flat, from which they only emerge to be escorted on shopping expeditions or, if they are lucky, for a brief visit to the park. Urban children, then, need big-muscle toys; although those who need them most, the youngest flat-dwellers, are least likely to get them.

Achieving muscular co-ordination is not just important as an end in itself, but because of the sense of mastery that goes with it. It seems a necessary part of the process of psychological growing-up, as well as physical growing-up, that a child should experience what it is like to be determined to acquire a bodily skill, to practise it in a way that demands thought, persistence and emotional involvement, and eventually to succeed; there is a very basic satisfaction in gaining control of one's own bodily movements, particularly if it costs some effort, and children need to be given plenty of scope for such experiences which enhance their own self-knowledge and self-respect. One writer on children's physical play, Alison Stallibrass, has in fact entitled her book *The Self-Respecting Child*;[1] her observations come both from her own playgroup and from working in the children's gymnasium at the famous Peckham experimental Health Centre. Her concern has been not to *teach* a child skills, but to 'see to it that children have, at every stage, the opportunity to learn to do what they have become newly capable of learning to do . . . [a young child] needs and wants to acquire a more and more precise control over his movement and co-ordination of his sensory, muscular and nervous systems, and he can only do this by moving – in a progressively more adventurous manner – for several hours a day. He needs to encounter all sorts of hazards, obstacles and challenges to his skill, and to be able to decide for himself which to overcome and which to circumvent, and to be entirely responsible for where and how he moves.' Stallibrass describes a toddler climbing and scrambling: 'He is deciding for himself where to place his hands and feet and how to hold his body in order to balance, and he is deciding how far and exactly where to climb; moreover, he is deciding what he will do with his whole body and not only with his hands and his eyes. He feels self-respectingly responsible for himself.'

In some ways these descriptions sound very self-absorbed and indeed we are talking about children at a supremely egotistic period of development, when they are deeply concerned with testing their own possibilities and learning to know their own relationship with their environment, rather than other people's; but in her account of rather older children in the gymnasium, where children were encouraged to do what they liked without adult direction, Stallibrass makes an interesting point about children's social development: that when children were given responsibility and self-confidence in this way, 'a diversity of spontaneous actions resulted in a harmonious whole'. She quotes the initiators of the 'Peckham experiment' in a passage which is worth re-quoting at some length:

Let us study this hub of activity (the gymnasium) from the point of view of a child who goes into it. He goes in and learns unaided to swing and to climb, to balance, to leap. As he does all these things he is acquiring facility in the use of his body. The boy who swings from rope to horse, leaping back again to the swinging rope, is learning by his eyes, muscles, joints and by every sense organ he has, to judge, to estimate, to *know*. The other twenty-nine boys and girls in the gymnasium are all as active as he, some of them in his immediate vicinity. But as he swings he does not *avoid*. He swings *where there is space* – a very important distinction – and in so doing he threads his way among his twenty-nine fellows. Using all his faculties, he is aware of the total situation in that gymnasium – of his own swinging and of his fellows' actions. He does not shout to the others to stop, to wait or to move from him – not that there is silence, for running conversations across the hall are kept up as he speeds through the air.

But this 'education' in the live use of all his senses can only come if his twenty-nine fellows are also free and active. If the room were cleared and twenty-nine boys sat at the side silent while he swung, we should in effect be saying to him – to his legs, body, eyes – 'You give all your attention to swinging; we'll keep the rest of the world away' – in fact – 'Be as egotistical as you like.' By so reducing the diversity in the environment we should be preventing his learning to apprehend and to move in a complex situation. We should in effect be saying – 'Only this and this do; you can't be expected to do more.'

Over and above the experience of mastery and growing self-confidence, big-muscle toys offer sensory experiences which may otherwise be difficult to achieve, but which enrich the child's sensual range. The delicious giddiness after a really good 'twizzy' on a swing with ropes long enough to twist many times round so that the rapid unwinding retwists them in the opposite direction; the pounding of blood to the head as one hangs by the knees from the climbing frame and stays there just a little too long; the vertigo of climbing higher than ever before, and the butterflies in the stomach before jumping off into the deepest space yet; the rush of wind past the ears on a toboggan or go-cart, or furiously pedalling one's first bike; the delicate apprehension of keeping a precarious balance on scooter, roller skates or skate-board, or negotiating a last-minute turn on a tricycle when the brakes don't work: all these experiences (including the jolt and judder of mistimed landings) extend the dimensions of the child's bodily awareness. In the same way, the ambivalence of the child to so many of these stomach-turning sensations – 'Ooh, it was horrible, I'll do it again' – gives him a practical but non-threatening insight into the complexity of human emotions.

For most households there will be limitations, in terms of both money and space, on the amount of big-muscle equipment that can be provided. In deciding what to choose, it may be helpful to consider what kinds of experience different toys basically provide, so that the different kinds of physical activities can all be catered for in one way or another. Thinking about big-muscle toys in these terms, it is soon clear that some toys are more versatile than others, some overlap with others, while some are not very versatile (like roller skates) but at least take up little room. It is also worth taking some thought about which toys are likely to be used in conjunction and thus extend each others' possibilities.

Basically, then, we are looking at toys which offer the experience of climbing; swinging, rocking and bouncing; balance; speed; and precision of movement, as in aiming or the body manoeuvres of complex skipping.

Climbing Equipment

A climbing frame may seem an enormous expense, and indeed an enormous object; it is worth serious consideration, though, especially for a large family, because it is so versatile, so durable, so extendable, and may even prolong its useful life into its owners' adolescence if it has a platform for solitary lazing (or sulking), or if it will support a hammock. Obviously it is there to be climbed upon; but the addition of ropes will give both swinging and a different kind of climbing, planks secured horizontally or set up as a slide will provide extra opportunities

for balancing and sliding, and a hammock gives a gentle rocking motion. There is no need to buy an expensive slide attachment; a smooth plank or two, held safely by a block screwed on under one end, is both more versatile and encourages more adventurous and inventive balancing. Alison Stallibrass described the effects of such a 'makeshift slide' in her playgroup:

> The planks are narrow (8 inches wide) and have no raised edges. This means that the child can go down them in any position – even sideways – and he can control his speed by holding on to the edges of the plank with his hands. If, however, he prefers not to hold on, he must balance on the narrow plank and this requires considerable control and skill, especially in a sitting position ... The children go up in many different ways, crouching, walking, on their stomachs pulling with their hands and pushing with their toes, on their knees pulling with their hands ... [One day two children aged four] had placed the two planks close together ... and had discovered how to slide, first crouching low and finally standing upright on their stockinged feet – neither shoes nor bare feet being slippery enough – in exactly the same manner as a skier descends a snow slope. In the days that followed, as one or two of the other children imitated them, the new 'trick' became one of the traditional skills of the group (and still was eighteen months later).[1]

In choosing a climbing frame, we need to check how possible it is to attach these various accessories; equally important, we should look at its potentiality for imaginative, role-playing activities. Some climbing frames have a hinged door set into them at a low level, encouraging children to use the structure as a house; more useful, in our experience, is a platform higher up with the possibility of making some kind of roof over it. Good-Wood of Sussex, a firm which, alas, no longer exists, used to make a 'climbing cottage': a well-thought-out example whose basic structure included platforms with a rope ladder as an alternative way of reaching them, and a sloping roof frame above; a tent to fit this could be bought as an optional extra, or one could simply use a blanket to enclose the cottage-on-stilts. Even quite a small climbing frame can be adapted as a play house, provided its shape allows; the very basic ESA tent frame, as its name implies, lends itself well to such use, but also allows for a low slide and toddler's swing. But there seems to be special pleasure in a play house whose height gives it a feeling of inaccessibility to outsiders; we shall say more about this in the next chapter.

To be a house or a castle is not the only function of a climbing frame in children's fantasy play, however. For instance, Kathleen Manning and Ann Sharp, who write on play from a much more interventionist viewpoint than Alison Stallibrass, describe a sequence of activities initiated one morning by the same group of nine five-year-olds: first the climbing frame was a cage, in which some of the children were lions while others fed them with red pieces of Lego for meat; then the scene shifted to the climbing frame as boat, in which the lions were being taken home to Africa (not without some uncertainty as to role):

Warren: Come on, we're taking the lions home. No, you can't come on the ship.
Ann: Why? I'm playing with you – I'm one of the lions.
Andrew: You don't get girls on ships.[2]

Finally there was a further metamorphosis into a rocket going to Mars to fight monsters. In our own Research Unit playroom, we have seen the climbing frame become a hospital, a jungle, a prison, a throne, a mountain, a tree, a look-out post and a sheriff's office – as well as, quite simply, a climbing frame.

Our playroom climbing frame, a large one, is nevertheless not as dominating as we expected it to be; one need not be immediately put off by not having a garden. Some designers have incorporated children's

beds, or desks and cupboards, into the structure of a climbing frame for a child's room, and it's certainly worth looking at the room with this in mind; probably most rooms waste the top four feet of space. Even if you have neither the skill nor the money to design and build-in from scratch, imaginative making-over of battered but solid junk (taken apart if necessary) will probably cost less than conventional new furniture and have immeasurably more play value, and this applies equally to small rooms. For instance, faced with a nine-foot square room for two children, we made staggered six-foot bunks in a strong wood framework, filled the spaces underneath with two cupboards, two big drawers and two little drawers (drawers and cupboard doors taken from an old and ugly chest), and thus crammed sleeping and storage all into two and a half feet along one wall; fitted with a ladder, staggered bunks give considerably more play scope than ordinary ones. We might well have left the top cupboard doorless as a hidey-hole for this 'climbing frame', but our children chose to set it out as a dolls' room; we might also have used a much stouter post, perhaps extending to the ceiling, and set pegs in it for climbing. We did have a slide for a while, alongside the ladder as an alternative, but later the children preferred to use it as a quick way out from the (ground-floor!) window-sill to the garden. Add an old mattress on the floor, and you have a soft landing, a bouncing/rolling/somersaulting place, and, once again, a potential boat or bus or magic carpet at will.

Swinging and Bouncing

Swings, rope ladders and ropes all give opportunities for both swinging and climbing, and can as well be attached to a tree, as a climbing frame, if a big enough one is available. It is infinitely preferable to have several hung side by side, both for companionable swinging and for up-one-down-the-other possibilities; if this really can't be arranged, at least have fastenings that allow interchange. Within reason, the longer the ropes of a swing the better (and they should also be thick enough to get a good grip on), since they can then be used for climbing up (one hand and one foot on each rope), or for turning somersaults between the ropes. Alternative seats are old car or scooter tyres, hung either vertically or horizontally. A hammock makes a successful swing, hung either in its normal position or doubled up. Strong elastic luggage grips, used several thicknesses at a time for additional strength and incorporated at the upper end of a rope, add an exciting bouncing movement: not only babies like bouncers.

See-saws are one of those 'natural' toys that must have been around for as long as there have been planks to borrow and solid objects to pivot them on. They teach a child useful lessons about balance and distribution of weight, but they need supervision where children too young to be thoughtful about the consequences of their actions are playing together: both because the 'bottom' child is very apt to jump off on impulse, leaving the top child to come crashing down, and because one child may equally jump on without looking, making the other end swing violently up to crack the chin of his prospective partner. See-saws as such also take up a great deal of room if they are permanently set up, and our own feeling would be to provide the materials for building makeshift see-saws, leaving the excitement of the real thing to be enjoyed on a trip to the park. Rocking boats are another matter: they have a similar action to see-saws, involve two children together, and can be endlessly used as an adjunct to fantasy play. The rocking horse, a more private toy, is discussed in our final chapter.

Getting Around

The sensations of travelling at speed, while approached briefly by swings and slides, come most vividly by way of wheeled toys; although we must also mention the toboggan. Most child owners of toboggans in temperate climates will have experienced the frustration of waiting all winter through for a good crisp snow which never comes, or having come will not last; perhaps, if you cannot count on snow, it is better to spend the money on an all-weather go-cart, and make sure you have a good big tin tray stacked away to greet the snow if it does arrive. One of us at least can testify that a tin tray gives an extremely exciting ride, not least because there is very little to hold on to; it can also be used successfully on grass slopes and sandhills, where toboggans tend to dig themselves in.

Go-carts are the nearest thing to toboggans on wheels, traditionally being made without brakes and steered partly by a rope to the front axle and partly by a lurch of the body and a ramming of one or many feet against the road surface: braking is achieved in a similar way, which is one reason why parents with a respect for shoe-leather tend to have an antipathy for 'proper' go-carts. A proper go-cart is home-made with old pramwheels and spare lumber; it is thus usually owned by older children who expect to live dangerously, and is essentially a street toy. One can also buy very grand commercial models in steel on a similar scale. So classic is the traditional design, however, that nursery toy manufacturers have sensibly been glad to copy it in wood with minor changes: for instance, Good-Wood's Nipper train (no longer available) allows several to be coupled together. While this hardly approaches the rakish panache of the original, it has the advantage of not falling to pieces at the bottom of the hill, an exciting habit of the older model.

Tricycles, scooters and bicycles are probably the most widely used vehicles during childhood. The first tricycle is often powered by a scooting action of foot to ground, having no pedals: it hardly qualifies as a 'speed' toy, usually moving rather more slowly than its driver would walk, but it gives a first introduction to the joys of steering a vehicle rather than just one's own feet. Pedals, the next stage in nursery tricycles, are usually attached to the front wheel in these small trikes: one of us still remembers in her bones the stiffness and resistance of their action, and what a joy it was to move on to a proper chain-driven tricycle. Scooters form an introduction to the more certain balance required by a real bicycle, though some of them cheat by having two wheels instead of one at the back. These are in fact useful for children whose co-ordination and balance are rather poor, but most will quickly learn to cope with the ordinary version, which is a better preparation for a bicycle. The very best have bouncy balloon tyres with an inner tube; avoided by playgroups because of the nuisance of punctures under very hard wear, they are more expensive but much more fun* (and less likely to be despised by those neighbourhood children who already have bicycles). It is worth advertising for a second-hand one if money is short, because they are durable and will usually outlast several children.

When we were studying 700 Nottingham children at the age of

* These scooters are fun for adults, too, as you can see if you go to Copenhagen airport, where they are provided for aircrew and passengers as an exciting and functional alternative to walking along those long covered avenues to and from the planes.

seven, we found that riding around on bikes or scooters was the single most popular outdoor activity at this age; however, very few of the children were actually allowed to go anywhere on them, and we concluded that the main purpose of having a bike at seven is not to travel from one place to another, but simply for the exhilaration of 'just swizzing round the close', as one mother put it.[3]

For very young children, there are of course a number of other 'vehicles' which can be scooted along while sitting astride, and whose point, like the first tricycle, lies not in speed but simply in being perched upon wheels. These come in the form of large engines, airplanes, lorries, tractors or simple trucks. To take a child's weight, solid wood is much more durable than plastic, and correspondingly more expensive; there are also a few metal vehicles that can be sat on, the Canadian firm of Tonka being outstanding. Apart from general durability, look at the wheels: hollow plastic will probably crack before the child outgrows the toy, while some wheels are so set that it is extremely difficult to manoeuvre the vehicle round a curve or steer it out of corners. The same applies to couplings if the vehicle has a trailer: make sure they allow room for the vehicle to take a curve easily. These problems are sometimes solved by replacing all or some wheels with castors or designing one axle to swivel, which certainly makes for a less frustrated driver. Huntercraft make a beautifully sturdy two-person bus, using both castors and wheels. It is worth considering that any kind of platform on castors is a lot of fun for a small child; one might try copying the old tyre on castors which appears (expensively) in the nursery school catalogues, or fixing castors to any solid piece of wood available – rounding the corners or buffering them if used indoors. A skateboard is a joy, even if the child uses it on his tummy rather than upright. (The obvious danger of skateboards used without protective clothing and in busy streets is another question.)

Finally there are the toys which are accessories to big-muscle activity and take up little room in themselves. Most children will have access to a ball and a skipping rope; fewer have roller skates, hoops and stilts.

Balls develop the skill of aiming, whether in throwing, catching or kicking. In general, remember that a variety of balls will help the child to adapt his skill to different weights and sizes, and that the younger the child, the larger the ball he will need to make up for his lack of accuracy.

If there is a shortage of people to play ball with him, he may appreciate something to aim at: a set of giant plastic skittles, or later a target chalked on the back wall or a 'goal' net strung up in the garden. Balloons and bubbles add a slow-motion dimension to aiming; most children love to pop bubbles as they float down.

In choosing a skipping rope, its length must be suitable to the user: he should be able to stand on the rope while holding the handles in either hand, arms horizontal. Most skipping ropes can be shortened at the handle; they are so cheap that it is worth spending a little bit extra for ball bearings in the handles which make the rope turn freely. Both balls and skipping ropes have a long history of solitary play as well as group play (see page 235); both have gathered a multitude of rhymes and incantations to accompany the turning of the rope or bouncing of ball against wall.[4] In our study we found that boys tended to play group games of ball, such as football, whereas it was the girls who played the more solitary chanting-and-bouncing games. Both ball-bouncing and skipping seem to be considered 'girls'' games by boys – we found skipping second-favourite outdoor activity for girls at seven, but nowhere for boys – so it is interesting that Strutt, who wrote a description of the *Sports and Pastimes of the People of England* in 1801, says that 'boys often contend for superiority of skill in this game [skipping], and he who passes the rope about most times, without interruption, is conqueror'.

Stilts and roller skates both add power to the user: the former in terms of height and stride, the latter in speed (once he is in control!). Roller skates are usually made in metal with ball-bearing wheels finished with a layer of hard rubber. They should be adjustable both in length and in width. We have seen small-sized ones made in strong plastic – not as unsuitable as it might seem, as the wheels are less free-running and therefore do not run away with a young child whose balance is less sure. Stilts should also be adjustable for height of the foot-piece; younger children will find them easier to balance on in the earlier stages if they straighten their arms to hold the stilts low down, allowing the top part to come behind the armpit. When we were young, we made things-to-walk-tall-on out of empty syrup tins, the lids hammered well on, holding them on to our feet as we walked with long loops of string threaded through holes pierced in the top of the sides. One firm (Orchard Toys) now produce a commercial version of this, which they call 'skilts': they are made from strong compressed-cardboard cylinders cut from the cores on which newsprint is rolled (which would otherwise go to waste), and very good substitutes for syrup tins they are.

Pogo sticks are an interesting variant of stilts: the single stick has a foot ledge on either side, above a rubber-tipped telescopic end controlled by a heavy spring, and the user, once he has got the hang of it, bounces along in fine style. In the twenties there was a craze for pogo sticks, akin to those for yo-yos and hula hoops in other years; nowadays they are seldom seen in the street, though they are still being made – indeed, the British toy trade directory listed four makers in 1977, compared with only two in 1970. A more recent invention, the Space-hopper, is a bouncing toy for the younger child: basically an enormous ball for sitting on, with handles on top, it gives the child irresistible kangaroo-power. Hoops have a long and oddly varied history; Breughel's famous picture of children's games (1560) shows a child prising one from a barrel in order to join his friends with theirs. A hundred years ago, boys rattled small iron hoops along, while girls made do with larger but more quietly ladylike wooden ones. Wood is rarely used today, but plastic has brought colour to hoops and kept them cheap, while its lightness makes it possible to use hoops for gyrations and skipping as well as for bowling along.

Alison Stallibrass in her book draws attention to the two-way interaction between child and environment and describes the child as 'digesting' through his activity the experiences he chooses to attend to: 'the product of this digestive process is new and original because it is specific to the unique personality of the child'.[1] She makes the important point that diversity in the environment promotes the growth of the individuality of each child, which in turn promotes the growth of environmental diversity and so onward: 'each child contributes to the total amount of nourishment available to all'. In budgeting for large play equipment, diversity is a useful concept to bear in mind: buy second-hand, extend possibilities with old rugs and planks and boxes and miscellaneous junk materials and brighten up the collection with a lick of paint or polyurethane and the odd new piece where you can manage it; far better than sinking every penny into one expensive slide or see-saw to stand alone in sterile grandeur.

Bricks

Parents who, as children, enjoyed playing with floor-bricks will probably take it for granted that bricks* must be provided as basic items of nursery equipment. Other parents might want to think carefully before buying them. An adequate set of bricks can be a fairly expensive investment (though no more so than a doll's pram or a tricycle); and the children who use them will demand a considerable amount of storage and floor space, both of which may be difficult to contrive.

Perhaps the first point to be made about any set of bricks is that there should be enough of them. It is very discouraging to set out on a grand design, only to discover, in the full flush of creativity, that one has run out of bricks. Experience with our own three children has led us to the conclusion that 100 bricks, plus halves, pillars and miscellaneous shapes, is an absolute minimum, and that a set of 200 enormously widens the child's scope.

The size and material of the individual bricks are also a matter of some practical importance. They need to be large enough to have the kind of weight and solidity that the child can feel in the hand, particularly when it comes to understanding why some structures are unstable, and how the fault can be corrected. Yet, at the same time, they must be small enough to be handled comfortably by younger children. For 'brick-shaped' bricks (and they must be brick-shaped: cubes, the easiest bricks to buy, are really only fit for babies to chew), a length of about four inches seems to be about right.

What does the child learn from playing with bricks? Probably a great variety of things, according to his age. One of the biggest learning achievements of the first three years is to use hands and eyes together in effortless co-operation, and to control the muscles so finely that this 'soft machine' – the body – will carry out the brain's order with a high degree of exactness. The toddler who picks up a brick delicately with a pincer movement of finger and thumb, transfers it accurately to a point in space immediately above another brick, and sets it down without upsetting the structure, is undergoing a highly distilled learning experience in a most complex skill.

* US usage: blocks.

Concentration and persistence are learned qualities which brick-play encourages; the more ambitious the building plans, the more time and effort and patience must be expended by the child. A set of bricks is not so much a toy as a raw material upon which the child imposes his personality and will. Parents who give bricks need to realize that such a present should also imply a promise of respect and tolerance for precious but half-finished creations, which must be left undisturbed until they are complete. If you want a tidy floor more than a creative child, don't give floor-bricks.

Wood still seems to be the only really practicable material in which to make floor-bricks, though a family we know did acquire a sack of marble off-cuts from a friendly stonemason. Hollow rubber and plastic should be avoided at any price: as bricks they are a contradiction in terms, their lightness frustrating the most painstaking attempt to build a stable structure. (This criticism does not apply to small interlocking plastic bricks, such as Lego; but interlocking bricks are a quite different kind of toy, anyway, and almost none of this applies to them. See p. 135.) Provided it is splinter-free, a good hardwood is better than a softwood, in terms of both weight and durability. Good hardwood bricks are expensive to buy, not just for the cost of the wood itself, but for the labour involved in sanding and polishing. One way of saving money is to get them cut to size by a machine-joiner, and then to sand

and polish them yourself – though you may find that this labour of love is not greatly prized by the recipients, particularly if they begin to play with them before you have finished.

One of the special virtues of floor-bricks is that they can be used as adjuncts to many different kinds of play. This is one reason why they are equally suitable for boys and girls, despite the fact that girls do tend to be less interested in constructional toys (see ch. 6, note 3). Our own daughters at eight and eleven often played a game in which they acted as teachers to their very large family of dolls; and every doll would be provided with a desk and chair made with floor-bricks. In the same way, bricks can be used by children of either sex to create the basic framework for a farm, a fairground, a museum or a landscape.

Bricks also have versatility over a very broad age-range. At nine months the baby bangs a brick on the floor, at a year he holds one in each hand and claps them together with a satisfying 'clonk'. At two he is making a tower or a train, at three he builds a bridge. We once watched our three children all playing together among the bricks: the baby banged away happily, and joyfully pushed down the towers which her father piled up for her; the four-year-old had made a roadway lay-out, and was organizing a heavy traffic-flow of Matchbox cars; and the seven-year-old also had a road-system – but in his case the removal of a paving-stone revealed a complicated arrangement of sewage-pipes and manholes underneath. Bricks adapt themselves most flexibly to the conceptual level of the child playing with them. And, with an age-range of roughly twelve months to twelve years, they probably have the longest life of any toy (barring the beloved teddy or favourite doll); this means that, in terms of hours of play for money spent, they are a very good investment indeed.

Abstract Thinking

The 'nondescript' quality of bricks moreover allows the child to give substance and shape to his imaginative ideas – in a sense, offers him a technique for expressing himself. Adults at the dining-table sometimes adopt a similar technique when they use the cutlery and tableware to illustrate a wartime campaign or to give complicated geographical directions. In our own research playroom, we recently saw a university teacher using a set of miniature bricks in precisely this way to explain some theoretical point to a student. Alan, a gifted three-year-old, invented maps for himself using floor-bricks to plan out his neighbourhood; his parents did not realize what they were until he started drawing the same patterns on paper. In fact, this ability to represent our thinking about 'real' events by the use of maps or models, in which the elements are arranged to symbolize various things in complex relationships, is exceptionally important biologically. It seems to form the basis for all scientific and mathematical thinking.

Of course, it would be ridiculous to suggest that the possession of a set of bricks will automatically induce a high level of conceptual skill in a child. But it is probably true that children who learn to play imaginatively with this sort of material will get a lot of useful practice in that kind of thinking from a comparatively early age.

Both for their effectiveness as building units and for their ability to spark off conceptual insights, the most satisfactory bricks are those which have simple modular properties, so that they can be made to fit together in an exceptionally large variety of ways. From this point of view, the majority of the bricks in a set should have the same basic shape. Cubes are impractical and unsatisfying in all sorts of ways; our own choice would be oblong bricks of the special type which H. G. Wells invented for his children (and for himself). The proportions in H. G. Wells's bricks are such that the length is twice the width, and the width is twice the thickness; and, although this results in bricks with oblong faces which may fail to satisfy the aesthetic purist because they do not correspond very closely to the 'golden section' (width = 0.618 of the length), these bricks undoubtedly score over other types in terms of the flexibility and versatility of the structures which can be built with them. The clarity and simplicity of their modular principle ($1 : \frac{1}{2} : \frac{1}{4}$) assumes even greater importance when we look at bricks from the strictly educational standpoint, as materials with built-in mathematical properties. Many modern educationists take the view that a conceptually rich play environment is essential for the successful mastery of formal mathematical concepts later on. Following Piaget, they suggest that children need to have *played with* mathematical ideas as part of their practical concrete experience, before they are ready to cope with a more abstract presentation.

Geoffrey Matthews, who organized the Nuffield Mathematics

Project for five to thirteen-year-olds, was asked how a set of bricks might help a child understand mathematical ideas; this was his reply:

The important thing to realise is that the understanding of certain mathematical ideas cannot be achieved through teaching. Children have to arrive at them through years of varied experience with many kinds of materials. Bricks are a very powerful tool in their hands.

To give some examples: before children grasp what numbers mean they need practical experience of 'ordering' and 'inclusion': as when three bricks are part of a collection of five bricks. This understanding precedes knowing that three is less than five. Primary schools provide activities like sorting out spills into size order to see whether children can make a comparison of length. A set of bricks gives children experiences of inequalities early on – this wall is longer than that one, but not as long as that.

They encounter addition by using two bricks to make the same height as one larger brick: this and this together make up that. And so do these. This is the same kind of activity that primary school children will be doing when they use several combinations of weights to weigh five ounces: five one-ounce weights, a four and a one, two two's and a one. And it's part of the understanding of measurement to accept a system whereby differing numbers of small units are equivalent to a larger unit. Children have direct experience of this when they build two pillars to support an arch – one made up of a single long pillar, the other made up of four squat ones.

Then again, 'invariance' or 'conservation' is a very difficult concept for children to grasp – conservation of number, that five sweets are always five whether they're in a small pile or spread out in a long line; of length, that two rods are the same length whether you place them like this ———— or like this ————; of area, that six plywood slats have the same covering power no matter how they are placed; of volume, that six small cubes take up the same amount of space however they are arranged. As children play with bricks they naturally use these ideas in making structures. They don't elicit the mathematical idea from the situation, of course. But when they meet the idea later on at school, this background of practical experience makes it probable that they'll grasp it fairly easily.

Finally, it's clear that children need to build up a vocabulary of words to describe different mathematical situations and relationships. All children use the word 'big'. They need to refine this, so that high, low, far, near, long, deep, wide, tall, up and down, are also meaningful to them. Language growth is fostered in play situations. If a mother encourages a child to talk about the structures he builds with bricks, this vocabulary can be built up. A child who can say that this tower is tall, but that another tower is taller, is getting to grips with mathematics.

But the best possible reason for investing in a set of floor-bricks is surely the simplest one: that it will give the children so many hours of pleasure all through the years of childhood. There are just a few toys – the swing, the sandpit – which seem to appeal at a very basic level to children of all ages, who return to them with fresh enthusiasm over and over again. A well-designed set of wooden bricks belongs in this select company.

Not only can they be used to build conventional isolated structures such as houses: they can be extended to produce whole layouts for use with other toys. They are ideal for noisy games in which elaborate structures are blown up or blasted down with a delicious crash. But they are equally suitable for quiet play where the enjoyment lies entirely in invention and construction. Beyond this, resourceful children will devise endless games in which bricks find uses as stepping-stones, pathways in a maze, skittles or marble alleys.

Perhaps one should add, though, that it is only by having bricks around, and by taking their existence for granted as part of the essential furniture, that the child will learn to use them profitably in all these ingenious ways. To the child without experience in this form of play, a pile of similar pieces of wood may not seem immediately attractive. Sometimes the possibilities have to be demonstrated, at least to the extent of getting him started; though once bricks are in the family, the younger children will learn from the eldest. When a child gets hooked on floor-bricks, his pleasure in them is likely to be enduring, often right through to when he becomes a father, and the cycle begins all over again.

Dolls and Furry Creatures

Dolls, unlike other playthings, have always been recognized by adults as having special significance for their owner. Perhaps this is partly because, in many parts of the world, and over long periods of history, the ownership of dolls has been as much an adult characteristic as a childish one, and has been deeply bound up with adult beliefs, desires and fears. Most of the oldest 'dolls' still surviving in museums were never children's toys at all, nor intended to be, but were made and used for religious or magical purposes; such dolls would have been considered too sacred or too dangerous for a child to play with.[5] For instance, it would seem a little risky to hand over to their small sisters the fertility doll which is still tucked into the garments of hopeful young women in some parts of Africa; and the giving to children of religious images which have been used in holy places has usually been associated with the plundering of such shrines by enemies, and seen as a deliberate insult, although small votive dolls used in festivals have sometimes been passed on to children after the festival period has ended.

Because the primitive dolls that survive have usually been objects of adult veneration (which indeed explains their survival), some historians[6] have suggested that the doll as children's plaything only exists in civilized societies. It may well be that in primitive societies adults do not manufacture dolls for children; but this is a different issue from whether children play with doll-objects which they have fashioned for themselves. Given the enormous fascination which the pattern eyes-nose-mouth-in-a-face has for very young infants, and the early age at which small children are prepared to behave 'as if' peg-people had human qualities (as we shall see in chapter 5), it would be very surprising if children were *not* reminded of people by the human-shaped objects they come across – knobbed and forked twigs, a spoon, a pestle, a seed-head on its stalk – and if they did not proceed to develop such thoughts by walking the twig along the ground, wrapping the spoon in a rag, or piercing mouth and eyes into the seed-head. To be loved and used by a child is not conducive to survival, even for less makeshift dolls – as the well-kissed flattened mouths of some of the wax babies in our museums can testify.

The older civilizations have passed down manufactured dolls which are much more toylike in their everyday look and their jointed limbs to make dressing and undressing possible – together with some which are more ambiguous. For instance, dolls found in children's graves have been regarded as evidence of children's doll-play; but the fact that many of them represent adult female figures, often with children in their arms, suggests a more protective purpose than a plaything for a dead child. Some are, however, more like our own idea of the doll to whom the child can play mother. Perhaps a better source of evidence is literature, and both Greek and Roman literature includes references to the selling of dolls to children in the market place, and to children's play with their dolls. The comparatively frequent mention of dolls by these

writers emphasizes their recognized significance: indeed, for both Greek and Roman children, they symbolized childhood itself; girls were expected formally to relinquish them when they became betrothed, and to mark this moment of growing up by dedicating their dolls (and their dolls' belongings) to Artemis or Aphrodite, or (for Roman girls) Venus or the household gods. Moving nearer to our own times, it has been very usual, from the sixteenth century onward, for portraits of little girls (though seldom little boys) to show a doll in the child's hands; it seems reasonable to assume a happy agreement between painter and sitter, the painter appreciating the doll's function as an ikon of childhood, the child simply pleased to share the immortality of portraiture with her own darling child.

Gwen White, in her scholarly book of dolls for collectors, points out that 'The collecting of dolls is different from collecting inanimate objects such as plates or lace, for *dolls when looked at can look back,* and many hoard dolls simply because they cannot bear the idea of parting from them'[7] (authors' italics). Perhaps this is the crux of the doll's potency as a symbol, whether as a symbol of religious belief, or of childhood, or simply of life. There is a compelling ambiguity about the alive-ness of dolls, exemplified in the small girl who hushed someone's remark about her doll with the reproof, 'I've been trying all my life to keep that doll from knowing she's not real.' Adults themselves, as Gwen White suggests, are drawn into this ambiguity, and not only in the child's presence either. Parents find themselves putting clothes on dolls which have been left around naked by their owners, not just to tidy up, but because the dolls look so cold; one mother commented on how 'companionable' she found her child's Sasha doll, and remarks of this kind are common among parents buying dolls in this particular range.

At this point we must explicitly bring soft toy animals into the discussion; in so far as they are humanized, in the sense of being endowed by child and parents with human qualities, including the ability to 'look back', to communicate and to receive communications, they share the function of companion and friend, protector and protected, in the child's 'reference group' – that is, the group of people (or sort-of-people) to whom he turns for one need or another.

It is the very ambiguity of being a sort-of-person rather than an actual person which allows the child such freedom to make of the doll or creature whatever he wishes, to suit his moment-to-moment needs. Real people are not so accommodating: they have their own personalities and make their own demands. But dolls and teddy-bears are tolerant of their owners' whims. They will suffer neglect for a while without recrimination, so that the child need feel no guilt; they are there to respond lovingly to his affection and sympathetically to his miseries; they are discreet recipients of his confidences, including his anger about people to whom he may not show anger; if he feels nurturant and protective, they will reflect his warmth; if he is in bossy and domineering mood, they will not, like his human friends, resent him for it, but will accept the subservient role for as long as he needs them to. Similarly, just because the creature is a sort-of-person rather than a fully rounded personality in its own right, it is able to become identified with the child in ways which are useful to him, serving as an extension to the child's own personality and acting as mouthpiece or perhaps scapegoat for feelings that the child does not wish to acknowledge as his own: 'Teddy doesn't like that new baby.' One of our daughters at four years had a doll, Susanna (her own second name, incidentally), who was the constant subject of her conversation, to such an extent that we conceived the idea of interviewing her as a mother about her upbringing of Susanna, using the interview schedule that we were currently using with mothers of four-year-olds. The transcript of this interview is published as an appendix to that study;[8] it vividly illustrates the use that a small child can make of a doll in trying out and playing with her own and other people's feelings and behaviours. Who is talking about whom in this answer to the question, 'Is there anything else Susanna is afraid of?'?

'Er – yes – when she's in bed, she says "I'm frightened of a lion coming in the night!" – and that's not true. It won't, will it? She puts her head under the blanket so the lion can't get her; and I say "It's not true, there isn't a lion". And she really *knows* there aren't a lion, truly, and she's making a joke and *thinking* it is. So I try to tell her, there's *no* wolf and there's *no* animals, and they're not *anywhere*, and I know there perfectly *aren't*, I know very well, don't I?'

In this example the child takes a helpful look at her own fears from the brave standpoint of motherhood: in comforting her doll, she both opens up the subject to discussion without having to admit to fearing something which rationally she 'knows there perfectly aren't', and reassures her private self. Some children develop protective qualities in the creature itself, deriving their own strength from living in its aura. Elizabeth Longford described the youngest of her eight children as choosing 'a large grey donkey on wheels – his first Christmas present – on which to build his fantasy. "Donkey", as he was prosaically called, grew from being an ordinary toy into a kind of superman. He had a birthday every day, was several hundred years old (instead of being the youngest) and had millions of pennies of his own (instead of getting a penny a week).'[9]

There are very close parallels here between the uses children make of dolls and soft toys and the ways they will use real animals, if they have the opportunity, or totally imaginary creatures. Our own children were fortunate in having a wise old tabby cat to commune with, who would whisper kindly in their ear when they needed it; when she died, the rather flighty young cat who was left could not really substitute for her benevolence, although just as affectionate. One of the children we studied at four years old was very fond of a dog, Tilly, belonging to another family; his mother told us 'this is a terrific personality, this dog ... they're coming to stay and we said "Maybe while they're here we'll go out in the evening"; and he said "Oh, yes. Well, if I want anything I'll call Tilly and she'll make my cocoa".'[8] A child in our study of seven-year-olds had an imaginary 'mate' called Lion; his mother said,

'He had had to wait [for me] that evening – and he told me that Lion had said I wasn't dead – so you could tell which way *his* mind was made up! I was late coming in, and he thought I might have had an accident, but Lion told him that I hadn't, so it was a good job Lion was there.'[3]

But not all children have suitable real animals available, and not all are able to give form to their fantasies as clearly as Lion's protegé; dolls and soft toys continue to be needed. Children do, of course, differ in how much they want to play with them, and how far they get carried away by their fantasy; some are very down-to-earth and seem quite uninterested in this kind of play. Having provided opportunities, there is obviously no point in pressing fantasy on a child who merely regards you as foolish. There are also big differences in the kind of creature that appeals to the individual child: one of our daughters had an enormous family of dolls and was barely interested in animals, while the other could hardly squeeze into her bunk for the array of furry animals, and had others hibernating in every cranny of her room; and our son was moderately fond of four plush animals, but really lavished his affection and fantasy on a cheap vinyl glove-puppet cat picked up at a fairground. In making suggestions about what to look for in dolls and furry creatures, then, we must add the reminder not to be too disappointed if, having spent time, thought and money on choosing the perfect companion for your child, you find him in love with some lumpy monstrosity from a jumble-sale.

Choosing a Doll

Obviously parents have preferences as well as children, and much will depend on what appeals to you personally: we can only offer a few guidelines. If you are choosing a first doll for a child, you will be looking for safety, naturally; nowadays, this is usually covered by regulations. Think about the size of the child, and look for a doll which will fit the child's arms comfortably: that means, not so big that he will look like a hedge-sparrow coping with a baby cuckoo, but not so small that the doll makes an unsatisfying armful. For a first doll you will probably be looking for a baby or toddler that a small child can feel happy doing things for; older-looking dolls can follow.

Most dolls have hair nowadays, rather than just moulded indications of it; it is not always easy to tell how well the hair is going to stand up to wear and whether it will end up as sordid matting. The safest bet is recommendation of a manufacturer from someone who has had one of their dolls for a year or more. Sasha dolls' hair is particularly good, although the baby dolls are a little too small to be cuddly.

A difficult decision is whether to buy a soft-bodied doll. A doll with vinyl limbs and head and a cloth body combines practicality (for keeping clean the parts that are left uncovered) with cuddliness: these dolls settle naturally into their owners' arms. On the other hand, they cannot be bathed, which some children feel to be a distinct disadvantage. A rag doll is limited in the same way.

An ever-pressed toy trade yearly produces new and sensational features in its dolls, which can currently be bought with built-in bladder-systems, drinking, speaking, scowling, crying, walking, writing, hair-growing, dancing, singing, head-shaking and so on – though not all at once. Sleeping eyes were patented in 1854, although moving eyes were known as early as 1636; swimming dolls were produced a century ago. No doubt someone is working on perspiration. Although such dolls have novelty value (and maybe status value) for the older child, we would look for simplicity in the first and basic doll, in order to give more scope for the child's own imagination (and less mechanism to go wrong). Apart from sleeping eyes, the most useful and simple special feature we have seen in a doll is in the Matchbox gripping doll, which will hold small objects (even a piece of paper) in her hand. A few dolls are designed with joints tight enough to stop the bathwater getting inside: helpful if your child's dolls seem to spend most of the time legless and draining at the bathside.

As children get older, they are likely to develop very definite ideas about what they like and what they do not in a doll; so that, if the doll is to be a surprise, it may at least be sensible to make a conversational trip round the shops to sound out the child's preferences. These may not be at all obvious; our small daughter very early rejected the film-star wide-eyed look, and longed for 'peepy-eyed' dolls, which at the time were hardly being produced except in Italy; still more puritanical, she moved on to softly painted eyes well before the advent of Sasha dolls made sleeping eyes seem slightly exhibitionist. Sasha dolls were developed by the Designer Sasha Morgenthaler to represent a child of somewhat indeterminate race; their complexion has a delicate tan and their features are softly moulded with ambiguous expressions so that one can ascribe to them whatever personalities and emotions one pleases. Black dolls have now joined the family. The Sasha baby can be bought with clearly masculine genitalia; the boy doll, oddly enough, cannot. Sasha dolls must be the outstanding design to span the decades; they remain virtually unchanged since Morgenthaler's early productions of the fifties, and seem to be outside fashion.[10] The children who buy them have a single-minded air, and they are clearly habit-forming in child and parent.

We have not discussed here the smaller dolls directed at an older market which are basically designed to sell large numbers of accessories to their owners: Sindy, Barbie, Action Man and so on. Although these dolls certainly have a place in the child's life, they seem to us more in the nature of miniatures and collection objects than companions and friends; we shall return to them, therefore, in chapter 6.

Furry Creatures

Although children usually have room in their hearts for several toy animals, it is likely that one will become pre-eminent, retaining its special place in the child's affection even into his adulthood. We once asked a group of university students how many had brought their teddies or other animals to university with them, a question which produced a substantial number of shame-faced admissions. As with dolls, parents cannot decide which toy will be the most loved; it is rather likely to be one which arrived so early in the child's life that he can hardly remember being given it,[11] so that it is certainly worth taking some thought over such a gift to a very young child.

A cuddly toy must basically be cuddly; obvious, perhaps, but this means that the fit of the toy against the child's chest needs to be considered. If the animal has four stiff legs sticking out from the four corners of its abdomen, it will be very difficult to cuddle satisfactorily. This may be one reason why the teddy bear is so successful: built to stand on hind legs, nothing impedes a hug between itself and its owner. If the animal is likely to be the child's constant companion, it had better not be too big to fit into the bed (or to take in car or bus), but, like the basic doll, it needs to be big enough to be an armful for the toddler.

There is something to be said for extreme softness and floppiness – a shape that will mould to the shoulder, tuck under an arm or settle itself down in any position. Our own favourite as a long-term friend is a 'tiger' made by Vera Small; by reputation fierce, its expression is as soft as butter, as is its floppy body, and, hugged to a child's shoulder, it will arrange its arms comfortingly around his neck. One imagines it could also be a reassuringly brave companion if need arose.

This cuddly is made in modacrylic 'fur' with Dacron/polyester filling, and is washable and quick-drying; both will, of course, be important considerations for a toy that is going to be much used: to quote another mother in our study, 'His teddy bear's never left his side since he was nine months old – he dropped it in his bath once, and we couldn't get it dry; and for two nights we had to nurse him to sleep, he was in such a state.'

Later soft toys can be both less intimate and more physically unyielding. The beautiful lion made by Jungle Toys, his eyes apparently fixed on some distant savannah, is too dignified to be cuddly; his role is more like that of the wise old cat or the donkey on

wheels that we mentioned earlier, a mentor and power figure. At the other end of the scale, a pocket creature – mouse, lambkin or tiny teddy – can act as a secret and magical 'familiar'.

Not every child wants to talk bear-language, or to drift off to sleep in the arms of a tiger. Some, indeed, fill their beds with tractors and racing-cars. For those who do delight in cuddlies, whether dolls or animals, it seems a very fundamental need. Bel Mooney has written of the stillbirth of her second baby and how in the lonely night she borrowed her first child's teddy-bear to comfort her grief.[12] Children's griefs and angers – and their triumphs too – are sometimes not to be shared even with sympathetic humans, who may enquire too closely for comfort. It is as well for them to have the refuge of these undemanding friends in need.

5 Props for Fantasy

One of the delights of watching and listening to a three-or-four-year-old at play is that, although she may not actually invite the adult into the private world that she is creating for herself, she does usually make things easy for the eavesdropper. Three-to-four is certainly a peak age for children's fantasy play, in which they try out for size the roles of other people or other creatures; but it is also a time when their fantasies happen to be relatively open to observation. Speech is reaching new levels of competence – many children almost seem in love with the activity of speech, practising it to themselves all day long even when no one is obviously listening – and at the same time the child is still unselfconscious, or perhaps so egocentric that she does not think about what impression she is making on other people. Later on the child will probably grow shy about letting adults overhear the adventures she is acting out, and the commentary itself will become internalized as the child becomes better able to follow her own thoughts without actually giving voice to them; as the mother of one of the children in our study of seven-year-olds said, 'She's got to the age when she's aware that there are things in her that she likes to keep secret.'[1] Adults who have the opportunity of observing pre-school children must make the most of it while they can.

'As if . . .'

Although the golden age of fantasy is three and four, in this chapter we begin by looking back to the first two years in order to uncover the roots of the child's ability to take a side-step into someone else's role: to act 'as if' behaviour which is meaningful for someone else is now also meaningful for her, but at the same time to retain the quality of 'playing at' which makes the difference between fantasy play and the everyday learning of new stages of behaviour. If we trace back this ability far enough, we find ourselves looking also at early language development, and the ways in which the mother and father themselves behave 'as if' in their interchanges with their child. Let's take an example of such an incident.

At seven months, Tim is playing with a ball which rolls beyond his reach. His eyes follow it, and he stretches his arm towards it, straining and grunting with effort, but it is still out of his reach. Because his mother is watching, however, she naturally moves in to retrieve the ball for him. She hands it back, he begins to play with it again, his face relaxes and he is once more contented.

Tim's mother has treated his persistent looking, reaching and grunting *as if* they were a 'give me that back' communication. This pattern is likely to be repeated many times when things he is playing with move beyond arm's length. Very soon Tim will begin to reach and vocalize with some anticipation as to what will probably happen in consequence, and eventually he will do so quite deliberately, looking at his mother at the same time, as a command which is directed towards her and which is effective in getting her help when he needs it. He will also learn that there is no point in doing this when she is not there, and may well also begin to throw the ball away deliberately in order to have a reason to command her in this way. A distinct sequence of communication gestures with a quite complex meaning is thus built up. By treating Tim *as if* he already knew how to say 'Give me that back again', Tim's mother made it possible for him to begin to make deliberate and specific 'statements' *to her*, rather than merely throwing out expressions of desire to the world at large. Incidentally, she also made it possible for him to start sorting out certain rather fundamental distinctions between himself as an agent, the object he has lost, and the kind of feeling he is experiencing about it. As we said earlier on, actions without words must precede words without actions.

It is widely believed by developmental psychologists that a child's thinking evolves out of the actions which she can be seen to perform; what we are stressing here is that it is the *interpretation* put on the child's actions, by communicating individuals who already make use of language and symbolic thought, which matters in the evolution of similar thought in the child herself. Through the adult's willingness to transform into communication gestures the actions that arise from feeling-states, the child's experience of the world is given coherence, because this allows her to share with others all those kinds of thoughts and feelings which we ourselves as adults take for granted as a result of sharing a common language. When children start trying to make themselves understood in language, often they need to support what they say by pointing and other gestures, and a child's meaning may only be clear because the adult is in the same context and can use the clues provided by it. This means that in unfamiliar situations, or when the adult is unused to this particular child, communication may break down altogether.

Apart from the question of gesture, there is another sense in which actions precede thought: that what we *do* with things and how we *label* them in words are closely bound up together. For example, to define 'cup' we cannot just talk about its size, shape and the material from which it is made; fundamentally its definition is about what we do with it: that is, it is drinkable-from. One might fashion a makeshift cup by picking a large leaf and folding it in such a way as to produce a vessel capable of holding water and being drunk from: the definition of such an object comes essentially from what is done with it. Mankind is a tool-using animal as well as a language-using one, and it is the use to which a child puts objects that in the end decides how she comes to conceptualize them. A 'bag' can have almost any shape, size, colour or flexible texture, so long as it remains possible for a person to put things into it and carry them about; a chair is a chair so long as it can be sat on and supports the back. The child understands the essential hattiness of hats only when, like ladies at Ascot races, she realizes that they include anything which she chooses to wear on her head. So it is an important human characteristic that we expect babies to accept as meaningful an action like spoon-feeding, even though spoons may come in many kinds, from a silver dessert-spoon to a wooden icecream spatula: we expect understanding at the intuitive level of action long before the child is able to walk or talk.

Let's take another example, this time of a baby coming up to her first birthday and how she was initiated into the shared concept of brushes and brushing.

At eleven months, Jane is having her hair brushed by her father. Perhaps in mild irritation, she reaches up to grasp the brush handle, and clings on to it while the brushing continues. Hair-brushing is a well-worn ritual which happens most days, and Jane participates at first willy-nilly, and later in a more cooperative and relaxed way, apparently enjoying the rhythm and feel of the action in which she has found herself involved. Soon Jane comes to pull down the hairbrush in anticipation of the next downward stroke, and her father, sensing this, says 'You do it, then' – finally letting go and leaving Jane holding the brush for herself. When Jane then perseveres with the brushing action, producing a few more downward strokes, her father reacts with a delighted smile: 'Are you brushing your *own* hair, then?' Later on, merely presenting the brush to Jane may be enough to induce her to begin to brush her own hair, and the fact that she can do this will be proudly shown off to other adults.

In this example, the mere presentation of the hairbrush comes to symbolize or stand for the appropriate action; and a mutual understanding of the whole idea of brushes and brushing, as well as the difference between doing things to yourself and having things done to you, becomes consolidated.

The Russian psychologist, Vygotsky, has argued that children need to act out ideas symbolically, rather than just in real life, in order to clarify them to themselves.[2] The idea of riding a horse is fully appreciated when the child is no longer limited to real horses but can *pretend* that the stick she bestraddles is a horse. Similarly, a toddler may have had many experiences of being driven in a car, but it is not until she can dispense with a real car and 'play at' driving – perhaps becoming a car herself, cornering bends with her whole body and simulating engine noises with one of the commonest of modern children's early words, 'brrm-brrm' – that she really masters the notions of cars and driving. To arrive at this point demands an amazing capacity to empathize with both the movements and the intentions of other people. But this is the point at which what we call symbolic play begins to be established. One more example will complete the series.

At 12 months Andrew is quite used to holding and eating his own rusks, and clearly enjoys the experience. His mother says 'Is that nice? Give me a bite', conveying her meaning by an appreciative look and lip-smacking gestures, followed by an approach movement by her partly open mouth towards the rusk in his hand. Andrew offers her the opportunity of a bite, which is in fact responded to by his mother only in mime, because the soggy end of sucked rusk is not as attractive to her as she pretends. This is a give-and-take routine which they have practised many times before; both know how to play their parts and anticipate each other's actions.

One day Andrew happens to be playing with a plate and a small wooden brick which is vaguely the same shape as a rusk. His mother notices this and says 'Is that your biscuit?' simultaneously going into her well-understood 'Give me a bite' routine: that is, she is inviting him to offer it to her *as if* it were a rusk. Andrew responds to this with the appropriate offering gesture, but at the same time it is clear from his amused expression that he appreciates that this is just a joke; he already knows from experience that one cannot really enjoy eating a piece of wood. Yet Andrew acts out his realization that the wooden brick can stand for the rusk in this kind of play. He is well on the way to sharing the 'as if' symbolism which his mother is proposing. Soon he will begin to demonstrate this understanding in other more original ways – for example, by 'feeding' Teddy with a wooden brick as if it were a rusk and, moreover, as if Teddy were a person who could gesture back.

These examples are all rather typical of the kinds of interchanges that naturally take place between parents and children by the end of the first year. Most parents repeatedly set up these 'as if' situations with their children, and the effect is to build up cumulatively a whole repertoire of shared understandings on a symbolic level.

The ability to use symbolic objects in play to represent real objects seems to be a human characteristic that appears surprisingly early, and is probably of fundamental importance in 'learning how to mean'. Certainly during the second year children can copy fairly complex actions which they have only seen other people do. We were once filming a thirteen-month-old girl who could barely walk steadily, when she came across a toy iron and ironing board for the very first time, and amazed us by giving a delightfully accurate performance of 'doing the ironing', though her mother assured us she had never seen such a toy before and had naturally never been allowed to handle the real iron at home.

At about the same time children also become able to recognize familiar objects in picture form; and, as the first words appear, a word like 'duh' (for duck) may consistently be used not only to generalize about three-dimensional ducks (real ducks, plastic duck, plush duck), but also to refer to pictures of ducks in story-books, even when these are stylized or monochrome sketches and hence very much less a 'copy' of a duck than a colour photo would be. The child's ability to recognize and take pleasure in the drawing of a duck, in much the same way as she would react to a real duck, reminds us that humans have evolved an extraordinary capacity to respond in a very immediate way to visual symbols, and that this capacity to treat symbols as *both rationally and emotionally meaningful* is the cornerstone of literature, art and religion, and possibly of science as well.

Equally mysterious and remarkable is the very young child's willingness to accept highly abstract object-symbols such as wooden peg-men to stand for little people – even though they may have been simplified down to a formalized token-shape, a spherical head at the end of a cylinder body, with no identifiable arms or legs, and only a few blobs of paint to suggest eyes, mouth and hair. Once again it is true that adults give children a good deal of encouragement to treat peg-men *as if* they were people, ascribing human thoughts and feeling to these small lumps of wood as they play with the child: 'Ah, poor little man, is he left all on his own?' – 'Oh, you've put him upside down in his car, he won't like that!' – 'Don't bite the poor man.' What is so striking is that the child accepts this symbolism so very readily as a working convention, and proceeds actively to incorporate it into her own spontaneous play. Soon she is herself 'walking' the pegs along the table-edge, making them fight or kiss, and deliberately courting adult expressions of horror by upsetting their vehicle so that they all fall out.*

We shall be returning in the next chapter to the ways in which toys are used to represent real-world objects for the child and thence to create private, imaginary worlds in miniature; so far we have been simply looking at the beginnings of the process which makes such symbolism possible. For the remainder of this chapter, we will look at the ways in which young children act out in their own person the roles and activities which they see being played out around them by parents and other adults with whom they come in contact; how this kind of play contributes towards their understanding of the world and of their relationship to it; and what kinds of toys help to sustain such play.

'Playing at Being ...'

It is an odd irony that what we think of as 'fantasy play' in children is in fact the very means by which they sort out the nature of reality and explore possibilities and impossibilities in their situation; it allows them, as the psychologist Phyllis Hostler has written, to 'reduce the world to manageable proportions, and find their place in it'.[3]

Children are surrounded by people, both other children and adults, who, by their actions and words, build up for them a notion of what the world is like and how the people in it are supposed to behave. Children do not know by nature what is expected of them or what are other people's accepted roles. Even in the basic parent-child relationship, all that is obviously built-in is the clear fact that parents are bigger and physically more powerful than children; this may have implications of protection or control or both, and the ways in which parents expect to use their common physical power will differ according to social trends, social class or individual personality.[4] Furthermore, how or whether

---

* Adults are not just humouring children when they play with them like this; they are themselves affected by the power of the symbol. It was an adult whom we saw removing the chute from the Matchbox musical slide and, with the most concentrated expression of glee, winding the handle that propelled the peg-children up the steps to the innocent refrain of 'Girls and boys come out to play', to see them tumble into space at the top; and it was other adults who watched fascinated through several repetitions.

mothers and fathers interpret their separate roles as different will also vary from generation to generation and from one place to another. Thus in the social roles most closely observable by the child there is plenty of room for ambiguity, and this may be increased by widening experience of other children's parents, who may behave in rather different ways from her own. We have elsewhere quoted one of our own children at the age of four telling us darkly that 'Philippa's mother is *not as nice as you might think*'; her remark showed her growing awareness both that Philippa's mother had a public face for other adults and a more private face for Philippa and her friends, and that mothers differ in personality; and it came at a time when she was much occupied by games of 'playing mothers and fathers' and trying out the feel of being different kinds of mother, nice and nasty. If we spend time watching and listening to children's imaginative play, we will soon find that there are a number of different ways in which this 'trying out' process is used by the child, and it is perhaps worth distinguishing between them here.

When the child *tries out her notions of roles*, she uses the picture she has built up so far to define the role which she then acts out; and through the reaction of others who object to or accept her definitions she will adjust her understanding. When children put this into words, we can see it happening in a very explicit way; but of course there will be many incidents in which roles are implied rather than actually stated. It is a major complaint of the Women's Movement that little girls are constantly subjected to role-definition which restricts them: Andrew's blithe assertion that 'You don't get girls on ships' (page 75) is an explicit example, but the girl who always finds herself playing nurse to her brother's doctor absorbs an equally powerful message. One might, however, wonder who is the loser when a little boy is seen wandering disconsolately round and round the play house, waiting to be allowed to 'come back from work', while the girls cook the dinner, dress the baby and have a party.

Other roles than sex roles will be explored in similar ways. 'I'm the policeman, I've come to take you to prison'; '*Don't* call me darling, I'm the *shop*man!'; 'I'll just go home and smack my children for getting out of bed' (a father drinking at the pub); 'But I *must* smack you, I'm your *mummy*!'; 'Be a good prisoner and I'll bring you breakfast in bed'; 'Do kings *have* to be cross?' – these are all remarks made by children between four and six during fantasy play. Sometimes arguments develop: 'Don't push me, daleks* don't push people', protested a four-year-old, to be countered by another four-year-old – 'Well, but they exterminate people!'

The role that is constantly before the pre-school child's eyes is the domestic one acted out by her own parents; the importance to her of these two adults and the familiarity of the things they do in the house combines to make their activities attractive subjects for imitation. Play here takes the form of *identifying with the adult model*. Phyllis Hostler makes the point that, early on, the child has feelings of conflict between her wish to be a separate independent person and her wish to stay close to her mother; the 'serious mimicry' by which children adopt their parents' activities is one way of resolving this conflict. So the child will delight in sweeping, cooking and polishing, baby-bathing, carpentering and painting, vacuum cleaning, mowing the lawn and tinkering with the car, either side by side with a parent, or as play-house play; the nearer her own equipment comes to mirroring that of her parents, the better she will be pleased. The element of identification and mimicry is often all too obvious to parents by the mannerisms, or even the nagging tones, which they unwillingly recognize as their own.

In an important sense, though, cooking side by side in the kitchen with mother or father is reality play, while cooking pretend cakes in the play house is fantasy play. The distinction is not just in the reality of flour and eggs, however; it lies in the difference between helping the parent, still in her own role as child, and taking for herself the parent role. A better example of such a distinction in domestic play is in baby care. The mother may ask the child to help her with the new baby, encouraging her to take pleasure in amusing him as he baths and in helping to dry and powder his skin; but the child is not so much identifying with motherhood as learning the joys of the reality of being a big sister. On another occasion, the mother may suggest that the child brings her doll and a washing-up bowl, and may provide her with a morsel of soap, a tiny flannel and a nappy for a towel, so that they can both bath their babies side by side; in doing this, the mother deliberately invites her daughter to identify with her in motherhood,

* Daleks were robot-like characters in a very popular children's television serial. Their easily-imitated droning chant of 'We-shall-ex-term-in-ate-you!' with which they advanced on their captives, combined with an oddly attractive shape, made them quite irresistible to small children.

and for the moment their actual relationship becomes secondary to their equal complicity.

Identifying with adults also carries the possibility of *trying out more powerful roles.* Listening to children playing at being mothers and fathers, doctors and nurses, teachers and policemen, one is struck by how much more blatantly bossy they are in these roles, and for how much more of the time, than one knows their adult models to be. Perhaps they are just less skilled than adults at conveying authority with subtlety; perhaps they are more honest; perhaps, given the opportunity to exert power, they have no intention of wasting it; maybe a little of all three. Children's comics depict a similar world, where parents are heavy-handed and unreasonable, teachers are wholly repressive and doctors are out to remove as many bits of you as they can.

In many ways children are likely to feel powerless compared with adults. In a battle of wills, parents often take care to make it seem that they have won, even though in fact the child has carried the day. Adults' ability to foresee consequences must sometimes seem like magical power to the child: 'Careful, you'll hurt yourself!... There, I *told* you you would', cries the mother – did she make it happen? Adults have a mental scheme of what is planned for the next few days; children, whose time sense is poor, are constantly astonished by the arrival of events, in a way which would seem intolerable to adults. Susan Isaacs described the supreme function of play as an activity which 'brings the child psychic equilibrium in the early years'. Playing at being powerful, even though one's power may be only over dolls, teddy-bears and peg-men, redresses the balance of powerlessness and makes the child's limitations tolerable to her. It is also true that identifying with the very people who have most real power in the child's life, her parents, can allow her to see their power as benign and protective, a source of strength in which she may share.

Because it is understood by everyone that play is not 'for real', play offers the child an opportunity to *try out real emotions in a protected context.* Children can feel passionately angry, destructive, even murderous at times, and the violence of their own feelings may frighten them, because they do not yet know how capable they are of controlling them and they do know that adults disapprove of them. By choosing a play context in which to express these emotions, the child can disown them at the moment when they become too threatening: 'I was only playing!' – and until that moment he can practise the art which all of us have to learn if we are to be regarded as sane members of society, the achievement of flexible control over our feelings.

One emotion that can sometimes get out of hand during a child's fantasy play is fear. When we were studying the imaginary companions of four-year-olds, we found that some who had started out as friendly creatures had become gradually frightening in the child's imagination; or that the imaginary dragon who played with the child during the day changed in character as it got dark: 'The dragon might get me if I go upstairs, won't you Dragon?' Older children in groups or in pairs often enjoy scaring each other with stories of the uncanny told at twilight, only to find themselves taken over during the night by the fears that earlier they were 'only playing' with. Although four-year-olds often have very real and terrifying fears, we also found at that age many examples of

a flirtation with fear (as sometimes with other emotions) in which the child relies, not always successfully, on being able to withdraw at the critical moment. Glen's mother, with some insight, commented on her son's sudden fear of the wallpaper in his bedroom, 'I think it's a bit of a lark, really'; and Glen confirmed this diagnosis with 'Well, I thought there were lions on it, but there weren't, so I like it after all.' Craig was ambivalent about fire-engines; to his mother's mention of fire-engine sirens as his chief fear, he protested 'I *like* fire-engine sirens!' 'Well, you always run in crying when they come'; 'I *do* like them, though.' Rosemary tried to play with her mother's fears as well as her own: 'She's frightened of mice, but she's never seen any.' (Are you – is that where she's got it from?) 'No – she thinks *I'm* frightened of cats. That's why she makes mewing noises at me – to try and make me frightened!'[4]

Another way in which children use the 'protected context' of play is to make it a vehicle for forbidden activities. For instance, many children are taught from a very early age that the 'private parts' of their own bodies are forbidden territory, and those without brothers and sisters of similar age may find it, in practice, very difficult to discover just what are the fascinating differences between their own bodies and those of the opposite sex. 'Playing doctors and nurses' may be recognized by the child as an ideal opportunity for making the physical examination which is sometimes difficult to carry out under a parent's eye. Unfortunately for the spirit of exploration, in this particular area the cry of 'we were only playing' often cuts little ice, as we discovered when we asked four-year-olds' mothers whether there was any sort of play they didn't allow, and received many answers to do with 'playing hospitals' where it was clear that it was precisely this aspect that they objected to.[5] Telling lies is another example of a forbidden activity which can quickly be transformed into a tolerated one, when the going gets rough, by giving it the quality of play: 'I was just joking!' – 'I was tricking you!'; and we have argued that it is important for children's understanding of the subtle gradations between truth and falsehood that they should have some opportunity for playing with such notions of fantasy, lies, stories, jokes and teasing.[6]

Freud saw in play the means by which the child not only rehearsed the roles of adult life, but also repeated life experiences in order *to gain emotional mastery of them*. It is perhaps true that by going over worrying experiences (including experiences of worry which have not yet become true experiences), they can at least become familiar and to that extent less frightening. Perhaps this is one of the reasons why children play school so untiringly between four and seven years: by trying out roles of teacher and pupil in every permutation, the potentially alarming world of school is safely stowed under their belts, so to speak. Adults do much the same thing when, after a hospital stay, they go on and on about their operations to anyone who will listen. When our own children were little, the departure of a neighbour's child to the eye infirmary was the signal for a protracted game of hospital in which, this time, all examinations centred on the head area; the child's taxi had hardly moved off before the dolls' beds were ranged on the playroom floor, where they stayed for the full week Paul was away as his sister and our own children played out their anxieties about what had happened to him.

Psychologists have tended to emphasize the child's need to use fantasy play in a therapeutic way, to cope with difficulties and troubles, and perhaps this is partly because these are the kinds of examples which make a big impact on psychologists' observation. But it is important to remember too that children 'play at being' just because it's fun to do so. Surrounded by things and by people, in a world which astonishes by its newness and changeability, what more natural than that the child should find trying out playing with people just as interesting as trying out playing with things? To slip out of one's own skin into the skin of a shopkeeper, astronaut, mummy, monster, traindriver, dustman or teacher at will – this is something we all might envy, but do not find easy to achieve as adults except, perhaps, in our dreams.

What Props?

So what kind of toys or equipment can we provide as props for the child's fantasy, whether she is playing alone or with a group of friends? Children will, of course, make use of anything that is around, and we have already discussed ways in which climbing frames, dolls, toy animals and bricks can contribute to the child's fantasy play; in the next chapter we shall be looking at the worlds to which the child plays the role of God – the dolls' house and the layout. What else can serve the cause of fantasy?

Domestic Toys and the Tools of Trades

Although children mimicking mother and father in household jobs can well use the ordinary household dusters, dishmops and brushes, some domestic tools are unwieldy for a small child to use; and, as we have seen, there is a great pleasure for the child in working alongside mother or father in the same task, when it will be both inconvenient and expensive to have two full-size brooms sweeping clean together. Most child-size household tools are in fact at the inexpensive end of the toy range, and will be needed later if you decide to furnish a play house or domestic corner. A small basket and purse should not be forgotten, both for playing at shops indoors, and for real excursions; toy money is fun, but not very easy to buy except from educational suppliers. Toy vacuum cleaners, lawn mowers and shopping bags on wheels are a delight to the right child but can sink like a stone for the wrong one; probably if the child is much past the age when she will enjoy a pushalong, it is already too late. A tea-set is basic equipment for any family-play or doll-play, and needs to be a compromise between doll-size and child-size; the spout and handle of the teapot are vulnerable areas, so make sure these are well-made. For a child on her own, china may be the best material because she will handle it with greater care; for a playgroup, we have found that the combination of a stainless steel 'morning tea' set (tiny teapot, jug and sugar basin) with melamine coffee-cups, all in fact sold for the use of adults, has outlasted several quite expensive plastic tea-sets – worth considering for a family of children, too.

Things to beware of are toy tools which are idle mimics of the real thing, incapable of use. This is particularly likely for toy carpentry tools, few of which are strong enough to be used effectively, and some of which crumple dangerously if much pressure is put on them. Some toy hammers are in plastic, and may have no weight in the head, so that it is impossible for the child to learn the proper wrist action. It is much easier to teach a child to use tools safely and skilfully if they are properly balanced and made to do a job, not for show; it is worth buying small-size tools from the tool-counter, rather than children's sets from a toyshop.

The most important piece of equipment for hospital play, apart from the nurses' cap, is a toy stethoscope, and these too are cheaply bought, and useful anyway to familiarize children with medical examinations. For gardening or other kinds of excavations, small-size real tools again are usually better than toy ones, and the child will need some kind of wheelbarrow or truck if she is to shift things around. Car mechanics will need spanners and an oilcan for 'oiling' with water. Small children will enjoy being house-painters with an old brush and a tin of water; if you choose a matt surface, the mark of the water will probably last long enough to satisfy the painter. Sometimes the success of 'tools of the trade' depends very much upon their being the right thing at the right time; a child may have weeks of pleasure from a post office set, with tiny stamps and envelopes, telegraph forms and postal orders and a franking stamp, or from a bus conductor's ticket machine, and some children have had their lives changed by the gift of an old typewriter or a printing set.

Dressing-up Things

There are some roles which seem absolutely dependent on having the right hat! How can you be a policeman without a proper helmet or peaked cap with a glinting silver badge, or a nurse without at least a big white hanky fashioned into a cap? A hat transforms its wearer as nothing else can; one of the most successful presents we have ever given (to a three-year-old) was a carrier bag full of different hats. So, whether or not you intend to go on to establish a dressing-up box in time, start off with things to go on the head and move downward from there. In our research playroom, next to the dressing-up box, we have a row of wooden pegs on which hang a police helmet, cowboy hats (more than one needed!), a big straw hat with flowers on it for a fine lady, a Viking helmet and a Roman one (plastic), an astronaut's helmet and a plastic 'tin hat', Red Indian feather head-dresses, a knitted helmet, numerous hats in velvet and straw from jumble sales, a crown and a coronet or two and a wedding veil. These are supported by an array of accessories which include a stethoscope, black eye-masks (for burglars and other villains), swords and spark-guns, binoculars and boxing-gloves, parasol, lengths of fur and chiffon, handbags, spectacles and goggles, beards and moustaches, and a collection of badges and gaudy jewellery.

Watching young children in dramatic play in this playroom, it is

clear that these are the parts of the dressing-up equipment that they like best, and often the actual clothes in the box are ignored. For a child at home who wants to spend long hours, perhaps whole days, playing out the role of nurse, astronaut, Red Indian or cowboy, it may be worth making or buying a complete set of clothes, but for most children it is the 'badge of office' – nurse's cap and apron, cowboy's hat and gun, Batman's cloak – which is important.

Probably the best dressing-up boxes are put together over the years, with some favourites (like Jo's russet leather boots in *Little Women*) which come out time and time again, in different roles. Remember, before you start a dressing-up box, to spray the box well with moth killer in order to avoid unpleasant surprises a few months later. Jumble sales and charity second-hand shops are a marvellous source of extraordinary clothes in velvets, lurex, brocade and other exciting materials (we even found a wedding dress in the Oxfam shop); but again it is worth taking the pile to the coin-op dry-cleaners before putting them into use. It doesn't matter that dresses are too big and trail on the ground a bit, so long as you have a few chiffon or silky scarves to tie them in at the waist and fill in a décolletage that reveals too much knitted jersey for romance. It may help to turn up a few sleeves permanently (or at least catch them up in big cuffs) since children find it difficult to do this themselves.

In sales and second-hand shops, or when grandparents are having a turn-out, keep your eyes open for: lengths of lace and fur, or net curtaining; string vests, especially knitted ones (they make wonderful chain mail if sprayed with silver paint); furry or glittery open-heeled sandals, which will fit anyone, more or less; junk jewellery, the more brassy or sparkly the better; wigs (we bought cheap lengths of false hair at Woolworths and made much-loved plaits for our short-haired daughter); long gloves – try making gaudy rings permanently fixed to their fingers from curtain rings or gold embroidery with brilliant buttons and beads for jewels; shawls, stoles and evening cloaks. Cloaks can be easily made out of an old curtain by pulling up the gathering string fairly tight and adding ribbons or a toggle and loop for fastening; a knitted helmet makes a good animal head if you stitch bits of fur (or feathers) over it; gum boots painted with silver paint are suitable footwear for space travel; strings of Christmas tinsel can be used in lots of ways.

As children grow older, some will graduate from fantasy play to putting on dramatic performances, either impromptu, or carefully worked out and rehearsed. Some families develop a whole tradition of such entertainments, sometimes evolving dramatic sagas in which well-loved (or well-hated) characters return year after year. For a family like this, the dressing-up box can go on being a central part of play equipment from one generation to the next.

Play Houses and Other Habitats

Most adults, if they remember their childhoods right back to the pre-school years, will recall the pleasures of having one's own little private place, usually rather cramped and confined, where one could not only 'play house' but also invite friends and exclude enemies, and which served as base for journeys and battles and other adventures. Very small children, like cats, will climb into grocery boxes or will make themselves nests under the table or behind the sofa; children of four upwards will try to find enough room for rather more active use of their house or den. If space can possibly be spared indoors or out, it is worth making an effort to create a reasonably permanent play house for the children, so that they can set it up as they want it and know that it will not be cleared away at bedtime.

Play houses can be bought for indoor or outdoor use in whatever degree of luxury you can afford; or they can be made, when their perfection will depend less on money and more on ingenuity and time. The best play house we ever saw was set up more-or-less permanently in the corner of a verandah; it was made using a large and solid second-hand table as its backbone, with a two-storey facade and side wall of hardboard on a light wooden frame around it. A door set in the lower part led into the ground floor room under the table, and from this a three-rung ladder went up through a large hole in the table-top into the upstairs room; enough light came through windows cut in the facade, and the house was roofed with hardboard, the whole being papered on the outside with wallpapers simulating tiles and bricks. Although the mother who made this house was a skilled craftswoman, the main skill needed was imagination rather than joinery.

Talking about tents on climbing frames in the last chapter, we mentioned the special appeal of a house built above ground. If you are lucky enough to have a suitable tree whose inner branches can be cut away to take a tree house, it will probably continue to be used, even if eventually just as a reading-platform, for years. One we have seen had a rope-ladder for access but a pulley-handgrip on a diagonal rope for a quick descent. We made our children a house on stilts, based on two enormous wooden crates fixed together mouth to mouth; this was set right into a tall hedge, so that the children got a view from the back window which was at other times invisible to them. If your hedge divides you from your neighbours' garden, of course, your children's surveillance may not be appreciated! Another play house in our road, also made basically of packing cases, had all the romance of a thatched roof: this turned out to be made of the stitched straw packing which (so we learned) champagne bottles are packed in, and had been begged from the grandest of the local wine merchants. It is always worth finding out what your local traders are throwing away!

As less permanent outside houses, tents are not to be despised; outside house-play is likely to be mainly a warm-weather activity anyway. A small tent or wigwam is like a magnet to small children; if you haven't got a proper one, you might try lowering your clothes line, hanging an old sheet across it, and holding the two sides apart with weights or bricks. A more fulltime solution will be to make pockets in the end of a sheet in which to put the weights (stones or bricks), or attaching guyropes to pegs in the grass, with extra bits of material sewn as tent-flaps on the ends. Inside or outside, a makeshift arrangement for very young children is a blanket or two over a framework of chairs. Much better than chairs is an old wooden playpen with two of the bars taken out for a door; playpens tend to be useful for their proper purpose only for a very limited time, because mobile babies get so frustrated by them, but they make up for this if they have a second life as a play house. In our family, for two generations, we have also used a playpen as a support for a blockboard ping-pong table; its *simultaneous* use as a play house leads to creative interpretations for the hammering on the roof, as one of us well remembers.

Whatever kind of playhouse your children have, there should be an unshakable rule of NO MATCHES, CANDLES OR OIL LANTERNS, even for older children. Play houses hold the child in a restricted space, difficult to get out of in a hurry or a panic, and fire accidents can happen fast. Make sure the child has some other means of light, even if it's expensive in batteries, so that she won't be tempted.

Some children may prefer other home bases than a house. If you have ever had a rowing-boat on chocks in the yard, you will know how difficult it is to keep children out of it. An old dinghy past its seafaring days would make a wonderful alternative to a house, especially if a makeshift cabin were rigged up at one end; or if a real boat is difficult to come by, a mock-up boat is probably as easy to make as a house, since children are quite happy to accept a flat-bottomed craft. Alternatively a silver-painted capsule of sorts, with a good complicated control panel inside, will make a spacecraft in which the child will feel less earthbound than she is. Similarly, she will not let a little thing like immobility destroy the fun of driving a packing-case car, so long as it has a steering wheel and instrument panel. If you have room, a junk-yard mini-sized real car with the doors taken off (to avoid crushed fingers), or a small trailer-caravan, has enormous possibilities for play.

If space is short, you may decide to choose a fold-away house, to be used mainly indoors. If so, look for one that can be used in other ways as well: the best are designed for alternative play as shop and puppet theatre. You may still decide that the most satisfactory thing is to make your own, especially if you have a particular alcove or corner in mind for the siting of it. Three main features are needed, which tends to mean three walls hinged together: a door (with bell or knocker), a window which should have a sill or hinged shelf wide enough to use as a counter for a shop, and shelves to hold the shop's stock or as kitchen dresser for the house. If you site it in a corner, you may be able to use an existing set of shelves or cupboard on the wall, and need only two sides for your house.

As for equipment to furnish house or shop, as usual anything is grist to the mill; but there are some things which we have found children use more than others. A cooker, or at least a cooker top, seems almost essential; they can be bought, but we made a perfectly good one by painting a cheap bedside cupboard white, drawing 'electric' rings in black and red on the top with a permanent felt marker, and adding knobs on the front in the form of cotton reels painted black. Kettles and pans can be bought at a toyshop, but the best frying pans we discovered in Woolworths in a size just right for a fried egg and a rasher of bacon – which can be found (and how they delight children) in any good joke shop. A doll's cradle or bed will be needed, and a stool is useful as it doubles as table or chair – but we don't find the children use tables much, preferring to stand at the window shelf. A telephone is important – preferably two, so that the second can be used from another corner of the room. Apart from the domestic equipment we have listed earlier, there probably won't be room for much else; but most children seem unworried by the space constrictions, and use their doorsteps and the 'pavement' outside to extend their living area in the old-fashioned way. Oddments which we have found particularly appreciated by children in 'making the house a home' have been a square of carpet, an old alarm clock, curtains that can be drawn and a plastic plant in a pot.

For a shop, a toy cash register is the favourite luxury, followed by scales for weighing out dried beans or chestnuts into paper bags saved from the real household shopping. Register and scales are a luxury compared with the necessity of having something to sell. Groceries are probably the most suitable goods, and tins and packets can be borrowed from the kitchen cupboard; for more permanent use, or for a playgroup, it is worth buying a stock of small tins (preferably those with pictures on their labels), as they last indefinitely and are satisfying to have on the shelves of both shop and house. Empty packets should be taped shut for verisimilitude, and they survive better that way. A basket of plastic fruit is another delight which will serve for both house and shop play.

Puppets

We cannot conclude a chapter on fantasy play without mentioning glove puppets, which are of special interest in that the child, in making them talk and move, is activating a creature which is separate yet not separate from herself. Even when she talks to the puppet, making it speak back to her, there is a knowledge that she herself is physically inside the puppet, and this perhaps makes the situation a different one in quality from making a doll talk, or even from using a string puppet. There is a slight ambiguity of identity – who is inside whom? – which has been explored in stories about ventriloquists being taken over by

their dummies; whereas the worst string puppets can do is to become independent of their masters.

Sometimes a child who is very shy can be liberated from her self-consciousness by using puppets: almost as if she did not have to be responsible for what was said by someone who was, after all, literally at arm's length from her. In our clinic we have found that a child overcome by shyness may be quite happy for a whole afternoon's session if she is allowed to talk through a puppet; one five-year-old girl recently spent two hours here with an emu on her hand and arm, and an emu playing lotto and doing puzzles is, we can vouch for it, a very edifying sight. Children who have difficulties with speech can often be helped by the introduction of puppets, which removes the focus of attention away from their own remarks and on to what the puppet is saying; one remedial programme is built around the use of puppets in this way.[7]

What particular puppet will inspire a child is not altogether predictable by adults, as we pointed out when we were discussing dolls and soft toys. There does seem to be something special about hand-

and-arm puppets, however. We have always had a basket of puppets in our research playroom – as many different ones as we could find; but the year we introduced our first hand-arm puppets (beautiful animals made by Merrythought) the children's interest in them, and the volume of speech and fantasy play which they generated, much more than doubled. They are of course more expensive than ordinary glove puppets; for our special use they more than justify their price, for a child at home they might well become a favourite soft toy, and there is, of course, no reason why they should not be home-made.

Finally, having spent some pages discussing toys for fantasy play, we should remind ourselves that fantasy play is quite capable of happening without any equipment at all; it is indeed the 'all in the mind' element which makes it fantasy. One of us spent a happy wartime year at the age of ten in cramped living conditions which necessitated sleeping three-to-a-big-bed with her younger sisters. Three little girls went to bed each night; but, in the twinkling of an eye, they were transformed, under the blankets, to three intrepid ladies named Mrs White, Mrs Brown and Mrs Brigstock, who pursued the most harrowing adventures as they foiled the wicked machinations of the villainous Mrs Singer – a real but maligned lady who would have been horrified to know how she was portrayed in these dramas. No, children don't *need* props for their fantasies. It's nice to have a few, though.

6   Miniature Worlds

(with a look at collections)

We quoted earlier one designer's definition of a toy: 'anything is a toy if I choose to describe what I am doing with it as play'. That is all very well, but, as we have already seen in considering dolls, it does not help us very much when it comes to identifying what objects were originally made with the purpose of play in mind. To some extent, the historian or archaeologist has to rely on circumstantial knowledge of the life styles of the period when deciding on whether a particular object had a play function or some other use. But is there such a thing as a toylike quality? What makes an object a toy?

One group of toys is easy to classify as such, because what they do serves little purpose other than play. A rubber ball is an example: so long as its surface is unbroken, the archaeologist finding it can be fairly certain that it was a play object because nothing much else could be done with it. As soon as there is some evidence of it having been attached to something, of course, it might have been a float, a lavatory chain handle or a barrow 'wheel', according to size: but the object in itself has a fundamental play capacity. Similarly a plastic rattle, while it might have conceivable functions as a bird-scarer or a musical instrument, is intrinsically most suitable for the amusement of babies and might be assumed to have been designed with this in mind, failing other evidence.

These are toys which *are* themselves and nothing else. But there is a much bigger group of toys which imitate for children some more 'real' form: not only do dolls imitate live babies and teddies imitate bears, but toy tractors imitate real farmers' tractors, toy stethoscopes and cash registers mimic the tools of proper doctors and shopkeepers, and toy guns simulate the power to kill. And at this point other factors enter the issue: question of scale and of precise replication.

Toys that imitate tend to change their scale to suit the different scale of the child. Usually, of course, they become smaller, corresponding to the child's smallness in relation to the adult. Occasionally they enlarge, adapting a concept that normally includes smallness to the child's purpose or dexterity: carpenters' nails and screws are translated into thick wooden pegs for hammering and twisting; the Fisher Price 'record-player' music box has its arm scaled up to fit a child's clumsy grasp; a toy ladybird or mouse is produced as a cuddly but gigantic version of the natural creature. As well as changing scale, most toys are simplified transformations of the objects they represent, and often this fact that they *suggest* rather than replicate the original is the strongest characteristic of toyishness that they have. In this sense the wooden popgun has more of the toy about it than a toy grey metal revolver (which may indeed be used as a real object in terrifying and threatening people); still more, the toy horse on wheels or rockers is clearly a toy rather than a statue, in that it attempts to suggest the movement of the real horse but at the expense of adopting a certain absurdity of form. A wheeled pullalong boat (Escor, Matchbox) or a wheel-less train (Abbatt) are equally absurd as representations: yet they are accepted by the playing child as boat and train because other elements in them (boat-shape, coupled units) offer as much realism as a *toy* requires.

The nearer we come to an exact copy of the original, the more we begin to be concerned with models rather than toys. Obviously it would be nonsense to say that a model cannot be a toy in the sense of a focus for play; indeed, many objects which came to be produced as toys were originally made as models for adult purposes: for instance the forerunners of dolls' houses, the 'Nuremberg kitchens' of the seventeenth century, were intended as instruction models in domestic science; early dolls' houses were filled with furniture and other artefacts made in silver to display adults' wealth, and many of the early dressable paper dolls served to display fashions to adult customers, though it would be natural for such things to fall into the hands of children. The distinction between model and toy is perhaps a pedantic one; nonetheless, while accepting considerable overlap between these functions, it is a point which must be made to the extent that we also distinguish between adult play and children's play (and also allow for overlap here). The issue arises with particular force in the area of miniature toys and models, because reduction of scale when combined with exactness of replication of the original seems to exert a unique fascination upon both children and adults. It is here in particular that the fantasy world created originally by and for the child (often, significantly, with the avid help of his parents) is most likely to persist and develop into his adult life: the battlefield or dolls' house or railway lay-out of childhood, surviving the uncertainties of adolescence, emerges as the adult collector's pride, to be touched by children at their peril.

Whose World?

The difference between the props for fantasy that we discussed in the last chapter (which were on the whole child-size and therefore not miniature in his terms), and the miniature worlds of dolls' house and lay-out, lies in the kind of participation which they encourage in the child. Child-size accoutrements of fantasy involve the child as a full member of the cast; he *is* the shopman, the teacher, Batman or a cowboy, and personally lives through their difficulties, triumphs and defeats. Furthermore, because so often there will be other members of the cast to consider, in the person of other children taking their own parts (or maybe competing for his part), much of the emotion generated

will be inescapably his own. In manipulating tiny people and animals in a world laid out before him, however, he is both distanced from the action and in greater control of it. The 'sorrows, passions and alarms' of his world's inhabitants are least partly decided by himself. He may well identify with their feelings and behaviour – these have clearly come out of his experience in one way or another, and may or may not be relevant to his own feelings and how he is coping with them – but he does not have to acknowledge any of them as his, and he can bring the action to a halt or turn it in another direction at any time he wishes.

Many psychologists, particularly those of the psycho-analytic school of thought, have used the child's readiness to absorb himself in these little worlds (and also children's habit of talking to themselves as they play) to come to a closer understanding of the individual child's inner feelings, often in order to help him through difficulties which he cannot resolve for himself. Looking at some of the records which have been made of children playing in this way, we can see how clues to some of the child's preoccupations easily emerge from this kind of observation, whereas it would be very difficult for the young child actually to explain his worries in words, and he might not even wish to do so explicitly. A famous account of a series of therapeutic play sessions with a disturbed five-year-old boy called Dibs was written in the sixties by the American psychologist Virginia Axline; it has many examples of the way in which play can offer a 'safe' context for the half-expression of thoughts which cannot yet be openly stated.

Dibs broke off his play and sat there quietly looking at the world he was building. He sighed. He took other figures out of the suitcase.

'Here are the children and their mother', he said. 'They live together on a farm in a friendly house. Here are some little lambs and chickens. And here is mother going down the road, down the street to the city. I wonder where she is going? Maybe she is going to the butcher shop to get some meat. No. She is going down the street and on and on until she is right beside the hospital. Now I wonder why she is standing there by the hospital?'

'I wonder, too', I said.

Dibs sat very still for a long time, looking at the mother figure. 'Well', he said at last. 'There she is and she is right beside the hospital. There are a lot of cars running down the streets and a fire engine. Everything has to get out of the way of the fire engine.' He shoved the cars and the fire engine up and down the streets, making noises for them.

'Now then, where are the children? Oh, here is one child. He is going down to the river alone. Poor little child so all alone. And the alligator swims in that river. And here is a big snake. Sometimes snakes live in the water. The boy goes down closer and closer to the river. Closer to the river. Closer to the danger.'

Once again Dibs stopped his activity and looked over his world. Suddenly he smiled. 'I am a builder of cities', he said.[1]

The richness of the observations that come out of this kind of play has led some psychologists to work out complicated techniques both for presenting the material to the child and for interpreting what the child does with it; others have relied on their own experience of children and a more intuitive insight in making their interpretations.[2] Undoubtedly there are insights to be gained from watching the child. Our own view, however, is that adult observers, whether parents, teachers or therapists, need to be more cautious than they often are in jumping to conclusions about what a child's world-play 'means'. Although what a child does must come *in some sense* from his experience, we cannot necessarily be sure to what extent it comes from actual experience, private fantasy or experience of fiction (stories and comics); nor can we always be certain whether the thoughts he is playing out are emotionally loaded or matter-of-fact. Sometimes, indeed, one suspects that interpretations are made on the basis of the adult's emotional feelings rather than the child's. For instance, children whose information about where babies come from has been straightforwardly and openly given may bring this knowledge into their play in casual, down-to-earth ways, making their dolls give birth (or giving birth themselves) with the same kind of common-sense air that they would bring to setting out a doll's teaparty; the observing adult, however, usually has a personal history of deep and complicated emotions about sex and birth which can hardly fail to colour how the child's actions are perceived. In the same way, the symbolization which adults may see in a child's arrangement of objects *might* have meaning for the child; but it might entirely depend upon the adult's own acquaintance with the common symbols encountered in art, conversation and jokes, and be quite unavailable to the child as yet, either from his cultural experience or in terms of his understanding. It can be very tempting to interpret children's play, action for action, with great assurance, both because it gives it meaning for us, and perhaps because in adult terms it makes it more exciting; but, just because massive interpretation can be sheer self-indulgence on the adult's part, such 'insights' need to be approached with self-discipline and in a very tentative spirit.

From the child's point of view, nonetheless, what is important about the miniature world in terms of his emotional and social development is that it gives him the opportunity to experiment with actions, relationships, happenings and feelings at one remove from himself, to play with threatening ideas without being actively threatened, to try out a scenario of events without having to carry it through or take responsibility for the outcome, and in general to sort out his ideas, both intellectual and emotive, on the safe play level. By the very process of losing himself in this kind of play, he is enabled gradually to find himself as a person.

Dolls' Houses

As we have briefly mentioned, some of the earliest apparent dolls' houses were not intended for play at all, but were simply cabinets filled with miniatures made in silver and other precious materials; a collection of such objects would naturally come to be arranged by its adult owner with increasing verisimilitude, the cabinet itself being adapted to resemble a house, the more effectively to display its contents. These cabinets originated in the Low Countries, and Dutch jewellers and gift shops still maintain the tradition of keeping a range of such miniatures in silver or imitation silver.

Perhaps a real dolls' house, however, should be defined as a house designed as a home for dolls; the Dutch cabinets would have been as unsuitable for actually living in as Midas's palace after he acquired the golden touch. Once dolls moved in, they clearly needed comfortable beds, food that at least looked edible and books that would open. And as soon as ordinary materials were used, the furnishing of a dolls' house (or baby house, as they were originally called) could become a long-term project for both parents and child. One of the great pleasures of looking at old dolls' houses is the evidence they give of having been added to bit by bit, with different degrees of skill, often over generations or throughout a lifetime: Mrs Graham Montgomery, whose eighteen-room dolls' house is in the Museum of Childhood at Edinburgh, started to furnish it in 1897 at the age of four, and continued to do so all her life. A dolls' house that grows with the family also has a happy element of luck to it: the delicate glass jug and goblets for which pocket money was hoarded are set alongside a tiny pair of scissors which was a charm from a cracker, an ornate gilt bowl that once lidded a perfume bottle and half-finished dolls' knitting worked out of embroidery thread on a pair of pins. Our daughter's dolls' house has an Art Nouveau screen, a pile of records and a shelf-full of books all owing part of their existence to the sumptuous advertisements of the colour supplements. This quality of serendipity is also the quality of warm and lived-in real households; the most luxurious collectors' dolls' houses, such as Queen Mary's famous mansion, while they produce gasps of wonder from all of us for their beauty and craftsmanship, are stately homes for stately dolls and seem too perfect to absorb the silver paper mirror or matchbox chest of drawers of a child's making.

Girls have tended to be given dolls' houses while boys receive farms, forts and lay-outs. While this difference probably reflects their preferences (developed not entirely as a result of environmental pressures),[3] children are individuals: many boys, given the chance, enjoy the intimate quality of dolls' house play just as girls often appreciate the wider-ranging adventures afforded by a lay-out. In the Bethnal Green Museum in London, that marvellous treasure-house of miniature worlds on many scales, there is a house called Dingley Hall which was 'made in 1874 for Laurence and Isaac Currie as school-boys'; the family that inhabits it has a distinctly masculine and indeed military tendency, but this is not true of every boy's dolls' house that we know. It seems more sensible, then, to discuss dolls' houses and lay-outs in terms of what each has to offer, rather than as being more 'suitable' for one sex or the other.

In choosing a dolls' house, it is important to think a little about the use to which it will be put. The major difference is between playgroup use and individual use. Children in a playgroup will have no permanent relationship with the doll family that inhabits the house; they cannot afford to have, since the dolls can have no loyalty to one child, but must be played with by whichever child turns up. Thus each child will re-arrange the furniture, perceive the family in a different way, arrange them in new attitudes, re-invent their relationships and their dialogues and put them through peaceful interludes or astounding adventures according to his whim. Often several children will play at once. For this

kind of use, the first necessity is strength and durability of house, furniture and dolls, since the physical survival of the dolls' house is not the child's first care, and since it is likely to be re-arranged by every child in turn. The second necessity is that the inside of the dolls' house should be easily accessible to the child, preferably to two or three at the same time.

Ten years' bitter experience taught us to furnish the dolls' house in our research playroom with furniture in chunky wood, eschewing the spindly legs, removable drawers and stuck-on ornamentation which make for realism but soon reduce the dolls' house to a realistic disaster area. The Woodpecker range of furniture survived its second hard year completely intact; we mitigated the ascetic plain-wood look by painting or colour-staining some of the surfaces, which improved it greatly in the children's eyes, though probably not in the designer's. We added details cheap enough to be regarded as consumable: little pictures cut, frames and all, from colour supplement advertisements, and transparent-taped on to card; blankets and carpets from squares of coloured felt; plastic tea-sets; and the whole came alive when we added plenty of plastic pots of flowers, still costing only a penny each. The house itself is a series of boxes, each one a room, heavy enough to sit stably on top of each other or side by side in a number of possible arrangements, and this allows the child or children easy access. Another suitable design for playgroup use is Roger Limbrick's Openside dolls' house, designed for Galt, which has eight inter-communicating rooms on two floors and internal walls only, so that children can play with it from every side.

Galt's catalogue claims that this dolls' house 'encourages frequent re-arranging of the furniture – the primary play purpose of a dolls' house'; but in our view this is the 'primary play purpose' only of the communal dolls' house. For the child who owns his own dolls' house, the primary purpose is to establish another family life alongside his own, another household that partly mirrors, partly contrasts with, the one which he belongs to. And whereas the household he inhabits is organized according to other, older people's decisions, in the dolls' house he calls the tune. Decisions will certainly have to be made about the arrangement of the furniture, and he may well try out different arrangements and move things around for a change, as real families do; but because there is permanence in his ownership of the dolls' house, this is likely to be reflected in the way things settle down and become an established pattern of life in the doll household, as in the real one. At this point he will probably object very much if another child starts playing with the house and shifting things around in cavalier fashion, just as adults can feel a sense of outrage if their friends try to alter patterns with which they have become satisfied and comfortable. In the same way, the dolls themselves become established in their own relationships and personalities, some of them perhaps bearing some likeness in his mind to real people, others only to fantasy personalities. The permanence of the doll household makes it possible for the child to slip into play with it without having to make preliminary decisions as to what kind of environment to make and what kind of people to put in it: each day it is waiting for him ready to take up where he left off last time. It is inherent in the nature of private dolls' house play that the dolls' house and its contents should be left undisturbed from one day to the next: for the real dolls' house enthusiast, the doll family continues its secret life between the visits of its patron, which it can hardly do if everything is packed away on top of the wardrobe at teatime. As the child grows older and more skilful in making the necessities and luxuries of dolls' house life, it will of course no longer be possible to put the house away, unless for good: each table and sideboard will hold its clutter of tiny objects, requiring more and more delicate movements from the giant hands that hover so lovingly over them.

The care that a single child can take with his own things means that the private dolls' house can be furnished with less consideration for strength and more of what pleases the child's taste and fancy. Depending on the child's age when first he is given the house, furniture can start basic and sturdy and become increasingly fragile with time, to match the child's skill in handling it. Although it has to be possible for the child to reach inside, open accessibility is less important than in the playgroup house: the child is probably playing alone, the furniture is moved around much less, and indeed there needs to be some feeling for the privacy of the dolls. If things are to be left in place for long periods, there will have to be some protection from dust; and what better than a front that can be taken off and put back on, thus giving the extra excitement of peering through the windows at life continuing inside the closed house. With the refinement of electric light the magic is complete.

Dolls' houses come in many sizes, qualities and prices, and one cannot always be certain, of course, that any one child is going to be an enthusiast. With a family of several children, it is probably safe to buy or make a reasonably good one for the first child and refurbish it for a later child if the first one loses interest. If you have little faith, there are ways of trying out the enthusiasm before spending too much: for instance, there are cheap and pretty cardboard houses on the market, together with cardboard cut-out-and-slot-together furniture, which won't last long but can at least give some indication of whether you've got a dolls'-house-type child. Or your child may have been trying to make dolls' houses with every grocery carton for months, which makes him a good bet. Another way is to advertise for the dolls' house someone else's child is tired of, being ready to paint and alter if necessary. A very hideous stockbroker's Tudor house can be made realistically pretty by pebbledashing: paint with a thick oil paint, while still wet *blow* dry sand or bird-cage grit (from a pet shop) off your palm and on to the sticky paint, let it dry and paint again. Velvet ribbon makes a beautiful staircarpet, wooden floors can be shoe-polished and scored with a ballpoint pen to make floorboards, or a floor can be given a new surface with a cork tile or sticky plastic sheeting. There are a

number of houses made with four rooms: convenient for the manufacturer but inadequate, since they allow for kitchen, living-room,
parents' bedroom and children's room but no bathroom – and every
child setting up house on a permanent basis very properly wants a
bathroom with a proper lavatory in it. However, it is often possible to
put in a dividing wall, even if it means that the bathroom can only be
approached through the bedroom.

If you are buying new, you *can* spend almost enough to need a
mortgage, depending on whether you are buying for posterity or not.
Some of the most beautiful houses are made by John and Gil
Honeychurch in wood; they can be finished in a variety of ways. You
may have to make a choice between a house with two or three storeys or
a bungalow; some children feel deprived without stairs, so long as they
actually lead to the upper floor convincingly; others like the way the
roof lifts off a bungalow, giving a fine God's-eye-view of the whole
house. Of the two kinds of houses which we had to make for the two
out of our three children who are enthusiasts, the bungalow is the
permanent success. You are likely to find that the best bargains in new
houses come from makers who also make a full range of furniture: the
houses tend to be relatively cheap because they are a come-on for the
more expensive furniture and accessories – and, after all, you don't
have to buy the whole range.

In fact it seems to us important to encourage the child right from the
beginning to make things for his dolls' house, both by helping him and
giving him ideas, but also by contributing some home-made bits and
pieces oneself. It is very easy, if one can afford it, to buy a house with a
complete set of furniture and accessories just like the show-pieces in the
shop, but leaving nothing to the imagination. In a way, this can be
another drawback of the playgroup dolls' house: it has to be ready-
furnished, because children of playgroup age find it difficult to make
furniture durable enough to survive other children. With the help of
parents or older brothers and sisters, though, quite a young child can
make chairs and table out of conkers* and pins and wool, cradles out of
walnuts, pictures drawn by himself and buckets and bowls out of found
objects like bottle tops and acorn cups; having placed them carefully in

* Inedible fruit of the horse-chestnut, a common tree in England. They are much
harder and smoother than chestnuts, and therefore prized by English children for uses
like this and in the ancient game of conkers (see p. 21).

his own house, he is likely to take care of them, the more so as his house becomes increasingly personal to himself.

From time to time other kinds of dolls' habitats come on the market: those we have seen lately include hospital wards, school-rooms and shops. They are clearly less permanently satisfying as a self-contained home for a long-term group of dolls, but they have very good play value both as a basis for making things to improve them and as a focus for fantasy play; they would have obvious use for helping children come to terms with difficult school or hospital experiences, and are therefore particularly valuable to have around in a communal setting to meet individual children's needs. Shops have a long history as children's playthings; some of the old drapers' shops are particularly charming (and copiable) with their bolts of cloth, tiny buttons on cards and dolls' garments. The fact that butchers' shops seem to predominate in surviving examples is probably due to their having been particularly useful as educational aids, to teach young ladies about the different cuts and joints of meat (as the Nuremburg kitchens were used to explain kitchen tools and techniques); certainly the butchers' wares were made with exceptional realism and in great variety.* The Bethnal Green Museum has several butchers' shops dating between 1840 and 1880, with upstairs living quarters (not all of which are usable); one of them was made by the butcher himself, a Mr Fernley, and includes an adjoining slaughter house as well as living space. Enterprising parents with a dolls'-house-minded child might consider making a shop with upstairs flat – a baker's† or a toyshop, for example; if the basic joinery seems daunting, it is worth looking round the second-hand dealers' for a small cupboard with a single shelf, to be turned upside down and roofed, using the cut-down legs as chimney-stacks. Further inspiration can be found by looking at the series of shops made by Mrs Greg, mainly in the 1920s, and now at Bethnal Green; or at the wares of the pedlar dolls, of which many museums have examples.

Most dolls' houses and furniture are made on a scale of roughly an inch to a foot; but another idea is to make a dolls' bed-sitting-room on a rather larger scale. John and Gil Honeychurch make a most beautiful fold-away room consisting of a shallow box with hinged lid which makes two walls at right angles, fitted with a panelled door and sash window; bed, chest of drawers, table and chairs all fit into the box and can be arranged freely by the child when it is opened up. The dolls to fit this room are about nine inches high (adult) and we have found it enormously productive of rich imaginative play. Our own daughters made such a room in a cupboard and peopled it with a group of children of about their own ages at the time – between eight and fourteen – who led independent lives apparently untrammelled by adults.

There are also a number of shops, schools and domestic rooms available, made and furnished in moulded plastic and inhabited by peg-people; Fisher Price and Matchbox produce good examples. These are rather different in purpose from the miniature worlds we have been talking about so far, in that they are much more constraining of what the child can do with them. It is not easy to arrange them in novel ways

---

* In 1977 the Craft Centre in London exhibited a very beautiful modern version of the toy butcher's shop, designed and made by artist-craftsmen Frank and Bridget Egerton (well known for their beautiful and witty 'toys' in wood); selling at £80, it was presumably intended for the adult toy-fancier rather than for a child.

† Very successful cakes and pastries, as well as other 'food', can be made with a hardening artifical modelling clay such as Das; or the flour and salt recipe given on page 220 can be hardened in the oven and then painted.

because the moulded accessories usually have pre-arranged sockets or pegs to which they are supposed to be fitted; the peg-people tend to have communal rather than individual characteristics. Their play value is therefore rather limited so far as continuing fantasy play is concerned.* On the other hand, they can certainly extend a young child's play with the wider world of a lay-out by being added as inhabited buildings to the roadways on which he runs his cars: can give him stopping places, as it were, for social life to go on, as a punctuation to what sometimes seems to parents a nursery take-over by the internal combustion engine.

Lay-outs

We can define a lay-out as, basically, a ground-plan upon which a small world can be built; this can be as simple as a chalked pattern of roadways. Obviously a ground-plan can lend itself to the addition of parks, fields, rivers, lakes, airfields, and so on; very quickly it can become three-dimensional as buildings and bridges, trees and hedges, personnel, animals and machinery are added. At the upper end of the range we have the enormous, complicated lay-outs to exact scale that are the result of someone's lifetime enthusiasm and expenditure of time and money, or specialist lay-outs, built perhaps for commercial purposes – like Legoland in Denmark, the world built of Lego construction units as a demonstration of that system's versatility.

A child is ready for a simple lay-out as soon as he begins to run his toy car along the border pattern of a rug or a line in a tiled floor, instead of merely randomly. Chalked roadways are not in fact very practical, as they get rubbed out by the child crawling over them as he plays; it may seem a good idea to paint a basic lay-out on the floor if the surface is suitable and if the permanence of it does not deter you. Or you may be able to buy a playmat which has a lay-out printed on it; Matchbox make

* 'Playpeople', invented by the German designer Hans Beck in 1974, are a considerable improvement on peg-people because of the mobility of their limbs and their ability to hold objects in their hands; they add enormously to the imaginative possibilities of the first lay-out or play-building. Their introduction to the British market in 1976 was followed in 1978 by play environments for them to inhabit. Their excellent design was somewhat marred by there being only one female figure included, a nurse.

rather flimsy ones, and others are available from time to time in heavier
gauge material which stands up better to active but perhaps clumsy
play. As the child gains in skill and adventurousness in handling things,
however, he will probably want to plan his own lay-out; from about
four onward, he will enjoy lengths of roadway that fit together in
patterns of his own devising. We used four-inch strips of plywood, with
beading on the edge as kerb and narrow pavement, for our children;
but manufactured alternatives are now available, such as Matchbox's
excellent tough card roadways with white lines, parking spaces and
crossings marked, and a good jigsaw fit between lengths. This can be
usefully combined with a simple railway track for a pushalong train
(Brio, expensive in wood, or almost-as-good plastic copies),
remembering to include bridges and flyovers so that the two tracks can
cross and re-cross. Given the two basic tracks, a boxful of useful
accessories can be put together over time; strips, squares and
irregularly-shaped pieces of felt or card in blue, green and brown will
be useful to make rivers, lakes and fields; road signs and other street
furniture can be bought gradually from model shops; bits of loofah
dyed green or pieces of plastic sponge will make believable bushes and
hedges; fences can be made of stuck-together lolly-sticks and
occasional lumps of plasticene will make them stand up; and so on. At
this stage parents and children begin to look at waste packaging with
new eyes as cornflakes packets become high-rise flats and corrugated
paper makes the roof to a factory; in our family the moulded
polystyrene box that had protected a radio became a magnificent
swimming pool, while the cardboard protective tubes disappeared
wholesale from boxes of tampons to create a drainpipe system.

Because mothers and fathers find miniature worlds attractive and are
easily drawn into the child's play, it is perhaps important to remember
that scale and accuracy of reproduction are of less importance to the
young child than they are to the adult participant, and that adult values
should not be pressed on the child to the exclusion of his own. There is
no reason why parents should not communicate to the child their own
enthusiasm for the perfection of a model engine's detail; but they
should also understand that the child sees nothing bizarre in combining
chalk-drawn pavements, over-size plastic houses inhabited by peg-
people, mixed-scale vehicles, cereal-box bridges and the odd dinosaur
found in a puffed-wheat packet, to make a satisfactory world through

which the engine may run. It would seem a pity to dismiss or undervalue a multiform world to which the child can contribute so much of his own imaginative construction, for the sake of bringing him prematurely to an insistence upon accuracy. Soon enough children lose their tolerance of approximation and suggestion, and begin to demand the kind of precision of replication which cannot without difficulty be achieved except by die-casting and other mass production processes: then scale models rather than toys take over. At that point, to make a scene as near as possible to the real thing, or to what it *would* be like if it *were* real, becomes an ambition in its own right. Interestingly enough, a similar development takes place in children's drawing. At the age of five to seven in particular, children paint pictures which are notable for their free and imaginative use of form and colour; but there comes a time when they begin to value (perhaps because they find they are praised for it) a photographic exactness in drawing, and their attempts to achieve this often results in inhibition and the loss of their former spontaneity.[4]

We do not want to suggest that, when a lay-out begins to be planned with special regard for accuracy and scale, this in itself makes it incapable of acting as a framework for the child's fantasy. The child may still in imagination walk the streets of his private city, control his airport or tie up his sailing boat on the further beaches of his offshore island, playing with half-formulated feelings and anxieties in the way Dibs was doing in the example we gave earlier. What perhaps we are saying is that lay-outs mean different kinds of play to different children; that an absorption with precision tends to move the child away from creating his own artefacts and towards collecting the commercially available objects which are provided in such profusion and with such explicit pressure to build up sets and systems; and that the illustrated catalogues, those seductive invitations to covetousness, tend to focus the child upon the collecting aspect of miniature worlds rather than on the rounding out of private dreams and sagas.

Building Systems

This brings us to a brief consideration of the major constructional toys which are devised as sets of basic units, massively supported by accessory kits which increase the interest and versatility of the system. The most successful forerunner of modern constructional kits in the United Kingdom was Meccano; patented by its designer Frank Hornby as 'Mechanics Made Easy' in 1901, the name changed to the more familiar one in 1907, still on the market seventy years later. The great attraction of Meccano, as with the systems which have successfully competed with it, Lego and Fischer-Technik, was that it was based on simple units of the nondescript quality that we described in relation to floor-bricks, which with the addition of multiples, halves and corner-pieces could be built up into ever more complicated structures, merely by increasing the number of units. Accessories such as wheels, cogs, axles and basic battery-powered motors made possible working models of greater sophistication. Meccano's uncompromising metal-girder look of heavy engineering, ideal for bridges and cranes but less well suited to more domestic structures, was overtaken by Lego's interlocking brick system in ABS plastic, a more versatile and cosy image: the villages and cities built as special Lego displays have something of the contrived angular coyness of Swiss chalet design,

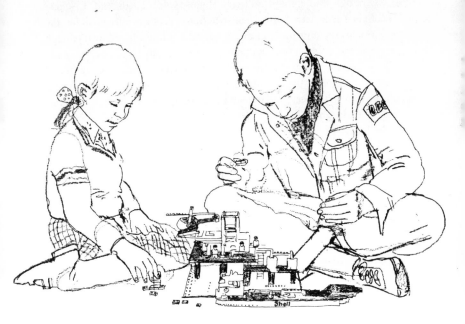

while their more streamlined models of planes and liners manage, with similar units, to seem modern in conception. Fischer-Technik owes something to both.

These building systems, along with the less sophisticated first constructional toys in wood or plastic, are interesting for their *mixture* of the precision and abstraction which we have up to now been contrasting. They cannot be said to be realistic likenesses of the objects in the real world which they purport to represent; at the same time, because they are essentially made up of predetermined modules, they have an internal precision and accuracy of scale of their own, maintained from one model to the next – and indeed they do not mix very comfortably or convincingly with other models on a lay-out. They are convincing *as a total system* because they express a powerful idiom or style – the Meccano style, the Lego idiom and so on – within which the child makes a contract to perceive reality; it is not just because the units from different systems do not fit, but because their idioms do not translate, that the child is likely to form an allegiance to one system to the exclusion of the others.

Although the major publicity displays for Lego and Fischer-Technik suggest that these constructional sets are intended for the creation of lay-outs in themselves, not many children will own enough to make more than a few small models or one really large one; it is most likely, therefore, that children will use their sets to build, take apart and re-build, more for the sake of the puzzle of construction than for the use of the finished object; and indeed Lego recognize and capitalize on this in their slogan 'Lego is a new toy every day'. None the less, the possibility of bigger and better models is always in prospect: if only one had a hundred more bricks – a few more baseplates – a couple of lighting bricks and an articulated joint – what wonders might one not achieve! So the catalogues and building plans are pored over, and pocket money mortgaged weeks in advance. Once again, the acquisitiveness of the collector is as striking as the creativity of the builder.

Collections

The collector's instinct is, of course, very strong in middle childhood anyway; it certainly cannot be blamed entirely on commercial manipulation, which makes use of interest which is already there. When we were looking at the playthings and pastimes of the 700 seven-year-olds in our study, we found that 73 per cent of them had collections of specific kinds of objects, not counting the children who were undiscriminating magpies. To quote what we wrote then;

> The following are *some* of the things collected by children in our sample: silver paper, acorns, matchboxes, string, buttons, tins, nuts and bolts, stones, conkers, tickets, boxes, religious texts, cigarette cartons, toffee-papers, makeup, matchsticks, free gifts, bottle-tops, nails, cheese-boxes, handbags, handkerchiefs, pens and pencils, plastic gardens, jigsaws, golliwogs, caterpillars, car numbers, marbles, model planes, soft toy animals, leaves, coins, chemistry set equipment, records, Meccano, costume dolls, dolls' clothes, books, little cars, feathers, Action Man sets, comics, jewellery, magazines, scraps, beermats, dolls' house furniture, labels, postcards, ornaments, railway accessories, drawings, badges, fir cones, tea cards, Lego parts, stamps, soldiers, bubble-gum cards, bricks, cactuses, footballers (*sic*), sweets, insects, Premium bonds, Scalectrix accessories, shells, 'anything that's weird or ghastly', and pictures of Cliff Richard.

The most collected objects at seven were picture-cards from packets of tea and bubble-gum, mainly collected by boys, and closely followed by Lego parts* and model cars. Dolls and their accessories were the most collected by girls.

Perhaps it is reassuring that children are still able to experience the pleasure of acquisition and possession without necessarily spending much money. We thought it strange that so few girls were collecting picture-cards, until our own daughters pointed out that most of the cards were on warlike themes which either did not interest or positively repelled them; it is true that the varied and gentler topics of the pre-war cigarette cards which delighted our own early childhoods (even with non-smoking parents) have given way to some extraordinarily bloodthirsty series – one of our sample children's mothers, the owner of a sweetshop, complained that they were 'unfit for human consumption', referring to the cards rather than the bubble-gum that they accompanied. In that sense, girls are more compelled than boys to spend money on the collecting items that interest them most.

---

* Fischer-Technik was not widely available at the time of the study. In toy-trade advertising, they claimed in 1976 to have increased their sales tenfold in three years.

The fact that dolls and their accessories emerged as the major subject of girls' collections is interesting, too, in that we were not asking what the children liked playing with or what were their most treasured possessions, but explicitly what they *collected*. It seems we are no longer now talking about dolls as the children or friends of their owners, the traditional function of the doll as we have discussed it in chapter 4, but as objects which can be built up in sets, together with the accessories that go with them. And in accessories we have the nub of it: although some children had built up collections of dolls in national costume, whose only accessories were the clothes they stood up in (probably the only characteristics which distinguished them from each other), for most children the doll was a focus for a whole wardrobe of clothes for all occasions, and often other possessions: furniture, equipment such as skates, radio and camera, and perhaps even a sports car or a pony.

These dolls with their expensive tastes are obviously very big business indeed, and they are promoted as such. Outstanding in their market are Barbie (Mattel) and Sindy (Pedigree), with many other competing young ladies, almost all apparently teen-age, though they sell to children well below puberty. Marketing needs insist that the doll be promoted by name; this creates an interesting phenomenon in itself, in that what is being sold is not a figure on to which the child can project a personality of his own idiosyncratic choosing, but a ready-made total package: the 'Sindy' or 'Barbie' persona. Long observation of this phenomenon suggests that children very rarely give the doll a private name, and it seems they are content to accept the public image; what is more, Sindy has been sold in considerably greater numbers than the UK female child population, so that there are many children who have two or more Sindies.[5] At this point the illusion of any individual personality is lost completely, and the corporate image takes over. While the doll's function as peg for a collection is a perfectly valid role, we clearly should not confuse it with our basic understanding of the doll as an almost-person.

The Barbie/Sindy phenomenon was barely approached in the pre-war history of dolls. The nearest similar situation was the promotion of Shirley Temple dolls in the image of the child star: again, the marketing of a ready-made personality which, however, because it was not so comprehensively sustained by a total accessory range, did not also include a ready-made life-style. One and a half million Shirley

Temple dolls were sold by the Ideal Toy Corporation in the 1930s. No recent child star seems to have had the magic for this kind of promotion, or perhaps commercial firms have preferred to manufacture their own dreams from scratch, which certainly allows them more scope; for instance, Sindy was at one time given the ultimate accessory of a boy-friend, Paul, who was quietly dropped as soon as it was clear that his clean-limbed but vacuous image lacked commercial impact. The use of real television and film stars as models for dolls has been almost entirely confined to male adventure characters identified mainly by their screen names: Starsky and Hutch, Kojak and so on. Some of these have accessory ranges in their own right, but they are also of a scale to use the extensive ranges provided for Action Man and his successors. These were originally an attempt to corner a new boys' market for an all-American fighting man, whose earlier accessories consisted almost exclusively of combat weapons and military uniforms; there was a considerable body of distaste for them among parents, and male dolls have now notably enlarged their sphere of action to include mountaineering, exploration, space travel and ecological conservation, which allows for an extremely attractive (and wholesome!) range of miniature cameras, sleeping-bags, tents, ropes and cagoules and the like.

With these last, there is a possibility of a return to a miniature world where things happen: dolls equipped for adventures can obviously go ahead and have them, accompanied and masterminded by the child. Although dolls on this scale do not easily fit on to a lay-out, which would need to be of very large and expensive proportions, children can happily use the furniture and rugs of their own home as mountains and seas. The realism of the tiny equipment somehow lends verisimilitude to the steep slopes of the settee; in the family living-room, the peaks of the Himalayas issue their ancient challenge.

7   Play and Playthings for the Handicapped Child

(Elizabeth Newson and Joan Head)

At this point, we are going to shift our focus a little and look more closely at children who for one reason or another have special needs. They may be physically or mentally handicapped, or both; they may have been born into deprived environments; they may be temporarily 'special', in that they are ill or immobilized for a while.

In some ways, 'special' needs are ordinary needs prolonged over time or intensified. In other ways, they are very idiosyncratic to the child concerned, but still demand the same kind of skills which parents of 'ordinary' children try to use all the time: an intimate, even if not very confident, knowledge of the child as she is; an ability to sort out priorities from her point of view and the family's; the insight and ingenuity to meet problems usefully as they arise; and the patience to make extra allowances and go to extra trouble during times of difficulty or crisis. From both these points of view, we hope that parents whose children are not handicapped will nonetheless find it interesting to consider how toys and play can serve these more specific purposes; and certainly professionals who work with children, whether handicapped or not, will (we believe) find here ideas that they can use.

The Implications of Handicap

To understand what it can mean in practical terms to be a handicapped baby or toddler, we must return once more to ordinary babies growing up in ordinary families. As we have already suggested, much of the so-called 'normal development' of non-handicapped children is probably only achieved as a by-product of the spontaneous busy activity, the ceaseless inquisitive restlessness, which is typical of the human infant's assault on her environment. As soon as she is physically able, with hands, feet and mouth the baby pulls and thrusts, pounds, nibbles and pokes at the surrounding world. Continually astonished, yet continually accepting, she devours with her eyes and ears the outcomes of her efforts, discovering in the process the form and nature of the diversity about her: what gives way and what resists, what is malleable and what disintegrates, what fights back at her and what eludes her grasp. It is only through this intense participation and involvement, both with things and with people, that she begins to structure conceptually the manifold characteristics of her perceptual world, and to make sense of it, both intellectually and in emotional, personal terms. The implication of this is that conceptual structuring and 'making sense' can by no means be taken for granted as the basic 'given' of experience, but is the end result of an essentially active, creative and social process of learning. This is also a circular process: patterns of activity simply reflect conceptual patterns, and we only perceive the world in terms of the patterns we are able to impose upon it – which, again, we arrive at *through* active involvement.

In contrast, young children who in one way or another are handicapped often seem to lack either the desire or the ability to play like other children. There are a number of reasons why this might happen.

Some kinds of handicap, such as spina bifida, cerebral palsy or blindness, restrict a child in very obvious ways. She cannot move around at will; she has trouble controlling the movement of limbs, so that toys cannot be reached for accurately, or may be swept off the table by a spasmodic arm movement; her ability to hold her head up may be poor, so that she finds it difficult to choose to look at anything not immediately in front of her eyes, and impossible to anticipate things arriving in her field of vision; she may have difficulty in grasping or in letting go of an object; she cannot judge distance, or perhaps cannot see her surroundings at all. These are fundamental problems which are immediately apparent to the onlooker. But it is important to look beyond the basic disability, and to consider some of the *implications* of the handicap for the child's total development.

For instance, if she cannot get about easily and at her own inclination, the child will be denied many of the taken-for-granted opportunities for exploring home and garden through which ordinary children learn and find out for themselves. A normally mobile baby can follow and retrieve a rolling toy, and so try out its properties again and again; discover the consequences of her actions and learn strategies for avoiding or exploiting them; hunt for some object to play with *in conjunction* with another object; turn out the kitchen cupboards to find out for herself about the size-ordering of saucepans and their lids (for example); and pursue an older member of the family in order to get help with something that is a little beyond her: but these are all activities for which the immobile child is very dependent upon other people and their ability to perceive need and spend time on helping to meet it. Lack of mobility is thus not only a *physical* handicap: it can quickly develop into an *intellectual* deprivation.

The immobile child is also restricted emotionally and socially. The normal active toddler, though she may at times enjoy being 'babied' and tenderly protected, feels intense emotional satisfaction in doing things independently: not for nothing does the word 'no' usually appear before the word 'yes', and often this will be in response to offers of help. The pleasure children take in doing things for themselves is obviously an important part of the whole business of growing up; for the immobile child, for whom so many things have to be done by other people, opportunities for these satisfactions may have to be deliberately manufactured if they are not to become so rare that the child no longer looks for them. A child who accepts total passivity is not a learning, growing child. We have already suggested a social restriction, in that the immobile toddler cannot pursue or seek out members of her family, but must wait for them to come to her; almost equally handicapping is that she also misses the casual but valuable encounters with other people outside the family, which ordinary children get by running to the door at the postman's knock, chatting to the milkman on the way to the gate, or making their own purchases from the ice-cream man or sweet-shop.

These are four different areas in which the immobile child is restricted *as a consequence of immobility*; and it begins to become evident, perhaps, why it has sometimes been said that there are no singly handicapped children, but only multi-handicapped ones: one area of a child's life so easily spills over into another area. Other conditions have other implications.

Some children, especially those who are mentally handicapped, receive very little stimulation during the early months because they are unusually 'good' babies, content to lie passively in their cots; often we later learn that parents were congratulated on how little trouble the baby was, and the very word 'good' implies that we approve of babies who make no demands on people or on their surroundings. But inactivity itself retards; a baby who is mentally handicapped needs very positive encouragement to reach out and take hold of the world, and thus begin to move forward to whatever potential she may have, because she is not urged on by the excitement of her own thoughts as is a normal baby.

A rather different example, but with similar results in reducing the child's playing and learning experiences, is the hyperactive, often irritable child. Such children often have very great difficulty in attending and concentrating on anything for more than a minute or so, often less – although some are only hyperactive for parts of the day, and may have a longer concentration-span during their calmer periods. The point we are making here is that – although there may be many reasons

why a child should have a 'flitting' attention – once her body is literally flitting at speed, this on its own will reduce her ability to stay with a play activity and follow it through. Similarly, irritable children may give their whole attention to screaming or grizzling. Toys which give big results for little effort may be needed to hold the attention of distractible children, and offer a starting-point for a parent who is attempting to extend the child's attention*.

Another reason for a handicapped child's failure to play may be seen in terms of severe sensory deprivation: the baby who is both deaf and blind, for instance, is imprisoned in a dark and silent cocoon almost as inaccessibly as if she were still in the womb. How can such a child discover for herself that exploration is worth the effort, and the fear of what is beyond the limits of her touch, when she is not tempted outward by the sights and sounds that reward other babies?

Handicapped children often have no desire, or a very limited desire, to explore the unknown. Some take refuge in a private world in defence against anxiety. In particular this is true of the two groups of children who, for different reasons, have difficulty in making sense of the two kinds of communication that come before speech and are a prelude to it: facial expression and gesture. These are the blind and the autistic children. In retreat from the confusion and ambiguity of the 'world-out-there', both blind and autistic children may set up defensive barriers of repetitive mannerisms and rituals (more marked in autistic children, who have specific problems of coding speech as well): rocking movements, head banging or shaking, finger flicking, hand flapping, and the flicking or spinning of objects close to the face. These seem to have a 'cutting-off' function for the child, keeping at bay the uncertainties of the world outside by filling her sensory input to the exclusion of less manageable messages; at the same time, however, their result is to stigmatize her still further as 'different' and 'odd', discouraging other people from trying to make social contact with the child, until she is indeed cut off from the social contact she so desperately requires. Here again, the child needs a very unambiguous

---

* An example is what we call a 'visual hurrah'. This is an array of Christmas tree lights on a frame, which can be turned on by mere pressure of a fist in the right place. Used as a 'way in' for very severely handicapped children, it can also be switched on and off as a reward for children from whom more is expected – hence its name.

stimulus from the outside world, which will entice her to move outward, away from her pre-occupation with her own body rituals, and towards interaction with her environment.

There are, of course, special problems for the institutionalized handicapped child. If she has lived in the more impersonal kind of institution from an early age, she may show the boredom, listlessness and apathy which we recognize as the signs of maternal deprivation: handicapped children are not immune from the deprivation that other children suffer in such circumstances. Perhaps it would be more accurate to talk in terms of deprivation of *personal* care, rather than maternal care; even the best institution finds difficulty in matching the ordinary family's ability to offer the child that sense of personal worth, of being *special for them*, which gives her both the security and the stimulus (person-centred as opposed to merely child-centred) to play as children do play in a family setting. Play sessions slotted into the time-table of institutional administration, while they are obviously helpful, do not have the potency of family play which capitalizes on a moment-by-moment loving orientation towards the child as an individual family member. Growing up in an institution, while it may be unavoidable in some cases, has to be recognized as constituting an additional handicap.

In the chapters that follow, we hope to show that play, and the toys which focus a child's play, can be used to draw a handicapped child outward and forward; to help her to interact with the world she lives in, both things and people; to enrich her limited experience so that, where the ordinary child learns by a sheer multiplicity of opportunities, she may learn through an intensified learning situation; and, by giving her a taste of exciting possibilities, to help her to push forward her own boundaries. At this point, perhaps it may be useful to give some quite specific examples of how toys might serve these purposes.

Tempting the Blind Child Outward

Sighted babies are spurred into activity by what they see: reaching is followed by kicking and swivelling, which develop into shunting, creeping and crawling. 'I see', 'I want', 'I can get', are a natural progression; take away 'I see', and the blind baby may be unaware of wanting anything, let alone of the possibility of going after it. Not yet mobile, and not knowing why it might be useful to be mobile, the blind child's psychological world, as well as her physical world, is extremely closely circumscribed.

Because she cannot see the attractive objects around her, she has no stimulus to reach out for them; but even if a toy is put in her hand, she cannot easily play with it as a sighted child would, and not just because of her inability to explore it with her eyes. For instance, a sighted baby with a ball will swipe and follow it, throw it and clamour for its return (making herself understood by 'eye-pointing'), and drop it into a box or basket. The blind child dares not let the ball roll away from her lest she lose it completely, nor will she drop it into a box, for she cannot see containers and therefore cannot 'see' their possible uses, even if she is prepared to let go of the ball. But every child seeks more stimulus than merely holding a toy in the hand; while the sighted child will gain this stimulus by alternately exploring visually and bringing the toy into contact with the environment (throwing, scraping, banging and so on), the blind child turns inward towards herself for this second stimulus, and bites or licks the ball, or rubs it against her face or eyes. Repeated endlessly during the child's day, this kind of play can begin to show the 'cutting-off' characteristics that we have already described, and can become an emotional withdrawal almost amounting to autism. Many children show a reluctance to handle objects at all. As we saw in the second chapter, an active wish for 'happenings' is as important for the child's development as the hunger for food and drink.

Toys are needed which have the deliberate and specific function of 'uncurling' the child, as it were, and making her aware of things beyond what can be contained between hand and mouth. At this early stage, a small collection of toys needs to be anchored for the child in some way, so that she can learn to risk dropping one in the knowledge that she can haul it in on its string when she wants it back; and items in the collection should include some things which activate others (drumstick and drum, spoon and tin mug, for example), so that the child learns to exploit one object in combination with another, rather than bringing each separately to her mouth. A container in the form of a small cage, so that the child can explore the contents with her fingers before going on to solve the problem of opening it, makes a rattle with far more possibilities than just rattling, especially as one can vary the object inside to suit the child's interest – a small toy, a bunch of keys, an

old scent bottle, a biscuit; a wooden cage can be specially made, using dowelling 'bars', but polythene storage jars can be easily adapted. As the child's mobility increases, play equipment which has its own boundaries (sandpit, baby-bath containing water or dried peas) can give her the security to feel free and relaxed within those bounds, and eventually to grow beyond them.

Stimulating Babble and Early Speech

In working with mute autistic children, there is an urgent need to get *utterance* started, by whatever means will work for the individual child: the 'chatty' child, even if she is chatty only in babble or jargon, has a head start on the child who is totally silent. Often the first problem is to make the child's utterance rewarding to her in other ways than the mere pleasure of communication, which is enough for the normal baby.

Many autistic children take great pleasure in mechanical objects, and most are fascinated by lights. Colleagues of ours were once inspired by these interests to invent an electronic projection kaleidoscope which changed its pattern (projected brightly on the screen) in response to one little boy's utterance. Because the child was delighted by the pattern, he would tend to make some sound of pleasure, which immediately was rewarded by a new pattern, which in turn became the stimulus for the next utterance; in this way, he became much more vocal very quickly indeed, giving us a structure of varied babble on which to build speech.[1] But the toy does not need to be nearly as sophisticated as this in order to serve its purpose. For instance, most of our work with this first child was done using a slide projector fitted with a cheap kaleidoscope in which the pattern was changed by hand in response to the child's babble. A variation is to project slides of everyday objects in slightly blurred focus, sharpening-up the focus as the reward for a vocal response; this is particularly useful, since what one demands of the child can be gradually stepped up to suit his increasing ability, from *any* vocal sound, through word approximations, to actual naming (cup!) or even two-word naming (blue cup!). We also use ordinary slide viewers to excite speech, again on the principle that pictures of a very high brightness level do seem much more stimulating for the child, and that children who have so far found people not stimulating enough (or possibly too confusingly stimulating, as with autistic children) need a different *kind* of exciting experience – almost as if one had to surprise utterance out of them. Obviously gadget-toys like these must be fully supported by other therapeutic procedures, but in individual cases they can have great value as a breakthrough technique.

Liberating Activity

A child who is very slow in understanding may also be slow in bodily activity and social response: there may be neurological reasons for a general clumsiness of movement, or it may be that her ability to see possibilities of action within situations is so limited that she becomes lethargic and listless. Similarly, a child whose physical capabilities are impaired may behave more passively than she need, because she has become accustomed to the tight limitations *for her* of an environment created by and for the unimpaired. For these children, sometimes a massive change in the nature of their environment can produce a liberation.

Jim Sandhu and his colleagues have devised and monitored many ways of changing the environment of handicapped children, both through play equipment and by other means (such as altering the levels of their play-space).[2] He and Roger Haydon experimented with large 'inflatables': some were just enormous air mattresses or sausages, others were enclosed by low inflatable walls rather like paddling pools, with the 'paddling' area itself a bouncy inflated floor; but perhaps the most exciting, both for the children and for those watching them, was an apparently endless tube of thin translucent plastic, which, when blown up with the wrong end of a vacuum cleaner, filled the room with its undulations. The large inflatables offer a way of transforming a room full of hard surfaces and sharp corners into a billowy sea of air and plastic: a place to roll and bounce, push and prod: to jump on one end of a sausage and see it astonish your friend on the other end, and to be astonished in turn by the effect of his bouncing; to experience the power of lifting huge shapes with ease – and to share these excitements with others.

Not surprisingly, children increase both in activity and in animation when they are playing in this way; for some, the experience seems to release them from physical passivity in other situations as well, and may even provoke an increase in speech. A swimming pool (or the sea), or piles of fallen leaves, give other opportunities for total experiences of this liberating kind; we should like, one day, to try out a room full of polystyrene 'worms' such as are used for packing. Since Jim Sandhu's first experiments, it has become easier to give children the experience of inflatables; not only can the big air mattresses be bought (expensively), but long unperforated polythene tubes are available (sold for cutting and sealing into bags), and many funfairs and amusement parks include an inflated bouncing area of truly gigantic proportions (under various names such as 'moonwalk'). These are strongly recommended as a *joint* experience for mentally handicapped children and the adults who care for them; but it is best to choose a time when the place is not full of large and noisy teenagers!

Helping the Child to Grasp Basic Concepts

The special intellectual needs of handicapped children can be well illustrated by the situation of the blind child. There are many concepts which the sighted child learns easily and gradually through innumerable experiences and self-demonstrations in his daily life: to take one example, the notion that objects may be classified and grouped in different kinds of categories. Through ordinary everyday play, children learn that things may 'belong' together because they are *functionally complementary* (bowl and spoon, chair and table, pram and blanket); or because they are *functionally inter-supportive* (milk goes in the mug, baby goes in the pram); or because they are *functionally equivalent though superficially different* (a dolls' house dining-chair, nine-inch doll's basket-chair, doll's deck-chair, kindergarten chair and doll's high chair can all be seen as equivalent by a normal two-year-old).

Concepts such as these are basic to intellectual development generally and to language development specifically. For example, it is almost useless for a child to learn the word 'chair' simply as a name for an object of such-and-such a shape (although her *first* encounter with the word may be tied to one particular object); to be useful, she must understand the word as applying to what chairs *do*, which is the essential 'chairiness' of chairs. We once filmed a normal two-year-old exploring a playroom: a constant feature of her behaviour was to scan the room to find things to 'go with' some other toy that she had already found. In this way, when she found an empty cradle, she looked around the room to find a doll to go in it, found it, fetched it and returned to the cradle; similarly, having found the first of the series of chairs listed above, she looked for other chairs, gradually found the rest of that series, and assembled them in a satisfying circle round a small table. For comparison, we then filmed an intelligent blind two-year-old in the same situation: she too found the cradle, found that it was empty, but had no possibility of scanning the room for a doll to go in it; and if she *had* found a doll in her explorations, what hope would she have had of finding the cradle again? In time, she too came upon chairs; some were difficult for her to identify by touch, but, more important, there was very little chance of her conceptualizing them as a group, since she could neither scan to find them nor make the quick visual comparison which would bring out the quality they had in common.

Because of the difficulties that a blind child has in amassing enough repeated experience to acquire everyday concepts, it may be necessary for family and teachers to find ways of deliberately demonstrating such concepts. In a situation like this, the so-called 'educational toy' (a posting-box, for instance), which children with a normally rich sensory experience do not particularly need, comes into its own as a means of helping handicapped children over their particular conceptual hurdles. We have come to think of these as 'concept-packed' toys, because they deliberately and almost selfconsciously set out to teach the understanding of a particular concept, and do so with great economy by being designed to make a specific impact. They do not take away the need for the child to reiterate her play-learning at leisure, but to some extent they make up for the handicapped child's diminished experience through their effectiveness.

Sometimes it is suggested that blind children should not be given

models to play with: that their experience should be entirely in terms of 'real' objects. Our own view is otherwise: that blind children should be encouraged to learn from any source available, and that there are some concepts about the 'real' world which they will have difficulty in learning at all except through models. Consider our understanding of 'car', for instance. Sighted children have many opportunities of conceptualizing cars as whole objects, for they see them approaching at a distance, gradually apparently becoming larger, until close to they become two doors flanked by two wheels. For the blind child, a car is an increasing engine noise until it becomes a door with a seat the other side of it. Even if the blind child is allowed to feel all over a real car, she will still find it difficult to conceptualize the whole of it correctly, since feeling it involves a *series* of actions in time rather than the reasonably integrated image that a visual glance gives. It is only the enclosing of different toy cars in her two hands, of course combined with experience inside and outside real cars, that will begin to make up for the loss of that distant view. Significantly, a blind adult once told us: 'I never realized that "upstairs" was *on top of* "downstairs" until I felt my children's dolls' house.' It can be a salutary shock for the sighted to be brought face to face with the misunderstanding of a concept so taken-for-granted that nobody had thought to explain it:* yet most sensorily-deprived people must suffer many similar misconceptions. And in the end it is the sensitivity and awareness and empathy of family, friends and teachers which will help handicapped children to become not-so-handicapped adults.

The Role of Adults

In brief, handicapped children, particularly when they are young, need to be lured, tempted, coaxed and sometimes even badgered into active involvement with things and people. They need exciting possibilities, not just as much as, but more than, ordinary children. But toys in

---

* It can be a shock to the blind person, too. A blind house-guest once apologized to one of the authors for coming down to breakfast before he had shaved, to which she replied 'That's all right, white stubble is rather nice to look at', and was surprised to see that he was taken aback: '*Is my stubble white?*' he said. He had been blinded as a young man more than forty years earlier.

themselves do not create exciting possibilities, however well designed
for their purpose; it is a constant anxiety for those who design toys for
handicapped children that this might encourage people to choose the
'right' toy, hand it to the child, and walk away. The purpose-designed
toy is not a substitute for adult involvement, but rather an *aid* to
involvement – a means of setting the stage for the child's more fruitful
interaction with parents and others. It is *the use adults make* of what the
toy produces that is important. The willing adult is an indispensable
part of the therapeutic play experience: toys on their own do not
produce dramatic results.

Probably nothing can really take the place of the interested mother –
except the interested father. We suggested at the beginning of this book
that the mother is the first and best toy; and 'therapeutic mothering',
by the man or woman who is most concerned with the child's care at the
time when developmental progress should be at its peak, is so valuable
that every effort should be made to support it effectively. Parents often
say that they lack information about what they can expect from their
handicapped child, and how best they can help her to progress. It is not
really helpful to send parents home with the well-meaning advice
'Stimulate your child', without any ideas as to how, and to what end.
Nor is it enough to advise parents on which toys to buy: they need also
to be aware of all the various learning opportunities that might be set up
with each toy, and to understand the aim and rationale behind any
particular routine so well that it is no longer a routine but a tailor-made
activity for their individual child. This is where a well-run 'toy library'
(see pp. 198 and 261–2) can help parents to assume their remedial role
with confidence.

Simply by playing with their children, parents re-structure the
child's whole activity in a way that the child herself, left to her own
devices, could never have done. This is true even at a point when
communication is pre-verbal; how much more so once language is
available to the child, even if that language is produced and received
with difficulty. Kay Mogford gives a vivid example from one of her
studies:

An intelligent but severely deaf child plays alone with her doll. She takes the
baby out of the cradle, kisses and hugs it. She then puts the pillow into the
cradle, but puts the doll in with the head towards the foot of the cradle. She
recognises her error and puts the doll's head to the head of the cradle. With the

doll fully dressed, she replaces the mattress and cover on top of the doll. Satisfied that she has finished, she moves on to another toy. Only when we see her mother playing with her, can we see the role that she plays in helping the child to learn how to treat the doll more appropriately. We can see just how in interaction the mother endeavours to teach her deaf child, through words, some of the ideas and qualities with which the normal child learns in play to endow her play and dolls. For example, her mother talks about the difference between the cover and the mattress and which goes in first. She suggests the child undresses the doll; that when naked the doll may be cold, when her eyes close she may be tired. (At the same time, the whole flow of the sequence is interrupted for the child, for her mother must physically stop and hold her so that they are face to face, before the child can understand her mother's words, and be drawn back to reflect on what she has just done. If her mother is too slow, the child's play has advanced far beyond the point at which her comment would be relevant.) We can surmise that only through interaction had the child already learned to realize that the doll sleeps with her head under the cradle canopy. It is especially in this imaginative play that language is needed to lift the play above the level of the actual physical possibilities of the play materials.[3]

Some handicapped children have an irrational dislike of anything new and it can be extremely difficult to introduce an unfamiliar toy to them. Here again, parents are all-important: often, simply playing with the toy calmly in front of the child is enough to draw her into the activity. Other children need rather more persuasion, especially if they are highly distractible. The mother's or father's own enthusiasm, shown in an exaggerated intonation or facial expression, will often serve; but gentle persistence, perhaps in the form of bringing out the toy for only a few minutes at a time, at a moment in the day when the parents know the child to be particularly receptive, is sometimes needed. It is surprising how successful a toy can be if 'rested' after an unsuccessful introduction and then reintroduced a month or so later, perhaps with co-operation from a brother or sister. Parents are likely to know their child's foibles well enough to carry this out with great sensitivity.

Once a child has acquired a new skill by using a certain toy, it is obviously essential that she then moves on to practise it outside the context of the toy itself: and the handicapped child may well need support in applying her skills adaptively to a different situation. Some mothers are exceptionally good at judging just when the child is ready to generalize a new skill. Again, this is very much a matter of awareness of aims, coupled with parents' intimate knowledge of their own individual child.

The intrinsic therapeutic value of the toy and the skills it stimulates is not the end of the story, then; a major reward for everyone concerned is the positive interaction that is fostered between parent and child, once parents are being adequately supported in understanding their child's special needs. Often their previous attempts to play with the child have been deeply discouraging and frustrating; sometimes they have begun to despair of their child's ability to play and of their own ability to help her. In a culture pattern that considers play to be childhood's birthright, not to play can seem to expel the child from the community of children, while not to achieve play for their child threatens parents in their accepted role. Play with a developmental purpose involves the family in a way which is clearly constructive and positive: progress made by the child is seen to be a direct result of that involvement, and all members of the family can be caught up in the impetus of creating a dynamic and lasting growth environment for their least able member.

Assessment for Remediation

If we are going to take seriously the idea of using toys and play activities for a remedial purpose, then we must also take seriously the way we set about doing so. Some toys are appropriate to an individual child's needs; others much less so. This is one major criticism of the injunction 'stimulate your child': it is insensitive to the child as a person. We can stimulate a dog by tying tin cans to its tail, but it is doubtful whether this will cause the dog to make developmental progress.

Thus it may be useful to start by thinking about the child's condition generally, as we have only begun to do in this chapter, and to ask ourselves what are the *implications* of being partially deaf, or totally blind, or slow-learning, or of having no control over our leg muscles: but we must then go on to look at the particular child we want to help, and ask what this means *for her*. What precisely has been the course of her experience in the past, and how has she reacted to it at different points? Are there times when she has been more able than she currently is, and in what ways? What is the picture now, and does it seem reasonably consistent from day to day, or are there big variations? If there are variations, under what conditions do they occur? Just what do the child's abilities appear to be, in the many different areas of behaviour, and have we any reason to believe that most of the time she is functioning at a much lower level than she is capable of? – and, if so, why might that be?

Unless we have made a determined attempt to assess this child's own needs, difficulties and possibilities, we shall not know how, or towards what goals, to direct our efforts for remediation. This should indeed be the major intention of assessment: that it should suggest guidelines as to what the priorities are for this child and what might be a fruitful way in. Too often in the past, assessments have unfortunately been carried out without any real consideration of what their practical implications might be: the main purpose has frequently seemed to be the *classification* of a child, often for rather ill-defined administrative reasons, and sometimes one is even left with the impression that labelling has merely made the child tidy enough to be set aside. One of the great advantages of parents and teachers being closely involved in the assessment process (in addition to the fact that this produces a better assessment) is that it forces psychologists and other professionals to consider the question that should be asked whenever a 'label' is given: 'so what?'. Parents and teachers have to live with that question '*so what – where do I go from here?*'

So assessment and remediation are two sides of the same coin: it is a waste of time to assess unless we have remediation firmly in mind, and remediation can only happen effectively if we have assessed what strategies are likely to be helpful for this child. But this is not just a simple matter of 'first assess, then remediate'. If assessment is to be productive, it must be a continuous process, in which the remediator does not cling to his first judgements, but remains open to new understandings. Early assessments will suggest what are the child's most urgent needs and how one might begin, and a start will be made on the basis of the information known; new assessments will be made *in the course of* remediation, and partly on the basis of how the child responds to these strategies. We choose our ways of working with the child *on the hypothesis* that our assessment of her need is correct: if these attempts are totally unsuccessful, however, we must always be prepared to admit that part of our assessment may have been mistaken, and modify it accordingly.

If the same person is carrying out both the assessment and the remediation programme, this monitoring of one against the other is reasonably simple. If, however, as often happens, professionals are assessing and parents are remediating, then it is absolutely essential that there should be free two-way communication about whether the programme suggested is working for the child or not. Ideally, the parents should be real (as opposed to notional) members of the assessment team.[4]

Whatever the division of roles, those working directly with the child need the opportunity to report back, secure in the knowledge that if they are not succeeding in attaining their goals, there will be a constructive consideration of how their methods (or, if need be, their goals) may be changed. Parents are vital members of the remedial team, and their child's progress or lack of it must be capable of discussion *as between members of a team*, without the parents feeling that the professionals may be threatened if their advice fails to work: to quote one paediatrician, who has been concerned about these problems of communication, 'Unfortunately, parents sometimes try to save their doctor distress.' The co-operative approach, which attempts to demystify and share professional expertise, makes communication more free and flexible; assessment immediately becomes more accurate, and remediation more reliably based and therefore more effective. Most of the understandings and ideas which are discussed in these chapters are the direct result of an approach which refuses to waste the resource we have in the interested parent: and it is normal for parents to be interested and ingenious and inventive where the needs of their own children are concerned!

8 Using Toys for Developmental Assessment

This chapter is of a rather different kind from the rest of this book. In it we want to open in more detail some of the work currently being done by psychologists on how play can be used to understand the child's current level of competence. Psychologists have tended in the past to be rather secretive about the methods they use to 'assess' children; sometimes this secretiveness has been defensive, reflecting the fact that their test results were often not very helpful in suggesting guidelines to parents and teachers as to what to do next. If psychologists are seriously to collaborate with parents and teachers as a remedial team, they must also devise assessment methods which they can share and use.

As psychologists and teachers have become more interested in assessment for remediation, and less in assessment for its own sake, people working with handicapped children have also begun to explore more *flexible* methods of mapping a child's difficulties and potentialities than formal tests provide. Very young children and handicapped children have in common that they are not very amenable to the social constraints involved in sitting down and doing an intelligence test; perhaps the inadequacy of these traditional 'psychometric' tools, when applied to a hyperactive or withdrawn child, has been a useful spur in forcing us to think about assessment in broader terms than scores on timed tests. Detailed and sensitive observation of a child's spontaneous or responsive play can be a potent source of information about him; psychologists in particular have been devising ways of setting up 'naturalistic' play sessions which will enable the child to demonstrate, not only his ability to solve formal problems, but his approach to, and strategies in, the kind of problem-solving that arises in play, his social and communicative behaviour towards an adult companion, his imaginative or innovative use of toys, his manipulative skills or his ability to circumvent his lack of skill, and so on.

In a sense, when we assess a child on formal tests we confine him within the tramlines of our own preconceptions about the nature of the abilities that he might show. This may or may not be a dangerous and misleading thing to do. For children with uneven development and for those with serious problems in behaviour and in social relationships, it is likely to be so, because they have already shown us that our tramlines are just what they cannot run on. Our only hope of approaching an understanding of their difficulties and possibilities is deliberately to stretch the constraints and be ready to follow the child wherever he leads.

Much of this work is still at the experimental stage; and too often creative and highly effective techniques of observation, although used very successfully in clinics and schools, remain unpublished because they can be more difficult to present than the standardized test. Learning how to use them is also a more lengthy process, since a *qualitative* understanding demands patience and experience: test scores offer the crutch of an apparently more precisely defined result, satisfying to the assessor, though it may tell us almost nothing useful about the child.

Two examples of attempts to come closer to the child's levels of functioning by observing his response to toys, rather than tests, will be described in this chapter; in both cases, the examples will be given in the form in which they currently exist, as practical working suggestions for professional colleagues, in order to keep the flavour of their authors' intentions. They therefore contain technical vocabulary which some non-specialist readers may not be familiar with – but this is not central to an understanding of the methods used. Both examples come from the Nottingham University Child Development Research Unit. The first is a series of notes written by Elizabeth Newson as a guide for trainee developmental and educational psychologists working in her assessment clinic;[1] the second example, part of a series of 'observational play repertoires', was devised by Kay Mogford together with Joan Head, as a tool for toy libraries for handicapped children.

Play-based Observation for Assessment of the Whole Child

(Elizabeth Newson)

These notes are intended to stimulate further ideas for ways of building up a useful picture of a child apparently showing delayed or uneven development. They are in no way comprehensive; nor could one use all these ideas in one assessment session. Many can usefully be incorporated into remediation activities, which it is assumed will follow an initial assessment.

Ideally, the person working with the child will be supported by at least one, preferably two, observers taking detailed notes behind a one-way screen if possible; parents or other caregivers will also be actively involved in contributing to the picture, preferably in conjunction with a third observer behind the screen. Parents may also work with the child if this seems helpful.

Formal tests may be used to investigate certain topics; they are likely to be more useful in later rather than preceding sessions.

1. Throughout Session

a) Keep tape-recorder switched *on*; not only for later checking of echolalia, analysis of sentence structure, analysis of speech distortions, but also for evidence of intonational patterns and prosody, consistent distortions, variety and range of phonemes, etc.

b) Observe gait, gross body movement, general muscle tone, as well as fine manipulation. Note handedness, and whether consistent.

c) Note any mannerisms.

d) Watch for level and span of attention; distractibility as opposed to hyperactivity; child's willingness to address itself to the task.

e) Note social behaviour, including amenability and sociable cooperation, eye contact and referential looking, social and non-social body contact, refusal of physical contact or shrinking from it.

f) Try to get the overall 'feel' of the child *re* level of arousal, depressive states, lability of mood, whether he is tolerant of pressure or has to be 'kid-gloved' to avoid tantrums or withdrawal.

2.　Initiation of Session

Convey by your manner that you expect the child to enjoy the session and to come with you into the playroom (i.e., don't cajole or over-persuade); if he won't, or wants his mother or father with him, be relaxed about this – a policy of gradual increase of separation distance, plus interest of playroom, will normally succeed. There's no objection to the child coming to find his mother behind the screen from time to time.

The following have well-tried efficacy in getting children's initial interest and response:

dried pea-tray:	almost *too* inviting, and it may have to be removed if the child gets too 'hooked' to give attention to anything else.
bubbles marble-run balloons	judicious use of these just inside playroom door can lure a reluctant child in.
pop-up cone-tree Pooh pop-up toy musical box humming top	and other novelty or surprise toys

Sometimes you can bring the child in by letting him push (or ride on) a wheeled toy, or roll and follow a rolling toy. Most children won't need special ruses.

Make sure throughout that the child is physically comfortable, as his attention and general competence will be reduced by discomfort. Invite him to remove his jersey, etc., if he seems hot. Watch for stiffness or wriggling indicating that he needs the lavatory; it helps if you have discovered beforehand what word for this he understands. Make sure his chair is high enough for a comfortable angle of gaze; that he is not slipping off it; that he has not shifted it too far from the table (which is an easier operation than pulling it back).

One advantage of having parents behind the screen is that you can quickly be given a message if you are trying something known to be aversive for this child – rewarding him with chocolate which he hates, for instance.

3. Investigating Special Topics

No special order is suggested; it is likely that topics will have to take a logically organized form in the subsequent report rather than in the actual session.

a) *Ability to Imitate*

A very basic ability which will be tested (or assumed) throughout the session in many different ways; main concern is for its quality (simple or complex) and whether immediate or delayed. (Complete absence of imitation is rare, though obviously significant.)

Move from simple to complex:

Simple – press button, throw ball, jump, bang drum, fill cup with peas, shout, thread beads on string.

More complex – press buttons in special order, bounce ball three times, jump legs apart then together, bang drum to modelled rhythm, put peas through funnel into cup, imitate phonemes or patterns of phonemes, thread beads to modelled pattern.

b) *Following Instructions*

Same general remarks as under imitation. Note child's ability with or without gestural/contextual cues. How *many* instructions can he carry, how *complex*, for how long without *visual cues*, how much is he thrown by the *unfamiliar* or unexpected? When testing child's understanding of pointing gesture, differentiate between ability to follow a pointing finger within his line of regard and the more symbolic use which

involves child turning when you point past him to what is behind him.

c) *Reciprocal Play*

Problems may arise at a fairly basic level, where child has difficulty relating to people in general or to you in particular.

Use 'slinky' or skipping rope to make wave patterns between you. Blow bubbles for child to pop, and try to reverse. Pour peas over each other's hands. Roll marbles in marble run, and hand him some to do likewise; encourage turntaking. Use hoop to catch and draw in child and involve him with you in hoop spinning and rolling. Roll, throw or bounce balls/beanbag between you. Use trundle stool or noise cylinders for reciprocal rolling. Use climbing frame, big armchairs, sagbag for physical play involving body contact – give him a jump and swing off climbing frame; bounce, burrow and cuddle. Dance to a noisy, lively record. (Both in this and when working more formally at table, watch for whether your touch is aversive to him; you can afford to [and should] push contact more in long-term remediation than in initial assessment.)

All this is useful both in initiating relationship and as a break between more structured tasks.

d) Manipulative Skills

Aiming and Fitting – pop bubbles, throw or roll ball to person or at skittle, fishing toys. Hammer toys; bead threading. Can he pour out his own glass of orange juice? Fitting without visual feedback at moment of fit (Escor toys, especially soldiers, small maypole, car merry-go-round). Fitting *in*, fitting *round;* various form-boards, including 'pastry cutter' type; Escor abacus; Escor boats and cars.

Balancing things – Escor carousel; wire carousel; wobbly pile-ups; hoop – roll and spin; slide see-saw; setting up toy farm (getting animals to stand). *Use of tools* – how does he pick up and re-adjust pencil, scissors? How well used?

Can he spin a small top or a coin? get a large top going by pumping? Can he turn key/knob/large handle/small handle of musical boxes? Pull music-box string? Can he put on a gramophone record without scratching it? Can he make quick movement of finger in, or hand over, his (or your) mouth to produce 'Red Indian' cry?

Independent use of fingers – try keyboard. Can he use fingers in sequence on keyboard or pop-up toy if you ask or demonstrate? If you stick a coloured star on one or two fingers, can he use them exclusively? Can he touch each finger separately to his thumb?

Note generally level of grasp; watch for intention tremor.

e) Gross Motor Function

Peculiarities of gait, generally clumsy impression, inhibition or hesitancy in movement, impulsivity or hyperactivity, inertia or lethargy, all to be noted throughout.

How far can he control whole-body movement adequately? Any difficulty in walking directly to where he aims to be? Standing still without falling over or swaying unduly? Jumping on the spot without deviating more than a few inches? Sitting down on a chair placed behind him? Climbing?

Does he overbalance when he jumps off a low stool? Can he run, touch and turn back without overshooting or overbalancing? Does he lose balance if you direct his gaze high up in different directions? Can he touch his toes (or thereabouts) without losing balance? Can he hop – on either foot? Walk a line?

Can he pedal the tractor or go-cart or trike? Does he steer adequately? Can he scoot?

Does he use brakes, controls on go-cart, pull up pram-hood and set lever?

Can he copy your actions – generally or precisely?

Can he perform body-actions of the 'Simon says' kind – hands on head, arms out, finger on nose, hands on tummy, touch your ears? Does he do this best when copying you face to face; or copying you as you stand beside him looking in the mirror; or following verbal instructions?

f) Speech and Communication

We are likely to get our most detailed evidence on speech and communication from a combination of parents' reports and the tape-recording now, plus (if appropriate) tape and observation later at home. However, useful observations can also be made in the session, over and above those noted in 1(a).

For children where there might be an elective element, it may be useful to defuse the face-to-face threat. Try speaking casually with your back to him (or sideways) – observe in mirror. Try using toy phones. Try puppets, or toy animals. Try role-playing – hats or helmets.

Make sure he has every opportunity to communicate to you, i.e., leave him *the spaces to do it in,* don't cut him off or rush in because you think he can't.

Watch for communication other than by speech. Does he use

gesture, mime, signing? If appropriate, it might be worth teaching him two simple signs to see if he can use this medium.

Active/passive vocabulary may be checked in a preliminary way, using pictures/collections of objects. Slides of common objects used in a viewer are more compelling than ordinary pictures, but difficult for observers to see. May be useful to try matching objects to pictures or to slides, with or without verbal mode: two levels can be tried, exact match (special apparatus) or conceptual match (two different flowers, for instance).

Understanding of special parts of speech may be investigated – for instance pronouns: put the mouse *in, under, beside, behind, on top of* the box, etc. The farmyard is useful here, or the doll's room. Make sure you are sitting beside the child when investigating 'behind', 'beside', otherwise you will not be certain whether he is taking your angle or his own.

Speech movements: if the child has no speech or very poor speech, what is his mouth control like? Does he bite and chew his biscuit? Does he drink his juice without spilling or dribbling? Does he manage his normal flow of saliva, or does he spit, dribble or drool? Can he put out his tongue? Touch tip of tongue to top of teeth? to top lip? to bottom lip? (demonstrate to him). Can he put tip of tongue in the corner of his mouth? Lick a lollipop? Put out his tongue to retrieve a crystal of sugar on your finger? Can he blow out a candle, or a pith ball across the table? Blow a bubble? Blow a mouth organ or trumpet or bird-call whistle; suck water through a straw, or retain a ping-pong ball on the end of a straw by sucking?

g) *Cognitive*

Many of the previous suggestions have cognitive components, obviously. The Piagetian schedule may also be referred to. Additionally:

Colour and Size Discrimination: sort pegs, buttons, etc., by size or colour or both. Pair coloured bricks in ESA truck. Colour-match Galt pop-up men, wobbly balls to sockets, Sio bus, Escor abacus, colour snap cards, colour twirler.

Size Ordering: various pile-ups, graded hammer toy, size-ordered form-boards. Beads, balls, dolls, animals, cups, spoons – almost anything can be used for trying concepts of 'big' and 'little'.

Number: abacuses of various kinds, poppet beads, peg boards, balls, skittles, dominoes, fitting 'number eggs'; simple games involving counting (hoop-la, dice game, number dominoes, board games).

Shape Discrimination: form-boards, jigsaws, posting-boxes.

Pattern Discrimination: single-shape form-boards (pattern put together without reference to shape of pieces); picture/pattern dominoes; card matching games; pre-reading material.

Shape Orientation: S–O dominoes; mirror-image form-boards.

Logical Ordering: toys which must be assembled in a certain order so as to fit correctly – tug-boat, contour toy, house-with-windows, logical pile-ups, etc. (Such toys are relatively rare commercially and almost all of ours are home-made.)

Child's level of drawing/scribbling may be noted – ability to copy figures, to draw symbolically, etc. Some children will finger-paint (perhaps on the glass of the mirror) when they won't draw. Avoid large wax crayons on the whole – few children can use them accurately, and they really only successfully test scribble-level.

Note whether child shows understanding of the oddity of the one-way screen by trying to look through the mirror once he has been shown that you can see through from the other side. If he does, ask him why he can't see through. Note whether, if he wants to go and see his parents, he finds his own way there – give him the chance to lead you!

Throughout, note strategies used in problem-solving; scanning, trial and error, use of social cues, verbal rehearsal, attempts at brute force, etc.

What strategies does he evolve to cope with *you?*

h) *Symbolic Play*

Use the dolls' house, doll's room, play house, farm, garage and roadways, doll's pram and dolls, toy animals and domestic play equipment such as tea-sets and cooking stove to see whether child can play games involving 'pretending'. Will he make dolls and animals 'do' things, will he give you imaginary tea and cake, will he tuck up a doll in the pram or cradle, or merely put it in the pram as he might a brick in a truck? Will he role-play using dressing-up things? (Go easy on first acquaintance – don't overwhelm him with your play-acting.) Will he talk 'for' puppets? Will he dance with a doll?

Some children are much more attracted by objects of one scale than another, which is why it's useful to have dolls' houses on two or three scales plus the play house. Don't assume that he is incapable of symbolic play if you've only tried him out on one scale of materials.

4. Note on Rewards

The child will usually do better if he is enjoying himself, and the session needs to be paced and varied in such a way that he can enjoy it.

Nonetheless, occasionally a child will seem to get most enjoyment out of avoiding everything you want him to do, and getting on with his own devices. If you can make use of these, do; but you may need to use extrinsic rewards to draw him into instruction-oriented activities, or even to get his attention at all. If so, use *small* rewards ($\frac{1}{4}$ Smarties) on a very precise schedule. *Don't* be trapped into holding out a Smartie as a lure: sit him down and at once pop it in his mouth, saying "Very good" or some such phrase. If he gets up, don't let him see the Smartie until he's sitting down again, even if you have to put him there. Similarly with tasks: decide on the task or subtask you will reward for, put him through it if necessary and reward immediately, without distracting him from the task by offering the reward in advance. Your message to him must be clear-cut, otherwise he cannot use it. Remember that we want to see his top performance, to know under what conditions he can produce it, and also to understand what he can't do however rewarding the conditions.

5. Finally ...

Remember that the end of the assessment session is not the end of opportunities for observation. The 'winding-down' period when people drink tea and stand about at the end of the session has a useful function in allowing us to observe the child's reunion with his parents and his reaction to a group of adults who are interested in him but not trying to get him to do anything special. Sometimes it is at this point that the child will suddenly display behaviour such as speech which may have been difficult to elicit in the circumstances of the assessment; sometimes in this more confused situation he will show intense hyperactivity or autistic mannerisms which were muted in the one-to-one situation. Note whether he shows or tells his parents what he has been doing; whether he indeed notices their arrival; what strategies they use and whether they are successful. (We have had a child whose *only* evidence of verbal comprehension was elicited by his mother in the course of putting his coat on and generally packing up to go home!)

The Observational Play Repertoires
(Kay Mogford)

Introduction

The Play Repertoires are not designed to function as either a measuring instrument or a test situation. They are an attempt to guide and focus observation on certain aspects of play development, and to aid the systematic observation of the child's spontaneous activity with a range of pre-selected toys.

One advantage of the type of service run by toy libraries is that it provides an opportunity for consistent and prolonged observation of the individual child over months or even years of pre-school development. This contact allows systematic observation, and a child's development and learning ability can be assessed in general terms. The OPRs are intended to be *an aid* in this process. There are several positive reasons for preferring this sort of assessment with the young handicapped child. In so far as the handicapped child's experiences differ from those of the normal child, it is perhaps unrealistic to expect to gain much insight into his functioning by placing him in the more formal situations which are used for children who develop along more normal lines. Comparing a handicapped child's achievements with age norms or stages in normal development may give a relative measure of current performance but may not give what may be more important information about the *nature* of the child's development. The unevenness of the child's development, when examined against a normal pattern, may also be striking, but again a mere score fails to make clear how this unevenness conspires to affect his competence in everyday living. By observing a handicapped child in play, we may see a child motivated to achieve ends of his own choosing, and so catch glimpses of the ways he can circumvent his handicap to achieve these ends. In addition, it is important to learn to infer his intentions in play (though he may fail in their execution), since these may give important information about his understanding of his environment. The final reason for laying stress on assessment through observation of play is that both assessment and counselling for remediation can go on in the *same* context and lead directly from one to another.

During the clinical experience gained in running a toy library, we have been able to observe a wide range of handicapped children playing with a standard series of toys. We noted that to a certain extent there was a core or relatively finite repertoire of play activities associated with any particular toy, which tended to unfold in a developmental sequence. Through experience, this repertoire and its sequence became so familiar that each child's position in the developmental sequence could be roughly located. In counselling the parents, it was suggested that, when the child's involvement and interest at the present level seemed to wane, they might invite, demonstrate, encourage and reward the child's attempts to play at the next level of involvement, or try to interest him in an alternative form of exploitation.

Initially our observation was shaped by our knowledge of developmental scales such as Gesell, Griffiths, and Psyche Cattell. For more precise reference we used a compendium of items compiled by Wood.[2] Few of these items, however, actually refer to behaviour which is spontaneously demonstrated in play. The framework expressed in Piagetian developmental stages (Woodward)[3] was more apposite and formed the basis of our observation and counselling. But play provides more and continuing complex problem-solving opportunities for the child, and many more continua in development, so that it can be a richer source of information. As many of the situations and developmental continua were commonly seen in spontaneous play with the same toy by different children, and as the variations observed provided valuable insights, it seemed a useful exercise to record these as an aid to further observation.

A study by Lunzer examined the development of play in children from two to five years, emphasizing intellectual development as demonstrated in play.[4] In this study he developed a nine-point scale which represented a measure of the organization of play, which he exemplified with behaviour from particular toys. We attempted to apply these criteria for each stage of play and derive relevant examples for our toys. We piloted this derived scale in an evening class for parents of children who belonged to the toy library. Our aim was to help parents to observe their own child's play as a means for giving them positive goals and expectations.

We found that the derived scale had certain limitations. Firstly, it failed to extend far enough downwards and to discriminate in early stages of play and exploration. The majority of children seen at the Nottingham toy library are in general below a three-year level of development. A second problem was that these parents found it difficult to apply abstract criteria or equate actual examples observed with examples given on the scale. On the positive side, we found that it did enable some parents to accept, recognize and make sense of low levels of exploration. More important, it helped to reinstate a developmental perspective with more positive expectations. In our experience, a proportion of the parents of severely handicapped children tend to lose hope and expectation of developmental progress. This happens especially when the child's behaviour violates their expectations in chronological terms and when progress is very slow and proceeds in small stages. Often developmental progress can be obscured by exaggerated traits or by the major handicap which may prevent the intention of the child's action from becoming clear. It seems that once parents are able to see a pattern to the behaviour and make sense of it in a developmental framework, they are able to participate more fully since they now know what to encourage. They also become more sensitive to obstacles which the child experiences, and are often able to develop methods of getting around them.

The Form of the OPRs

On the basis of this experience, we decided to assemble (from video-recording) observation of the play of a sample of normal children from approximately six months to five years on a standard set of toys. The four toys chosen for the repertoires were (a) the Escor four-horse roundabout, (b) Galt pop-up men, (c) Pedigree pop-up cone-tree (Mothercare Trigger-jigger), and (d) a baby doll (dressed in a dress, hat and pants) in a cradle with pillow, mattress and cover. (*Only the last two are included in this chapter.*) These toys were chosen because of their appeal to a wide age range, the large number of the sample who had played with them spontaneously, their suitability for handicapped children and because they are 'standards' as far as the toy market is concerned. Our intention at this stage was to establish the value of the Observational Play Repertoires as a tool in the observation of play; individual repertoires may be refined or constructed in time on different toys.

The play observations record four separate repertoires of play observed for each of the four toys, as they unfold in developmental sequence. This provides a structure of normal development observed directly from play with toys which can be made available and are suitable for handicapped children. The assembled repertoire records a number of different aspects of play actually observed and the various stages in the continua of development. Each repertoire is presented in two or three parts, each part corresponding to play with the toy as a whole, or play with individual parts. After each single observation item, an age level is given in brackets. This refers to the age at which this behaviour was first observed on the original sample.

Alongside the recorded repertoire, we set three blank columns to help in structuring observation. In the first column, headed *Child's approximation*, it is intended that a record be made not only of what play responses are observed, but how far the child achieves his intentions, noting any difficulties he appears to have. This directs the observer to be aware not only of successful attempts, but of *the gap between intentions and success,* and also to notice difficulties and to begin to think of ways of getting around these.

The second column is headed *Mother's or companion's invitation.* This column is intended to direct the observer's attention to both *what* is said and *how* the adult playmate suggests to the child further avenues of exploration – as well as whether the encouragement is successful. The observer can then see how the encouragement given matches the child's present capabilities and whether failure may be due to the form of communication used. This provides another starting point for counselling.

The final column, headed *Implications*, is again meant to provoke the observer into thinking about what the child's observed response could imply. For example, if a child replaces a peg-man upside down in a hole it could imply that he is unaware of the representational nature of the peg-men and hence that orientation matters. His lack of awareness may be because he simply has not yet developed to this cognitive level, and his attention has not yet been drawn to the face painted on the peg, or because his vision is too poor to see such detail. Only further observation will help decide the issue, but it will lead to a better understanding of the child's difficulties.

Following each section is a space to record behaviour not included in the repertoire. Each complete repertoire is preceded by a picture of the toy with glossary, and each is stapled as a separate leaflet.[5]

The OPRs in Use

The repertoires are at present used in the Nottingham Toy Library by library staff. It is suggested that they may be used elsewhere in a number of ways:

1. By the professional, whether therapist, teacher or psychologist, who interacts with the child himself in direct observation.
2. By the observer/counsellor to observe a handicapped child and adult playing together in direct observation.
3. By observer and parent as a joint exercise using video-tape recording of parent and child playing together.

It is envisaged that the OPRs can be used by both professional and voluntary personnel involved in play-based counselling.

There are three important points to be made about the OPRs. Firstly, these repertoires *only* record what a small sample of children did with these particular toys. Though few of their endeavours were idiosyncratic, it should be remembered that there are many things a child might do with the toy which do not appear on the repertoire. With the handicapped child, the observer may need to decide whether his activity represents productive and positive play or is stereotyped and unproductive, and respond accordingly.

Secondly, the age levels quoted after each unit *only* represent the age at which this was first observed in this sample. They are *not* standardized age norms: they serve only as a rough indicator of the age at which this play might normally be seen, and we have at present no intention to standardize. This is because we do not consider there is any justification for rigidly associating certain behavioural acts with an overall level of development. An achievement of a particular item may represent something entirely different in psychological or intellectual terms for any particular child.

Finally, although each repertoire is set out so as to indicate for counselling purposes the next stage of play, it is *not* intended as a *syllabus*. If it is treated as such, it may well negate the value of play for the child. One of the features of play observed in the construction of scales is the way it develops through more repetition and rehearsal of routines which only slowly are added to, elaborated and changed. There is presumably much to be gained by this elaboration on a theme (which is not the same as stereotyped repetition) and attempts to speed up or rush the child to the next stage may invalidate the experience for him: not only because the repetition and experiment are essential to the learning process, but because pressurizing turns play into a lesson or task, and so takes away from the child the opportunity to exercise his *own* initiative in the situation. The role of the adult is to suggest, demonstrate and encourage, and this only when the child's motivation wanes or when he meets barriers which he cannot overcome unaided. Whereas the normal child can and does seek assistance spontaneously, the handicapped child is often without this ability, and needs the participation of a knowledgeable adult with a sensitive understanding of his difficulties.

In summary, the OPRs are an attempt to construct a guide to the observation of the play of handicapped children with a range of four selected toys. The purpose is to offer a structure for the clinician who is trying to acquire experience in this skilled task, and to provide a method of pin-pointing a child's achievements and difficulties in play. It is hoped that they will be used to help the child's parents to observe his play and learn to respond in ways which will encourage his attempts to understand his world and make them more effective.

Pop-up Cone-tree or Trigger-jigger

A.   Toy as a Whole

Observed Repertoire of Play (Age first observed in sample)

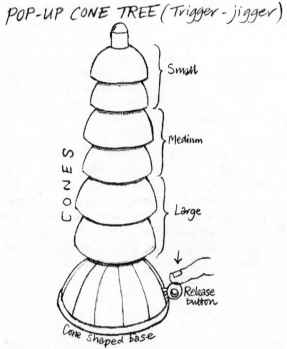

POP-UP CONE TREE (Trigger-jigger)

Small

Medium

CONES

Large

Release button

Cone shaped base

The cones fly off when release button is pressed.
After re-stacking, they must be set for release by
pushing the stack down against the setting mechanism.

1. (In prone position) Watches companion stack only, following their hand from floor to pole. (7m.)
2. (After companion gets attention) Watches cones spring off as companion releases. (7m.)
3. Watches whole sequence of stacking, setting and releasing cones, but *doesn't* watch companion's hand as it pushes release button. (7m.)
4. Watches whole sequence through to release but jumps in surprise. (7m.)
5. Watches stacking and makes anticipating noises – jumps at release but gurgles with pleasure. (7m.)
6. Pulls assembled cone-tree towards self by base. (7m.)
7. Reaches to assembled cone-tree, grasping for base or pole; pulls it over. (7m.)
8. Reaches to assembled cone-tree, feels and grasps cones. (7m.)
9. Lifts up base – results in cones accidentally sliding on to floor. Watches result. (9m.)
10. (Sitting on floor) Reaches out to the cones when they are released by companion and fly through the air. Watches them in the air and landing. (10m.)
11. Removes cone which companion has just stacked with right hand, pulling it up and off (looks at it briefly and discards). (10m.)
12. Grasps the top of the pole with one hand, while feeling with left hand. (10m.)
13. Removes the top cone with one hand, holding base steady with other hand. Drops the cone. (10m.)
14. Releases cones accidentally (with foot or another toy). Jumps but also vocalizes. Watches cones land and reaches for them. (10m.)
15. Presses release button deliberately with foot. (10m.)
16. Holding cone-tree at oblique angle, tries to pull cone off sideways. (10m.)
17. With cone-tree in horizontal position, scrabbles at cones until two fall off the end, vocalizes and inspects them. (10m.)
18. Plays game with companion, pulling off each cone immediately after stacking it. (10m.)
19. Grasps top end of the pole and lifts base into the air. Cones slide down to child's hand. Watches. (10m.)
20. Tries to remove cone with left hand, while holding the top of the

pole with the right. This prevents cone coming off – so tries pulling the cone sideways. (10m.)

21. Holds base, base upwards; lifts cone and tries to put it into the hollow base. (12m.)

22. Shouts with delight at first demonstration. (15m.)

23. Lifts full cone-tree and carries it. Places it base downwards on the floor. (15m.)

24. Attempts to stack a cone, misses top of the pole with the hole in the cone. Holds it by the lip and makes no attempt to look underneath and align hole and pole. Cone hangs on the pole by its lip. (16m.)

25. Attempts to stack a cone – misses altogether. Cone falls to floor. (16m.)

26. Presses release button when indicated by companion. (16m.)

27. Presses release button before cones are replaced or set. (16m.)

28. Presses release button on assembled tree but before cones have been set. (16m.)

29. Releases cones and laughs at the result. (20m.)

30. Turns the tree around to find the release button for self (20m.) or searches with hands for release button. (21m.)

31. Releases cones *and* attempts to replace them (unsuccessfully). (20m.)

32. Inspects hole in cone visually and with finger before attempting to place on the pole (after demonstration). Fails to align pole although watching intently. (20m.)

33. Successfully threads a cone on to the base using the pole as a large needle. Stands base upright on the floor successfully. (20m.)

34. Threads a cone on an upright base with no physical assistance. Presses release button, but no attempt made to set cones for self. (20m.)

35. Grasps a cone on the tree, knocks it off accidentally. Examines it and its hole before replacing successfully. (21m.)

36. Responds to the release of cones, saying 'go'. (21m.)

37. Attempts to replace *all* the cones himself. (Asks for assistance when attempts fail.) Does not 'set' cones for self. (21m.)

38. Replaces a cone holding base steady and aligning pole and hole entirely without aid or suggestion. (21m.)

39. Completes whole sequence of release and stacking despite diversion. Needs prompting to release again (still fails to set cones). (21m.)

40. Deliberate attempt to empty pole by tipping it over and pushing cones off. (21m.)

41. Grasps idea of threading cones after seeing only one cone replaced. (22m.)

42. Threads cones smoothly and accurately with very few 'misses'. (22m.)

43. Collects all cones together before completing the whole re-threading process of own accord (no sign of size grading). (22m.)

44. Completes whole sequence of release, collecting cones, re-threading and pressing release button without aid. Companion still needs to set cones. (22m.)

45. (At companion's suggestion) transfers all the cones on tree to another pole on another toy. (22m.)

46. Gets into difficulty threading. Feels central hole with fingers then uses both hands to align pole and hole (without suggestion from companion). (22m.)

47. Spins a cone round on the pole with one hand. (22m.)

48. Tries to transfer threading principle to another unsuitable toy. (22m.)

49. Replaces cones following instructions to select order by colour and size. Needs cues to know when correct. (2 : 4m.)

50. Threads cones with *no* misses and needs only to glance visually to align hole and pole. (2 : 4m.)

51. Systematically removes all cones, lifting off without upsetting base. (2 : 6m.)

52. Imitates naming of colours. (2 : 6m.)

53. Continues counting sequence initiated by companion (i.e., companion says, One! child, Two!) not related to actual quantity. (2 : 6m.)

54. Continues counting sequence initiated by companion but jumps from 3 to 7. (2 : 6m.)

55. While holding the cones on at the top, tips the assembled tree upside down and back again to create 'echo' sound (says, 'bang'). (2 : 6m.)

56. Sits listening to 'echo' sound created after stacking a cone. (2 : 6m.)
57. Stacks several cones dropping on to base to produce 'echo' sound. (2 : 6m.)
58. Re-threads cones with rough attempt at size grading (several errors). (2 : 6m.)
59. Strokes both hands down the contours of the assembled tree. (2 : 6m.)
60. Companion demonstrates setting by putting child's hands on cones and assistively pushing down; child imitates immediately. (2 : 6m.)
61. When failing to release cones (have not been 'set'), creates a springing movement by sweeping cones off into the air with both hands. (2 : 6m.)
62. Describes action of releasing, says, 'It's pretty.' (2 : 6m.)
63. Fails to thread cone in one orientation. Turns it up the other way and is successful. (2 : 7m.)
64. Imitates setting immediately after watching demonstration. (2 : 7m.)
65. Names colours correctly and spontaneously. (2 : 7m.)
66. Talks of 'two', using term accurately. (2 : 7m.)
67. Attempts to 'set' cones unprompted by instruction or immediate demonstration. (2 : 7m.)
68. Stacks, releases and sets without reminder from companion. (2 : 7m.)
69. Child accidentally prevents successful release by holding the top with one hand, while pressing the release button. (3 : 0m.)
70. Describes toy. Says. 'It's like a tree.' (3 : 1m.)
71. Comments verbally on how the toy operates, says, 'I have to press that button.' (3 : 2m.)
72. While stacking, rejects cones because they are the wrong size, but only after they are on the pole. (3 : 2m.)
73. When prompted, accurately estimates number of cones (up to four) without counting. (3 : 2m.)
74. Exchanges the order of stacking two cones because dissatisfied with size grading (actually are the same size). (3 : 2m.)
75. Verbal instruction and gesture in the air (not in relation to toy), used to teach setting motion. Child successfully performs setting. (3 : 3m.)

76. Predicts result of pressing release button. 'They go up, don't they?' Gives demonstration of action. (3 : 3m.)

77. When directed by companion, selects 'biggest' (without additional colour cues) and before placing on pole next to other cones. Makes errors doing this. (3 : 3m.)

78. Comments on action of cone. 'It's going down the bottom.' (3 : 3m.)

79. Selects biggest by opposing, side by side, the largest and medium size cones, prior to threading them on. (3 : 3m.)

80. Completes whole sequence, including setting and collecting cones, without prompting (no size grading). (3 : 3m.)

81. Before selecting to size grade, compares size of cones matching base to base (at companion's suggestion). (4 : 1m.)

82. Completes whole sequence, including size grading, without prompting. Makes errors in size grading. (4 : 1m.)

83. Removes a cone which fails to spring off at release. (4 : 1m.)

84. Size grades spontaneously without aid, making *one* error only. Two next in size reversed only. (4 : 1m.)

85. Comments on action, 'That one didn't come off, did it?' (4 : 1m.)

86. Deliberately places hand over cones to prevent them springing off. (4 : 10m.)

87. Decides to use one or two cones only before setting and releasing. (4 : 10m.)

88. Pauses during sequence to talk to companion about something else. Returns and completes sequence *un*prompted. (4 : 10m.)

(Other responses observed)

B.   Cones and Empty Base as Individual Items

Observed Repertoire of Play (Age first observed in sample)

1. Reaches for a loose cone (which companion has just touched). Mouths and examines with fingers. (7m.)
2. Fails to give up cone on request. (7m.)
3. Watches a cone, as it rocks on the ground (following release), but does not watch them in the air before landing. (7m.)
4. Reaches for empty pole and pulls towards self. (7m.)
5. Follows cones in the air and watches (7m.) Watches them land and roll along the floor. (9m.)
6. Guides top of pole into mouth. (9m.)
7. Moves base to side, out of way. (9m.)
8. Removes a cone, or picks up loose cone, explores with fingers and eyes – discards to left. (9m.)
9. Explores with finger, looking elsewhere. (9m.)
10. Picks up a small cone, transfers to other hand. (9m.)
11. Turns cone round and round in the air by rotating wrist. (9m.)
12. Mouths cone while exploring other toys with free hand. (9m.)
13. Drops cone to explore another toy. Notices it again and retrieves it. (9m.)
14. Lifts empty base by the release knob and drops it. (10m.)
15. Takes from companion's hand while she stacks. (10m.)
16. Fingers the end of the pole in an exploratory way; feels hole with finger. (10m.)
17. Lifts a cone in each hand and throws to the floor. (10m.)
18. Reaches to take cone from companion. Knocks it out of her hand accidentally. Watches it fall and reaches for it. (10m.)
19. Reaches out to catch cones as they bounce, or while in the air. (10m.)
20. Holding empty pole at the end, bangs the base on the floor. (12m.)
21. Holds base, base upwards. Explores with fingers and peers into hollow base. (12m.)
22. Pushes cone along the floor with the base held in one hand. (12m.)
23. Places base upright on the floor. (12m.)

24. Lifts empty base over shoulder and drops it. Turns around to find it. (12m.)
25. Bangs and sweeps other toys with base. (12m.)
26. Puts in a box and removes it, standing it on the floor. (12m.)
27. Lifts empty base and visually inspects the underside of the base. (20m.)
28. Tries to put part of another toy into the hole in the top of the pole. (20m.)
29. Squeezes cones in exploratory way with finger and thumb movement. (21m.)
30. Pushes down on the cone-shaped base as if it were a loose cone. (22m.)
31. Taps base on the floor to produce 'echo' sound of the spring. (22m.)
32. Holds base up to companion's ear (on request) to listen to 'echo' sound. (2:6m.)
33. Bangs empty base on the floor, on other toys, and plays with release button to create 'echo' noise. (2:6m.)
34. Places all cones base downwards on the floor, like a crop of mushrooms. (2:7m.)
35. Sorts cones from other plastic pieces. (2:7m.)
36. Calls biggest cone 'The big one'. (3:3m.)
37. Counts six cones with some prompting. (4:1m.)
38. Squeezes cone back to circular shape when deformed to an oval. (4:10m.)

(Other responses observed)

Doll in a Cradle

A.   Doll and Cradle as a Whole

Observed Repertoire of Play (Age first observed in sample)

1. Feels the edge of the cover with finger and thumb. (12m.)
2. Pulls off the cover. (12m.)
3. Feels the doll's clothing. (12m.)
4. Rocks cradle deliberately. (12m.)
5. Removes cradle cover and then removes doll from cradle (with some difficulty). (12m.)
6. Pulls cradle towards self and peers inside. (12m.)
7. Watches companion rock and talk about doll. (14m.)
8. Crawls to cradle, looks at the doll and exclaims. (14m.)
9. Pulls cradle towards self, touches doll and says, 'Oh! Ba!' (with intonation). (14m.)
10. Looks around to find the cradle cover. (14m.)
11. Removes cradle cover, covers face and removes (peep-bo!). (14m.)
12. Roughly replaces cradle cover so that it is across the length of the cradle. (14m.)
13. Indicates the empty cradle. (14m.)
14. Pulls mattress out of the cradle and wraps it roughly around the doll, and later pulls off. (14m.)
15. Looks into the cradle and removes the pillow, feels and inspects. (14m.)
16. Touches her face and neck with blankets. (14m.)
17. Rests head on the blanket as if going to sleep. Refers to companion. (14m.)
18. Removes mattress and/or pillow, looks at it and discards it. (15m.)
19. Drops a toy into the cradle, tips it up so that toy rolls to one end and then to the other. (15m.)

20. Puts doll back into the cradle but does not cover. (20m.)
21. Puts doll (fully clothed) into the cradle. Covers (at companion's suggestion). (22m.)
22. Attempts to tuck in cover. Folds inexpertly and ends up shifting it into the canopy area. (22m.)
23. Handles cover. Says, 'That's the blanket.' (22m.)
24. Rocks cot deliberately, in side-to-side motion. (22m.)
25. After placing doll in cradle says, 'Night, night, sleep tight.' (22m.)
26. Takes off cover, takes off the doll's hat, takes the doll out and brushes her hair and clothes (with toy brush). (22m.)
27. Cot falls over sideways. Stands it up by herself. (22m.)
28. Replaces pillow and cover – but stuffs them roughly into the canopy. Says, 'Can't get in.' (22m.)
29. Peels back the cover when removing doll. (2:4m.)
30. Replaces cot cover, along the lengthwise of cradle, but top to bottom. (2:4m.)
31. Makes a rough attempt to tuck in cover. (2:4m.)
32. Takes a rattle, shakes it and places it in the cot under the cover. (2:4m.)
33. Removes hat before 'putting her to bed' (i.e., an attempt to undress). (2:4m.)
34. Wakes up doll and takes out of the cot. (2:4m.)
35. Replaces the cover the right way up. (2:4m.)
36. Replaces the cover when accidentally knocked off. (2:4m.)
37. Replaces doll, covers with cover carefully and deftly tucks in (doll is fully clothed). (2:6m.)
38. Having replaced doll and tucked it in, rocks the cradle. (2:6m.)
39. Pushes cradle along floor (like a pram). (2:6m.)
40. Lifts cot and rocks it from end to end. (2:6m.)
41. Rocks doll in the cradle and sings 'Rock-a-baby'. (2:6m.)

(Other responses observed)

B.   Doll Only

Observed Repertoire of Play (Age first observed in sample)

1. Feels doll's clothing. (12m.)
2. Lifts doll from floor by its foot, in the hand. (12m.)
3. For convenience only, rests doll on knee (no mothering behaviour). (12m.)
4. Explores eyes, poking a finger in them. (12m.)
5. Lifts doll by the skirt. (12m.)
6. Holds doll by foot, inspecting the foot. (12m.)
7. Holds doll by foot, while exploring another toy. (12m.)
8. Watches companion rock and talk about a doll. (14m.)
9. Takes doll from companion (right way up) in two hands. (14m.)
10. Holds baby to her, rocks own body side to side, smiling (?hugging). (14m.)
11. Takes off hat and hands it to companion. (14m.)
12. Imitates kissing baby. (14m.)
13. Discards doll on to the floor to one side. (14m.)
14. Gives doll to companion to kiss. (14m.)
15. Kisses doll at companion's suggestion. (14m.)
16. Puts the doll down on the floor before going on to another toy. (14m.)
17. Without any suggestion being made, lifts doll and holds close to face (?hugging), refers to companion. (14m.)
18. Lifts doll and carries to companion. (15m.)
19. Removes doll's hat and drops it – looking backwards and forwards between doll and hat. (15m.)
20. Lifts doll, using inflected 'ah, eh'. (15m.)
21. Walks over doll, when going to another toy. (15m.)
22. Picks up the doll, hugs and kisses her without suggestion. (20m.)
23. At companion's suggestion, washes doll's face (with toy sponge). Uses additional prepared brush, sponge, cloth etc. (22m.)
24. At companion's suggestion 'washes', or otherwise tends, doll's feet. (22m.)
25. Pretends something is there in order to tend the doll, e.g., says,

'Water is in a bowl.' Drops real sponge into pretend water. (22m.)

26. Brushes doll's feet with large sweeping brush (inappropriate use). (22m.)

27. Turns doll the right way up in order to attempt putting doll's hat on. (22m.)

28. Attempts but fails to replace doll's hat. (22m.)

29. Over-extends an activity, brushing doll's hair using a hair brush, but also brushes clothes. (22m.)

30. Comments that the doll has no hat on. (2 : 4m.)

31. Pats the doll's back (at companion's suggestion), and hugs it on own initiative. (2 : 4m.)

32. Searches for the doll's hat which has come off. (2:4m.)

33. Replaces hat unaided. (2:4m.)

34. Walks doll along. (2:4m.)

35. Pretends giving doll a drink (using a plastic beaker), and talks about it. (2 : 4m.)

36. Gives doll a toy and says 'Babies like these.' (2 : 4m.)

37. Walks carrying doll out in front of self to look at it. (2 : 6m.)

38. Accidentally knocks off hat – picks it up and puts it on a table. (2 : 6m.)

39. Names or describes doll. Says, 'He's a little baby.' (2 : 6m.)

40. Swivels doll's head around to face the front. (2:6m.)

41. Places doll on companion's knee (as if a real child). (2 : 6m.)

42. Shows doll its face in mirror. (2 : 6m.)

43. Talks to doll. (2 : 6m.)

44. Makes repeated attempts to replace doll's hat. Wedges doll between knees to free both hands. (2 : 6m.)

45. Succeeds in replacing hat. Adjusts its position, says, 'There, nice dolly.' (2 : 6m.)

46. Adjust doll's limb position. (2 : 6m.)

47. Lifts telephone receiver to ear of doll. Holds two-way conversation, speaking for the doll. (3 : 1m.)

48. Refers to doll as 'he' or 'she'. (3 : 4m.)

(Other responses observed)

9   Using Toys and Play Remedially

(Joan Head and Kay Mogford)

Just as it is possible to map out and understand the handicapped child's difficulties in achieving spontaneous play, so we can also plan to compensate for them. The greater the child's limitations, the more pressing the need to make the most of her remaining opportunities by deliberately planning play experiences. Rather than providing for the child's play in a rather vague way, hoping that this may help, we need to work out a clear idea of how to make these experiences relevant and accessible to her.

In remedial or compensatory play, then, we aim to encourage and build upon the child's inclination to explore and play in a way which is tailor-made for her own requirements. At different times in the day, play may be *designed* for different remedial purposes, varying in the degree of selection and planning imposed upon it. It is probably as important a part of this planning to appreciate the different purposes involved as it is to choose and encourage particular kinds of play.

We said earlier that the needs of the handicapped child are in some ways only those of the ordinary child prolonged over time or intensified in some way. This becomes clear when we think again of the role of the adult in the child's play. Looking at the ordinary mother playing with her ordinary infant, we saw that the baby is highly dependent on her in a number of ways. In the earliest stages of its life, play is mainly initiated by the mother and is largely interpersonal. Gradually, with the mother's help and encouragement, play comes to include and focus on toys and playthings. At this stage the baby depends on her mother, or play partner, to make toys physically available to her and to return them if they fall or roll away from her. She is also rather dependent on her mother to draw attention to new playthings and to demonstrate their potential interest. As the baby becomes more familiar with an object, she needs a partner to reveal other possibilities for exploration which she cannot discover for herself. In this way the mother maintains and extends the baby's involvement with playthings. As ordinary children's abilities develop, mothers and other adults relinquish this close involvement, gradually withdrawing from direct physical intervention to verbal guidance, until the time when the child needs only a passive, approving presence offering occasional hints and suggestions.

For the handicapped child, the degree of dependence on an adult playmate is greater and extends over a longer period. Because each child varies, the adult who fills this role must be sensitive to the child's needs, intervening when necessary to make new experiences available, to provide just enough support to prevent discouragement and to develop the ideas which child and adult together create.

Without the attention and foresight of the adult, opportunities to learn and experience would be denied to the handicapped child. That does not mean, however, that *all* the child's play can or should be designed in this way, since she also needs to discover for herself how to come to grips with, and find ways round, her limitations. This simply underlines the point that the degree of moment-by-moment intervention by the adult depends on the purpose of the remedial play and the needs of the particular child. Successful remedial play depends on individual adults: their understanding of why a particular experience is valuable; their knowledge of the needs and abilities of the child; their sensitivity and judgement about when and how to intervene. This is achieved not only through intellectual understanding but also through willingness to identify with the child and communicate with her.

Therapists are often much concerned with the repetition of certain actions or skills to strengthen, extend or otherwise improve them; and one characteristic of play is in fact a natural tendency to repeat actions in a variety of slightly different ways. As play activities are chosen by the child, and often persist for long periods, they have been seen by therapists as an ideal vehicle for therapeutic procedures because their play quality ensures the child's active co-operation. Much of the work of speech therapists, occupational and physiotherapists in this field involves building the necessary stages in learning, and the practice these require, into games and activities. The aim is to persuade the child to co-operate fully and willingly, so that the repetition has meaning for her, and contains built-in rewards and pleasure.

If the child's understanding that she is playing is not to be destroyed, flexibility and imagination from the therapist is needed, together with the realization that the child must be allowed some freedom to digress. Play is not defined simply by the presence of toys, nor even by the child's manipulation of toys. The essence of play is the attitude the child brings to her activities and relationships with others: that is, play is playful. In play a child does not necessarily choose or find the most direct path to the solution of a problem or completion of her purpose; she may make many digressions, some of which may prove to be blind alleys. She may forget her first intention, or abandon it along the way as she sees other more interesting possibilities. Play may involve the child in peaks of real effort, persistence and concentration and there may be valleys of relaxed repetition with little apparent purpose other than sheer pleasure. In remedial play, it is possible to preserve the character of this experience for the child, sharing her pleasure, while at the same time having to some extent planned the activity and monitored her progress. Some parents whose handicapped child has seemed unable to play have found that thoughtful analysis, planning and even a degree of self-consciousness in playing with their child can enhance the pleasure of play for both parent and child, opening up for both a more rewarding relationship.

If real play is to be preserved and made accessible to the child, the role of the adult, *to invite, not to impose,* must be understood. If it is not understood, or forgotten in the anxiety of willing the child to achieve a particular task or step in development, the play element is lost and the activity becomes a tiresome drill. In a situation like this, the adult gives the impression of having taken over the activity, leaving the child to contribute the *minimum* she is capable of, rather than extending her capabilities.

In a study which looked at parents playing with their non-handicapped child, we found that parents only chose to encourage their child when her interest was lapsing. The most skilful parents were those who had a clear view of inherent possibilities and the order in which their child could tackle them as she became more proficient. Each child too had clear preferences and intentions which her parents usually encouraged her to achieve. Often this would lead to a game developing between parent and child, at first around simple imitative or turntaking activities. Gradually the child became able to initiate and expand these games herself. Here again, the child was showing a

growing self-sufficiency, and the need for adult participation decreased.

In our work with parents and handicapped children in the Nottingham Toy Library, we have seen this kind of interaction unfold between parents and children. Sometimes parents have found it difficult to play with their child, but this ability has gradually developed, enabling growth in the child's more general abilities to attend, co-operate and communicate – the ground skills for all later, more formal learning.

For the child, repeated opportunities to communicate with an adult are invaluable for the development of speech and language, since at first children learn best from clear adult speech which is vivid and full of meaning for them. The pleasure of play also gives them the maximum encouragement to speak freely. While any toy that creates a natural opportunity for sharing a child's play can foster speech, some are especially useful in allowing the same words and phrases to be repeated in slightly different ways, so that the child can hear the words over and over again and begin to use them appropriately herself.[1] Language learning needs a variety of topics in order to introduce new words and ideas naturally and meaningfully; some toys, like a toy farm or zoo, are particularly rich in this way. But even toys which at first sight seem more restricted in the activities they stimulate (such as jigsaw puzzles) can be the cue for practice in conversation.

To sum up our aims in using play remedially: these are, firstly, to compensate for restricted experience; secondly, by participating in the child's play, to expand her capabilities, especially the more general abilities of attention and co-operation which she will need for school; thirdly, to preserve the child's initiative so that she may develop that sense of mastery and achievement which is easily undermined in the handicapped; and finally, perhaps, to use the motivation of play to provide the exercise and development of necessary skills.

Two Approaches to Remedial Play

So far we have only discussed the purposes and benefits of remedial play, not methods or guidelines. It may appear simply a matter of following common-sense principles, which in many cases it is. Nonetheless, in the midst of coping with all the different demands of the child and the rest of the family, it can be difficult to see the wood for the trees. Parents may tell us that their child simply *does not* play; or, after many fruitless attempts to play with their child, they may have virtually given up, and looked for more passive pastimes to relieve the child's stress. This is not a happy solution for either parent or child. Other children have specific problems in play, and we are repeatedly asked for toys that will solve them; but the toy itself is only one element in the whole interaction between the child, her disabilities and her environment. In chapter 7, we saw that even children with single handicaps may be considered multi-handicapped because 'one area of a child's life so easily spills over into another area'; but, in practice, we rarely have the luxury of working within the needs of one specific condition. Very few children have a single handicap. Most handicapped children have clusters of disabilities in different proportions, affecting several areas of development, so that each child presents her own unique pattern of abilities and disabilities. Nonetheless, recurring behavioural difficulties arise, not necessarily confined to specific handicaps. Although no 'rule of thumb' solutions will work in every case, there are certain strategies that can usefully be tried. This is what we might call the *problem-oriented approach*.

Some difficulties are most likely to occur at particular stages in the child's development, and part of their solution may lie in choosing playthings that are appropriate to the child's developmental stage, rather than to her actual age. For a great many handicapped children – perhaps for most of them, most of the time – their main need is to be given extra opportunities for play geared to development which is both slower and less consistent than that of ordinary children. These children require a predominantly *developmental approach*, to supplement their own natural progress; we will look at this before returning to the problem-oriented approach.

The Developmental Approach

With the ordinary child whose development is relatively trouble-free, and proceeding at a steady rate, it is quite appropriate to refer to the different developmental stages in terms of age. For example, when we say a toy is suitable for an eighteen-month-old child, we mean a child just walking and just beginning to talk who can probably build a simple tower and may perhaps recognize simple pictures. This is a useful way of relating play activities to the appropriate level of ability. With the handicapped child, however, these age levels are misleading unless related to the appropriate developmental stages. In most cases the child's handicap affects some areas of development more than others. For example, the child whose major handicap is deafness will be most affected in the area of speech and language development. Depending on the cause of her deafness, other areas of development may be relatively unaffected. But if, for example, her deafness has been associated with extremely premature birth, her movement skills might also be slower to develop, though perhaps not as slow as her speech and language. In providing suitable playthings, we have to cater for her

particular needs: toys suitable for a lower level of understanding and slower motor development than her age might suggest. Her deafness requires toys with clear visual effects and perhaps a suitable sound, which she can hear through her hearing aid, to encourage her to listen; and all this must take into account her own particular likes and dislikes.

It will be obvious, then, that no single list of toys and activities in developmental order for a particular handicap or group of handicaps will suffice. The approach is always, in part, experimental, the initial choice of toys and activities being based on the child's own pattern of progress.

Assessing the child's developmental level and needs depends largely on learning to observe the significant aspects of the child's play and relating this to what we know of normal play development. This has already been discussed, both in the last chapter, and in chapters 2 and 3. Here we only emphasize that, in the end, the final choice of toys and activities is best made by looking at the child's response to them and asking four questions:

1. Does this toy or game, given careful demonstration and introduction to the child, catch her interest, tempt her to explore, or involve her in any way?
2. If the toy or activity does this, can I, or the child, develop this first response in one or more ways?
3. Does the toy, or can I, provide clear messages of success and achievement?
4. Does the toy allow the child to reach towards higher levels of achievement when she is ready? Does it present a challenge, and not simply a rehearsal of what she can already do?

If the answer to each of these questions is 'yes', then it is highly probable that the child herself is happy, excited and involved with the toy or play activity. If the answer to any of these questions is 'no', then it is likely that the child's interest will quickly disappear and that she will reject the toy – except, perhaps, as a focus for ritual and non-progressive activity.

The ability to answer these questions implies some knowledge of the stages in play development and, more important, the ability to gain and hold the child's attention and communicate with her. Whoever plays with the child must be able to give her an idea of what the toy is about, how it works, what it does: in short, to introduce her to its possibilities. As the child exhausts one possibility, she may not see others unless her playmate can indicate this to her in some way. Again, if the toy itself has no obvious built-in reward or satisfying climax, the playmate needs to supply or amplify this in a way that the child values and understands.

Most toys present a variety of opportunities for play. This makes any simple classification of the purpose or use of toys difficult. Whatever the primary point of a toy, we need to work out what other opportunities it offers so that we can encourage the child to take advantage of these.

An example is the Escor graded abacus. At first sight it is designed to introduce simple concepts of quantity in play. It also includes the opportunity for colour matching and sorting, as well as for practising skills of threading and co-ordinating hand movements. The wooden balls can also be threaded on to a string (more difficult), rolled along the floor or dropped into a suitable container. All or some of these activities

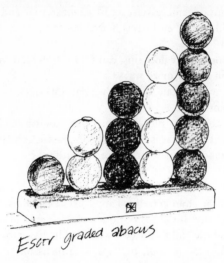

Esor graded abacus

may be chosen, depending on the child and her level of ability. For example, the first purposeful activity of a severely mentally handicapped boy, with partial sight, involved lifting the balls off the abacus and dropping them into a biscuit tin. Although he needed to be shown physically how to do this at first, the sound of the balls banging in the tin and the shiny reflections from inside the tin so fascinated him that he was soon tempted to reach for and retrieve them himself and offer them to his playmate. Many other toys can be equally versatile, given some thought about how the needs of the child can be related to the characteristics of the toy.

To allow for the individual preference of each child, to grade materials in small steps for slower learners, and to give variety and practice at each stage of development, demands a resource for toys which will be beyond the pockets of most families. This is why a toy library is a virtual necessity for a handicapped child. A toy library can provide a stock of carefully chosen toys to meet these needs and make full and economic use of expensive items. The toy library movement in England, which has received its major impetus from parents of handicapped children and individual professionals concerned with their welfare, was one of the most remarkable self-help initiatives of the seventies, developing from a mere handful of libraries at the beginning of the decade to 500 in 1977. This reflects parents' and professionals' growing awareness of the value of a knowledgeable adult playmate and purpose-planned toys.[2]

Many of the most suitable toys are more easily available through specialist catalogues than through shops. There are a number of successful, suitable and relatively inexpensive toys available, however, from the ordinary shops found in most shopping centres. To help parents and toy library organizers choose their own toys, we have compiled a list of those which are more easily available and which we have found useful for the children we have worked with. It is put together in more-or-less developmental sequence, and we have indicated what toys are helpful for particular skills. Toys are ephemeral and particular brands and varieties may come and go, but the basic successful formulas are repeated in different guise year after year. If a successful toy disappears, it often returns under a different name and made by another manufacturer. For this reason we describe the principle rather than give a brand name in most cases.

Toy List

1. Early Play

We include in this stage the first signs of interest that a baby shows in people and objects. It is important to recognize these signs – eye following, reaching out, babbling at an object or person. Some babies dislike loud or sudden noises: it is sensible to accept this rather than force frightening squeaky toys on them. Taking toys to the mouth is an important early stage in play and is significant for the later development of hand and spoon feeding; mouthing objects should be encouraged.

Toy	*Comment*
Things to Look At	
Mobiles (including tinkling and spring-hung mobiles)	Look for bright colours; some wind up for music
Toys that roll or move in an interesting way, e.g., wobbly balls, roll-back toys	Adults can play with these for a very young or handicapped child to watch

'Mirrors'	Not glass; plenty of safe types available to suspend from side of cot or playpen

To Handle and Finger

Cradle toys (especially the Swedish Semper toys which have easy pull action)	Any handleable toys that can be suspended over cot, pram, playpen
Rattles	Single or in pairs; look for contrasts in sounds
Toys to hold and manipulate	Look for light, easy-to-grip toys such as wooden ball cubes and teething rings
Textured toys	Interesting feel is important, even a soft 'prickle'
Sound-producing toys	Things that can be tied to a baby's ankle or wrist and sound when moved; musical balls in cot to encourage kicking; Semper musical cradle toy

When Sitting Up (or with enough head control to enable child to play with toys at a table, with support, or lying on a foam wedge)

Nesting and stacking toys	Colourful; encourage 'in' and 'out' concepts in play
Rag-covered foam bricks	Light, easily clutched
Kelly bounce-back dolls	Not for children who throw
Vehicles, etc., with peg 'occupants'	A first representational toy; very versatile

Bath and Water Play

Floating toys that also let water drain; boats with occupants	Allows child to experiment in a different medium; common fear of bath may be allayed

When Toddling

Interesting balls	Look for size, colour, texture; some have easy-grip hole/texture; some will take bell inside
Push along and pull along toys	Interesting sound or action motivates child to walk, crawl or roll

2. *Fascination Toys*

This category includes toys which provide maximum (and prompt) reward for minimum skill, which handicapped children will find less frustrating and more exciting.

Toys which move and respond at a touch, e.g., Fisher Price Chime ball, p. 50; Escor maypole, p. 51	Exciting because of the colour and movement; encourage *gentle* touching. Escor's range highly recommended, and spare parts available
'Remote control' toys: pressbutton or battery operated	Good practice for finger movement
Pop-up toys	Nice surprise element; mechanism presents puzzle to child

3. *To Encourage Mobility*

Tyre on castors	Child lies across on tummy and paddles with hands/feet. Look for one with good grip holds

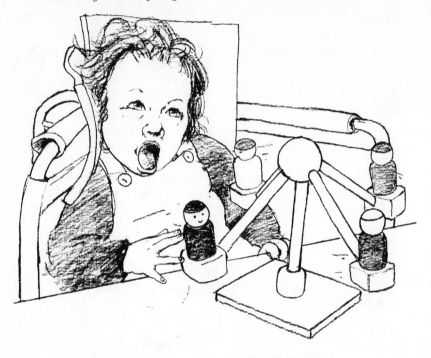

Lever Cart	Hand-operated vehicle with chair seat
Rocking toys	Tubular steel/wooden; varied in size and support given
Tricycles	Good back support important for some children
Baby walkers	Look for ones with handles adjustable to height, and a wide frame for stability

4. *To Encourage Hand-eye Co-ordination*

Toys which involve threading and lacing	Large and smaller scale; laces need long tags at ends
Stacking and nesting toys	Use for building, knocking down, hiding sweets, and for bath play
Constructional toys	Some demand screw movement; control rather than strength; ordered assembly
Bricks of all sorts	Both 'sets' and offcuts: see chapter 4
Constructional sets in plastics	Coloured perspex visually exciting. Some (Lego, Meccano, Fischer-Technik) produce larger-scale versions for less controlled handling
Two-handed 'drawing' (Etcha-sketch, Spiromatic)	Good for older children, especially if immobilized

5. *Toys to Develop Discrimination Skills*

These involve matching, sorting and grading in size, colour and shape

Posting/sorting boxes	Plain simple ones to begin with. Each shape should only enter one hole
Form-boards and shape-fitting puzzles	Introduction to inset trays and jig-saws: start with small number of large pieces

Lotto, snap	Look for clear pictures that make sense to child. Use for matching picture to object at first
Sorting kits	Can be home-made; look also at the commercially available ones
Insets and jigsaws (George Luck's especially beautiful)	Look for pictures of everyday situations (encourages conversation) and number of pieces. Wooden ones superior

6. *To Encourage Speech and Language Skills*

All games that involve other people encourage these skills: look for opportunities to extend a child's understanding in these situations.

Tea-sets	Small-sized adult ones probably best for younger children, especially those in tough polythene/melamine
See-inside jigsaws (p. 66) (Willis, Galt)	Surprise element stimulates speech exchange
Garage, airport, railway, farm lay-outs	Add to gradually: buying new additions gives focus for planning and shopping, as well as imaginative play
Pictures and photographs (best mounted)	Collect these at home, including some involving child and his family. Commercial sets also available: see educational catalogues
Lotto and snap	See section 5

Toy telephones	Can reduce tension in some children; buy two if possible. Go for stability, good bell.
Puppets, glove or finger	Especially look for family or animal puppets: but an authority figure (king, fierce animal) can lend a child confidence

The Problem-oriented Approach

With children who present their parents, therapists and teachers with behaviour that makes a normal sequence of playful interaction difficult or seemingly impossible, the developmental approach is not enough. We give here suggestions for experimenting to find a solution to these problems. Some will take time, persistence and effort to modify; there are no easy answers to these difficulties.

We have found it useful to pool ideas on these children with colleagues and parents, and to keep careful records of what has been observed and what we have decided to do, discarding an approach only when it can be seen to be unsuccessful after a fair trial, and if at all possible analysing and making a note of what made it impracticable.

Very Severely Handicapped Children

We mean here those children who are unable to sit or raise their heads and whose limb movements are abnormally restricted or uncontrolled. Their sight, hearing, touch or sense of their own movement may also be impaired, and they may show some degree of mental handicap. Because communication is at a very low level, and voluntary movement minimal, it is not at all easy to assess their intellectual capabilities.

In a way, these children still need a developmental approach, but this is difficult because at the lowest levels of development there are such limited possibilities for play. At this stage in the normal child's development, we tend to take rapid progress for granted and so fail to notice small details of development unless we make a particular effort to look out for them. Before planning experiences for these children,

such details need to be acutely observed so that each new sign of
interest or step forward can be encouraged and consistently rewarded.
Experiences with sensory impact can be designed so that responses are
stimulated into being. For example, one of the earliest responses a
normal infant makes is to follow a moving object with his eyes. When a
child can focus even momentarily, the next step is to encourage eye
following, for example by introducing a toy in brilliant luminous
colours, or tracking a torch-beam around a darkened room, or setting
up a lighted fish-tank with brightly coloured fish in the child's field of
view.

You may have to physically help a child explore a variety of bodily
sensations because she cannot achieve this for herself, and encourage
her to do a little more each time. An immobile child needs to have her
position changed frequently so that she can experience the world in
different physical relationships. While dramatic changes may stimulate
some children, others may be distressed by such contrasts and need
continued gentle persuasion to accept a greater range of sensation.

To enable a child to become aware of her own movements and of the
effects they produce, every source of feedback needs to be exploited,
though not all at the same time. There are many ways of doing this.
Mirrors that reflect body movement provide feedback; so do mobiles
hung where a child can see them, perhaps with a string attached to her
wrist for a while, so that she can move them at will. Toys with bells or
other sounds that respond to incidental movement are useful (for
instance, a bell ball in a cot which tinkles when kicked). Experiment to
find surfaces which amplify the effects of the child's own movements,
such as sag-bags, inflatable mattresses – and water. Some toys respond
to the smallest movement: the most simple might be a lightly inflated
balloon tied by twelve inches of string to ankle or wrist, but some
battery toys have been adapted to work on the simplest contact on/off
basis, i.e., they move as long as contact is maintained, and stop on
release. All these toys can be enhanced by the adult who talks to the
child and encourages her efforts.

. The most responsive plaything, of course, is the human being; the
social games based on rhymes and body movements which were
discussed in earlier chapters can be rewarding for both adult and child.
Rhymes which allow the child to join in, either imitating simple
movements or anticipating the climax, as in 'Round and round the

garden', help establish a simple form of co-operation. The child's part, at first, may be that of just watching and being astonished, as in Peep-bo. Adults may develop their own special games with each child, tailored to the sounds and movements and sensations which surprise, please and excite her. A severely deaf child loved to watch a hand creep towards him before it tweaked his nose, while another child learned to anticipate her father blowing in her ear. Ultimately the child may be able to take turns and swap roles in a game of this sort, but for the severely handicapped child this is a long-term aim, and we may actually have to teach her role reversals of this kind.[3]

Very Withdrawn or Passive Children, and the Child with Obsessional Play and Mannerisms

Although these problems are not identical, they often occur together and similar approaches have been used to overcome them. For example, a withdrawn child may use a mannerism to cut herself off from the world and resist attempts to prevent it. A child who is passive, rather than withdrawn, may develop a comforting repetitive activity which merely pleasantly stimulates her and replaces active exploration. The child who is truly obsessive in her play is blinkered and rigid in her choice of activity, incessantly repeating the same activity and resisting with surprising vigour efforts to change or deflect her. Only by observing what happens when someone comes between the child and her repetitive activity can it be decided which of these difficulties is involved. Generalization is misleading since every child is different. Instead, we will give three examples of specific problems and strategies.

Alan was a severely retarded boy of five years who repeatedly slapped his face with his hands, although he would sometimes pause to watch and listen to his mother or father, and might briefly push a dumper truck. He enjoyed having the back of his neck rubbed and allowed his mother to hold and stroke his hands. He liked to walk outside the house and ceased to slap his face if both his hands were held as he went for a walk. He allowed his mother or father to hold his arms down at waist level and, after initial fussing, he would reach out and touch a toy placed in front of him providing it had a simple and dramatic action or a sensation which he liked. We began by trickling sand over his hands and helping him to manipulate it, and later water was introduced in a similar way. After a brief interval, he would try to raise his hands to his face again. Each time his mother or father stopped him with an arm and told him sharply, 'No!'. When he returned his hands to the toy, sand or water, he was told warmly 'Good boy', and he was rubbed on the back of his neck. This approach was maintained systematically by his parents for periods every day, and they constantly looked out for new toys and playthings which might interest and divert him. Gradually a short 'No!' or a token movement of mother's or father's arm was enough to check his face-slapping. Probably more important, he began to develop his play with sand, water and small vehicles, so that these activities gradually replaced face-slapping except when he was frustrated, unhappy or unwell. We can assume that the slapping originally developed as an obsessive reaction to a frustrating and confusing world, but had already fallen to the level of a habit when we started trying to replace it.

Caroline was a mentally retarded three-year-old. She had an obsession with paper which totally absorbed her energies. Holding a sheet of paper in both hands, she tweaked it expertly and then tore it into small pieces. When that sheet of paper was gone, she could not rest until she had found another and started again. It was impossible to get through to her because she held the paper in front of her eyes, gazing at it unwaveringly. If you attempted to remove the paper, she threw herself in a tantrum on the floor, or rushed off to find another piece. Occasionally she would glance straight at you or at something you were playing with. When she found herself in a corridor or a large room she would run up and down with pleasure; she also liked to be lifted and cuddled by her parents. She did not respond to speech, however. Our approach was to remove from the room all available pieces of paper, including those she arrived with. We then waited until her tantrum had subsided and showed her a simple toy. At first she would look fleetingly, and very gradually this extended to her reaching for, taking and holding toys. We found we could develop her pleasure in running up and down by giving her a toy to push or pull behind her – if possible, one that had an interesting effect that would catch her attention: for example, a ringing bell or a whirling windmill. From these beginnings her play slowly developed and some simple communication was established. Eventually her obsession with paper disappeared, and, although it was replaced for a time by others, none was as striking, nor as effective in cutting herself off.

Mark was a retarded three-year-old and seemed withdrawn from other children in his nursery group. Sometimes he seemed to understand what was said to him; at other times he looked straight through you with a blank stare. He had a few words which he rarely used to any purpose, and he spent his time wandering around the room hugging a toy iron to his chest, coiling and uncoiling the flex. One holiday he developed an obsession with steps. At home he would scream and bang on the door to go outside and walk endlessly up and down some nearby steps. At his mother's suggestion we lent him some large wooden building bricks from the toy library, and with these she built his own 'steps'. From then on he began to try to build steps and demanded also that his parents and family build them. A student attached to him found he strongly resisted the removal of the bricks or the introduction of any other activity, so she decided to accept his activities with the bricks but to diversify them. She showed him how to make bridges and push cars underneath. This was the starting point for introducing other toys and other people into his play. The obsession with steps, bricks and coiling faded as it was built upon and his play repertoire was extended.

Children Who Persist in Chewing and Sucking Their Toys

During the normal course of development, all babies explore playthings by taking them to their mouths. This period may be prolonged in children whose development is in general slow, or it may appear late in those children who may have had difficulty in reaching their hands to their mouths at the usual stage. It is an important activity and can be encouraged at the appropriate time. The ordinary child usually ceases to mouth playthings at about the same time as she begins to build, stack and fit simple toys together. Some children use mouthing as a way of becoming familiar with a toy before they begin to play with it in a more consciously constructive way, while others may use their mouth as an extra hand. We recently saw a deaf child of twenty months removing the peg-men from the Galt pop-up toy with his mouth as he held the base firmly with his two hands.

With some children, however, mouthing seems to persist and becomes both irrelevant and a barrier to further progress. Mouthing and chewing can be a real nuisance if they are so removed from a developmental context that they limit the range of toys that can be given to a child. For example, children may be ready for some of the large, simple picture toys, but the toy may quickly become spoilt, or mothers may be reluctant to borrow them from the toy library because the child sucks them. Sometimes, like the face-slapping described above, sucking the hands or fingers interferes with play and, because it is habitual and intensive, causes sore places on the child's hands and face. We are not, of course, referring to the thumb or finger sucking used as a normal comfort habit.

If the child needs to chew on something because she is teething, we can look for suitable objects and provide plenty of variety. There are many teething toys that have other interesting features incorporated: where possible, encourage, develop and reward the positive aspects of the child's play, rather than attempt to stop her sucking or chewing. For example, a bell can be attached to the handle of a wooden or melamine spoon, so that a mere teething object acquires possibilities for play, and sucking can thus eventually be developed into spoon-feeding. At first, the chewing and sucking will return when the child loses interest in an activity or finds it too difficult or too easy. Just occasionally this habit will be so deeply ingrained that more drastic intervention will be needed, using techniques similar to those described with the boy who was face-slapping.

The Child Who Persists in Throwing

A similar approach applies to children who hurl toys rather than play with them. Again, this is a developmentally appropriate stage in babyhood. Children throw toys away from them, either from a height or along the floor, and watch them disappear; this often turns into a game with an adult, which further encourages it. This may sometimes be the source of the problem for the child whose ideas for moving on are limited: throwing a toy can bring immediate response, and, even if the response is disapproval, this can be rewarding for the child in the sense that she is showered with attention. Few parents are prepared to ignore a child throwing objects around their home.

Usually throwing becomes a nuisance when the child has few other alternatives in play and yet has moved on beyond simple sensory exploration. If we watch carefully we may see that she briefly explores a new object before throwing it, but throws familiar objects without hesitation. It may be better at this stage to put most of her toys on one side and concentrate on more active games and play. Some games channel the throwing into more acceptable forms, and may also be a first step to developing the child's play. An example is throwing soft foam bricks into a plastic laundry basket, turning them out and throwing them back again. This is both a developmentally appropriate activity to follow sensory exploration, and a more tolerable form of throwing. Children who throw often love banging, too, and toys such as hammer pegs may also help to develop more constructive play. Some children get stuck at this stage of throwing because they have no means of learning; they do not watch and imitate simple movements. Percussion instruments can be useful here, as these children are often immediately attracted to a xylophone or drum. Even better, a small portable electric organ can teach the child to use *gentle* movements to get a rewardingly loud response. Imitation can be encouraged by the adult first copying the child and then, when the child begins to show interest in the adult's activity, encouraging her to copy. Once she can copy she is ready to learn new kinds of play by following simple demonstrations.

Children Described as Destructive or Aggressive, and the Inattentive Child Sometimes Described as Hyperactive

These two problems are treated together here, since both seem to be made worse by inappropriate physical or social environments. In talking about destructive or aggressive children it is important to define terms. Usually a child described as destructive is one who tends to break up playthings, and an aggressive child is one who attacks other children without due provocation. Sometimes, however, the term 'aggressive' is applied to children who abuse toys because (it is assumed) they feel an anger which they might otherwise express towards other people, but turn towards their playthings. Over-aggressive behaviour is a complex problem which we cannot discuss here. We will confine ourselves to children who abuse playthings either as their form of play or through lack of comprehension. For example, a short-sighted or retarded child who treads on small, fragile toys is accidentally destructive, while a child who drags a doll by its foot usually fails to understand that dolls, like babies, are supposed to be treated kindly.

True destructiveness is where play consists totally in the pleasure of dismantling or destroying play objects. As we have seen, at a certain developmental stage children enjoy pushing over towers or castles of bricks, or squashing sandcastles made only for this purpose. But normally they quickly progress to more constructive activity: building up becomes more interesting to them than knocking down. Again, children may only become destructive when they have exhausted the interest of a play activity from their point of view. If they are encouraged to explore other features or introduced to more challenging activities, the destructiveness may cease. Sometimes children destroy toys that are too difficult for them in the same way that some people upset a games board when they are losing! This is where, again, careful observation and analysis of the precise circumstances in which the child is destructive will pay dividends. Much of what was said about children who throw, also applies here; in fact, children who throw toys are often themselves described as destructive.

One of the most common complaints about children who don't seem, to their parents, to play constructively at all is that they are 'hyperactive'. This term has a more precise clinical meaning, to describe a condition which is often the consequence of brain damage, but it is more loosely used to describe a child who, unlike the others we have discussed, is all beginnings and no endings. It is not so much that the child fails to be attracted to activities but that she moves away distractedly before she can finish what she has begun. For these children, a 'rich stimulating environment' can really exacerbate this characteristic to the full: the 'flitting' from one activity to another increases with the number of new sights and sounds. What sometimes happens is that parents meet with little success in the struggle to pin the child down to quieter and more reflective activities, and so begin to spend all their spare time with the child outdoors, running, walking and jumping, since these are the play activities in which they can naturally share. Consequently the child fails to learn habits of concentration and an understanding that activities *can* have ends and their own rewards.

Sometimes the solution is relatively simple – all the child needs is a more restricted environment, perhaps sitting at a table with nothing to distract her from the one toy she is playing with, and plenty of help and encouragement to achieve and appreciate results. At the other end of the scale are children who will need the help of drug treatment as well as well-planned handling. In between are a number of children who can learn to attend and co-operate in longer and longer play sequences, providing the presentation is carefully thought out, and repeated and persistent attempts made with toys at the right level of development. A child may need to be allowed to run off around the room after only a brief spell of attention, but in time she will find it more and more rewarding to return to an adult who never forces her, but who coaxes, gently restrains, and rewards every sign of attention and co-operation. Meanwhile, the demands on her concentration are extended week by week.

Most generalizations in this field are misleading, as we have said, but there is one exception to this rule. Whatever the profundity of the child's handicap, it is essential to home in on the positive elements of her behaviour, however minute these may be. Even the briefest response, if we look at it in the context of the child's development, can be taken up and built upon in the remedial approach to play.

10 Toys and Play for the Sick Child

During the past few years, people concerned with sick children have become increasingly aware (not least because parents have made them so) that, in concentrating on a child's physical needs, his emotional and psychological needs may well be forgotten. The necessity for children to have the comfort and support of their parents at a time when they are most vulnerable was long ago pinpointed by two epoch-making scientific films: *Grief: a Peril in Infancy,* made by Rene Spitz in 1945, and *A Two-year-old Goes to Hospital* made by James and Joyce Robertson in 1953; and the battle for parents to be freely welcomed on hospital wards has been substantially won, to the extent that medical staff are now regarded as rigid and old-fashioned if they still try to exclude parents. Side by side with this movement has emerged a similar concern with the sick child's contentment and adjustment, focused upon the positive importance of his play activities and of continuing to foster these while he is in hospital; and some specialists in this field have investigated ways of helping the child to come to terms with the frightening experience of hospital through 'therapeutic' play.

There are a number of books which give ideas for making the hospital ward a hospitable environment for play;[1] in this chapter, we intend to concentrate more upon how parents with a sick child at home can help to keep him interested and happy. Obviously, though, some of our suggestions for toys will be helpful to parents and others buying for a child in hospital. Because books on play therapy are less easy to find, we have also included a section by June Jolly (Nursing Officer, Paediatrics, Greenwich), who has made a study of hospitals where staff are doing particularly imaginative work in using play as a therapeutic medium.

Probably a child's first need when he is ill, even if he is in his own familiar surroundings, is to have mother or father available – perhaps especially his mother. In our own study of the upbringing of 700 children in the English Midlands,[2] both mothers and fathers tended to feel that, however participant the father was in the child's up-bringing, it was the mother whom the child most wanted for comfort when hurt or unwell. Asking our own children about this, they agreed – which surprised us, as we hadn't felt our own parent roles were very different. When we asked them why, they said that, first of all, mothers' hands are softer; and secondly, that mothers can be better trusted to wake up quickly in the night. It may well be true that mothers who have breast-fed, in particular, develop an internal alarm system to tiny distress noises that never wholly leaves them and that easily comes back into action on these occasions.

Be that as it may, it does seem important to children when they are ill to know that someone very familiar to them is close at hand; and it will be less frustrating for both child and caregiver if whoever is looking after him accepts cheerfully that this is going to take up some time and normal activities will have to be fitted in as best they can. For instance, it should be no one's priority to spring-clean the house to make it fit for the doctor to see – a good doctor would much prefer to see a comfortable and contented patient.

The second need for the sick child is that, in the early stages anyway, he should be allowed to go at his own pace. In discussing the child's need for play activities, we are *not* implying that a child who is feeling ill should be sat up and badgered to play. At the acute stage of even a minor illness, it is a self-healing reaction to withdraw into sleep or dozing, and children for whom bed has been a welcoming, comforting place will often prefer to curl up there and 'sleep it off', uninterrupted by demands to eat or wash, or unwanted efforts to amuse them – though they may like to have someone sitting quietly in the room, or to hear drowsily the reassuring tiptoe that tells them they are not forgotten by the family. As the child begins to feel a little better, his concentration is still likely to be less active and less lasting than usual, and a game begun with enthusiasm may soon pall as he slumps further down into the bed, languidly counting patterns on the wallpaper or drifting into a doze. Activities provided for the child must take his body's need for physical recuperation into account; it will not help the child if parents show annoyance that the delightful pastimes that they have devised are not yet fully appreciated! It is the caregiver's job to foster the reviving interests of the child in ways that suit his individual needs at the time, making relaxed allowance for his physically convalescent state, yet continually renewing the gentle movement forward that prevents the child from relapsing into the psychological apathy and passivity that can be the aftermath of illness for any of us. If in doubt as to whether the child's level of activity is appropriate for the illness he has undergone, obviously it is sensible to consult the doctor first.

Many doctors nowadays feel that, in the 'ordinary' illnesses of childhood, as soon as the child feels ready to get out of bed he should be allowed to do so – with the proviso that bed or a quiet sofa should be easily available for the moments when he suddenly feels more fragile than he had realized. Children who are up and about will probably be able to continue their usual play activities, though they may play with less persistence and skill than usual; children who are immobilized but otherwise well are likely to be happier in the family living-room, where they can still feel a part of everything that goes on. Much depends on whether the child's bedroom is a warm, pleasant place to be in, and whether it is within easy 'popping-in' distance for the rest of the family or is up a flight or two of stairs and feels isolated and lonely. Sometimes a flexible arrangement is the best idea, so that the child can join the family for most of the day but retreat into the quieter sanctuary of the bedroom when family life gets too noisy and demanding; a change of scene is itself a good way of breaking the monotony. Our own children have sometimes chosen our bedroom as a good place to be ill in during the day, and certainly a double bed solves many of the problems of finding the space to set out play equipment – especially if the household is short of such luxuries as bedside tables and trays on stands. It also allows another child, officially ill or not, to join the patient's play in comfort. If parents have an extension telephone by their bed, there are additional possibilities for amusement!

We will focus, then, on children who have to stay in bed, or are immobile, for one reason or another. For the young child this can be especially frustrating, not just because reading and the games of skill and chance are unavailable to him, but also because young children have a much higher normal level of physical activity than older ones. A PE instructor once tried the experiment of following his three-year-old around for a day, imitating her every action; by the end of the day he was physically exhausted, while she was still going strong. In trying to interest and occupy the child, obviously we shall have this physical frustration in mind; on the other hand, the reason that the child is immobilized will also be a factor in the activities we choose. For instance, for a child in plaster, the plaster itself is doing the work of keeping the limb or joint in place, so that we are mainly concerned to keep the child as active as possible within that physical constraint. But for a child who has simply been prescribed bed rest, for whatever reason, we need first to discuss with the doctor precisely what degree of rest is necessary, and then help the child, by finding him interesting yet quiet activities, to tolerate that amount of inaction; as Emma Plank points out, 'Permitting limited activities often results in more rest because the child relaxes and stops resisting the restriction.'

General Equipment

Some of the equipment that makes life easier when caring for a sick child needs to be bought specially; some can have a different use when nobody is ill; some can be made out of junk and waste. Obviously, if you are expecting a long haul of illness, it may be worth spending some money on items that are going to get a lot of use.

Bed-tables and bed-trays extend space both for playing on and for storing toys that aren't immediately wanted. Particularly useful are cantilever tables, which bring the surface in front of the child, especially if their height is adjustable and if they have a beading round the edge so that things don't easily roll off. Ordinary trays are useful in any number, as this makes it easy to remove an unfinished activity for a while and bring it back at will; improvise extra trays by using grocery boxes cut right down to a one-inch depth. Vegetable racks make very good storage beside the bed, and the expensive ones on castors are especially convenient; our children also got a lot of fun out of using oblong-shaped vegetable racks as dolls' bunks. A series of grocery boxes in different sizes ranged beside or under the bed will keep toys in reasonable order; string bags are also helpful, as their contents can be seen. Polythene washing-up bowls have many uses, for safely containing messy materials like clay, plasticene and mixtures of all sorts, for keeping together constructional toys, or materials for collage or sewing, and for general storage. Drugs and medicines, including junior aspirin, must NEVER be kept near the bed.

If the child is to be in bed long, it is certainly worth while investing in a large sheet of polythene to cover the bedclothes so that messy play can continue without anyone getting worried about it. Start collecting together a good pile of newspapers to protect the floor, and, if necessary, use *small* polythene bags, split at the bottom, as pyjama-cuff protectors, or envelope the child completely in an old shirt with the sleeves cut short. One of the most invaluable things for a long-term patient is a baby-bath on a stand which can be brought to the bedside or removed as necessary; with a few inches of warm water in it, boats can be sailed and containers filled and emptied; it can be used for sand-play, or can provide a base of damp sand for an older child to build a complete village or townscape; we've found that several pounds of dried peas, beans and lentils in such a container provide endless amusement for nursery-age children to pour, dabble in and sort, with an adult present to make sure that they are not poked into ears or up noses.

A change of angle is nearly as interesting as a change of scene, though both can usually be contrived. Perhaps the bed can be shifted into another position; or the child can be moved to an airbed or campbed on the floor, in the garden or on a balcony for a while. Sag-bags can be useful for a change, as they adjust to the child's shape, although they do not give much support. A hammock in the garden offers another possibility. Hammocks are useful in other ways; if it is possible to suspend them over the bed, they can provide additional storage space for the child to reach into, and also a means of tethering toys or tools that might otherwise get lost in the bed or roll out of reach. Similarly, hammocks or other nets can be strung across a young baby's cot, and interesting objects be hung on strings from them so that they are available when reached for. Look around the room for possibilities of hanging things safely, if the child is very immobile; some hospital workers have used a large ball enclosed in a net, hung above the bed, as a 'punchball' for children who don't otherwise get any opportunity for the violent movement that most children normally indulge in every day. If the ceiling has no safe anchor point, it may be possible to attach a rope from one wall to another, and hang things from that. A length of string running from a far hook down to the child's hand, and curtain rings to flick up its slope, will provide half an hour's amusement. Better still, a pulley attached to the wall above the bed-head, with a double cord running to a pulley on the opposite wall or door post, can give enormous pleasure, particularly if two children are ill at the same time, or if another child is just there for company; the exchange of notes and drawings, small objects or sweets, becomes an adventure when they are hauled in in a doll's basket tied to the cord – even a comb, delivered in such a way, may actually be used!

'Active' Toys

Once we decide not to be too inhibited by the fact that the child is in bed, but to protect the bedclothes and let him get on with it, all sorts of play becomes possible. We've mentioned clay and plasticene, but in fact dough is a better idea, being pleasant to handle, clean if a lump does get dropped between the sheets, and non-smelly. The classic kinder-garten recipe of a cup of flour to half a cup of salt (to prevent drying out), mixed to a stiff consistency with water and dusted with extra flour if necessary to prevent stickiness, makes a good malleable dough, which can be used again for several days if stored in the fridge in a plastic bag. Coloured doughs can be made by adding a few drops of food colouring to the water. The doughs can be simply squeezed, rolled and modelled between the hands; provision of an assortment of 'tools' (dead matchsticks, a plastic 'blade', a screw or other serrated or milled bits and pieces from wherever you keep your junk) makes all sorts of impressed patterns possible. With a board and rolling-pin, and small pastry-cutters perhaps, the child can produce beautiful doll's food, with painted 'jam' and decorations; or, while you're about it, proper pastry dough might be used, and the food cooked for tea. Now is the right time, too, to investigate all the instant cake mixes on the supermarket shelves; look for those that have their own small paper cases, packets of icing and decorations included.

Paint is easier to manage if it comes as thick poster-paint in little pots or in a paint-box; the well-known makes offer very good value, and the saving on the ultra-cheap paint-boxes is not worth the frustration caused by their watery grittiness. If you mix powder paints, or when providing water, a non-spill bottle is helpful; make your own by cutting off the top two inches and bottom four inches of a squeezy bottle, removing the whole cap fitting, and inserting the top part upside down

into the bottom part. For paint in bottles, a separate brush for each colour does save spills though it may seem extravagant. A shallow biscuit tin will hold the bottles safely together: wedge crumpled newspaper or kitchen paper between them to keep them steady inside it. Kitchen paper is useful for wiping the brushes, too. Use sticky tape to secure the drawing paper to a pastry-board, tray or sheet of cardboard; or the whole thing can be rested on an improvised bed-table made of a stout grocery box cut down to suitable height and turned upside-down, with arches cut to fit over the child's legs (he might enjoy covering this with a collage of sticky paper or plastic). Try finger painting, mixing the paint with a little tapwater paste; experiment with printing. Most of us have made potato-cuts, but this needs a sharp knife; instead, use a lump of plasticene, flattened on one side, with patterns pressed into it with any hard object (pencil, scissor handle, etc.) – this makes an excellent printing stamp which gradually changes as the impression becomes deformed. A wall pinboard is useful to display both these productions and magazine cut-outs, get-well cards and other oddments.

A box full of bits and pieces for making things can keep older children happy for hours, particularly if they can then use what they've made. Include bits of coloured felt, ribbon, lace, sticky tape, cotton print, sequins, wool, buttons, beads, pipecleaners (mixed colours if you can find them), crepe hair or fluffy wool, and clothes pegs: peg dolls are one of the easiest and most interesting things to make, and can keep the child company or go through elaborate adventures afterwards. Our children once helped organize an exhibition on 'People' in which the star attraction was a peg-doll-making stall, piled with the materials described above, where child and adult visitors stood bemused making doll after doll. Another idea is to make 'cone-people' – small paper cones with faces drawn on and dressed as simply or elaborately as you like. Pop each cone over a marble, and they will run races down a slightly tilted tray. For cutting material it's important to have round-ended but sharp scissors (blunt scissors are dangerous, because the child tends to compensate by putting too much power into his handling of them), and a good glue in manageable form. Fibre pens (water based) will be needed for drawing features on dolls or models; pasta with holes in it can be coloured and threaded into necklaces. If needle and cotton are to be allowed, attach a pin-cushion to something beside the bed, provide only one needle, and remind the child to put it *back* rather than just down when not using it. A stapler is a useful tool, especially if it has a narrow arm.

If the child is to be in bed for a long time, a model village or town, or a dolls' house, will provide a lasting and growing interest. We've suggested using a baby-bath for the village; another way is to use a piece of hardboard, gradually drawing and sticking the scenery on, and making models and people for it, adding cars and animals from the toy box. The child may need quite a lot of co-operation and enthusiasm from other people to keep this going, especially as he cannot go and look himself for the materials he needs. A dolls' house can be made from the ever-valuable grocery boxes, or a smaller one can be built up from shoe-boxes fastened together on their sides. Help will almost certainly be needed in making the construction look like a house in the early stages, but, as it begins to become more 'real', elaboration can be added at the child's own pace. The beauty of these little worlds at the child's bedside is that, in between busy periods, he can lie and project himself into them in his imagination, using them as a base for fantasy games of his own devising. If the child already has a dolls' house or model lay-out, there is, of course, no need to start from scratch.

Lots of musical instruments or toys will give pleasure, at least to the musician! A mouth organ is one of the best, since it can be played in any position and quite young children can produce some sort of tune to their own satisfaction after a day's practice. Music shops often have a surprising range of cheap and traditional instruments like jews' harps, ocarinas, kazoos and tin whistles; but a comb and paper, or even a couple of shakers made of tins quarter-filled with rice and played in conjunction with the radio, can enliven the bedroom. Toy pianos and xylophones, which often get put away and forgotten after the first birthday enthusiasm, may be returned to with a new zest at these times. The loan of a guitar or zither would be a delight for most children.

The presence of another child opens up possibilities as well as providing company. Many a good family project has been initiated out of the enforced idleness of two or more siblings; one of the authors at ten started a family newspaper during communal chicken-pox, which ran to five subsequent issues produced by a healthier editorial board. Loan of a typewriter can fire this kind of activity. We've mentioned the overhead pulley railway; equally, a toy telephone makes communication more interesting. If the children own a battery-powered phone, the pleasure of talking over the wire certainly has the edge over just shouting from room to room – for the rest of the family as well, maybe. If both are in bed in the same room, they can happily phone each other from under their respective bedclothes. A cheap but satisfying substitute is the old-fashioned cocoa-tin phone: all that is needed is a pair of cylindrical tins without lids and a length of fine string just long enough to be stretched taut between the positions of the two callers. A small nail-hole is punched in the centre of the base of each tin, and the two ends of the string passed through the two holes and held inside with a knot. Each speaks in turn into his tin, while the other listens into his, and the contraption works very well – especially if the caller blocks the other ear to complete the illusion of a long-distance call rather than a speaker in the same room! Obviously all the board and card games are opened up to older children by the presence of more than one; so are 'playing at' games to younger children – 'house', 'shop', 'spaceships', 'schools' and so on. Ball games, possible in theory, can easily become too difficult to control in a confined space; bean bags are more manageable, as are shuttlecocks and balloons, or the game can be restricted to ping-pong balls. (One child alone can enjoy a large balloon on a string, and this again makes quite a satisfactory punch ball if it is tethered.)

More 'Passive' Toys

There are times, both during acute illness, and in between the more active hours of convalescence, when the child needs just enough stimulus to keep his thoughts ticking over, as it were, but not enough to tax him. For these times, certain toys have a gentle fascination without making demands on his concentration or physical effort.

Toys that are familiar to the child and normally have a partly comforting function are especially important to him when he is ill. In our own study of 700 four-year-olds,[2] we found that a third of them had an insistent attachment to one particular soft toy or cloth which always had to be there at bedtime, and that half the children insisted on some bedtime comfort habit, including dummies but not counting bedtime rituals. Few hospitals are now insensitive enough to attempt to 'break' children of dummies or other comfort-objects at such a vulnerable moment, and one of the great advantages of home nursing is that the special love-objects and cuddlies of the child are known and can be provided. Favourite dolls and animals are not just comforting by being cuddly; they also give what one of our children called 'comforty', by which she meant the comfort of *company*, in that they can be talked to and maybe talk back. Apart from creatures that are already familiar, there is a strong attraction for the sick child in something that can be cradled in the hand and looked at close to without effort. A small palm-size woolly mouse or squirrel, a tiny teddy-bear three inches high, a pyjama-pocket-sized doll – such a companion makes a happy gift to a sick child because it is scaled down to his own temporarily contracted world.

Glove puppets can also give undemanding company to the child, and can become gradually more active in tune with the child's own inclinations. There are a great many on the market, from the beautiful hand-and-arm animals made by Merrythought, through smaller animals (some with four legs) and people, to finger puppets; but a successful puppet can easily be made from a plain coloured knitted mitt, by embroidering a face in wool and adding a halo of woolly or furry hair. Similarly, two whole families can be made of a pair of knitted gloves, embroidering a different face (and clothes, for still greater effect) on the inner surface of each finger. For a child in hospital, it might be interesting to make patients on one hand, and doctors, nurses and playlady on the other!

Toys that vary the view from the sickbed can be amusing without being too exciting. The kaleidoscope which one looks through rather than into, turning all one sees into a bright repeated prismatic pattern, transforms the familiar scene; so does coloured translucent plastic to look through, or a prism, or a toy telescope or binoculars (to be used either way round). A torch makes a mysterious cave of under-the-bedclothes, especially if it is the kind that changes colour to red and green light; one can experiment gently with the look of the beam as diffused by fingers or tongue. If you are giving a torch to a sick child, don't forget that some spare batteries will be appreciated. Any child with spots or swellings needs a hand-mirror to enjoy them fully. Lying still in bed also offers a great opportunity to try out and become talented at those skills so rightly prized by small boys and girls: winking, 'nose-crunching', tongue-to-nose touching and so on. The Puffin book of *Body Tricks*[3] is a useful primer, and again a mirror is needed. Mirrors are also invaluable for throwing a 'jack' of reflected light on ceiling and wall and learning to make it dance around at will.

Some children will appreciate toys or objects that suit a contemplative mood. A crystal ball or a 'snowstorm' in a dome can be gazed at and dozed over pleasurably. A polished stone egg, or piece of agate, is a double pleasure for touch and sight. A perspex block or disc containing 'liquid crystal', which changes its lucent colour and form at a touch, is a contribution from modern technology, and no doubt holographic glass is a delight to come. Old-fashioned kaleidoscopes are by no means obsolete, but there is also a new kind containing coloured oils which form and re-form into convoluted patterns as the tube is turned in the hand; the very slowness of its movement at once soothes and fascinates. You may be lucky enough to find a 'magnetic mouse game', which consists of a tray containing a mouse obstacle course (old

boot, carrot, wedge of cheese and so on) in and out of which the mouse can be made to run by means of a magnet moved underneath the tray; when one of our children was in hospital, such a toy kept a whole ward of sick children gently amused. If the child feels like making a little effort, bubble blowing alternates minimal activity with contemplation.

For both long-term and short-term illnesses, don't forget that pets are comforting and can also rouse an over-listless child's interest. Dr Hugh Jolly once introduced us to the ward guinea-pig as 'one of the most important members of my staff' – and he meant it. Family pets can be allowed into the room as convenient; for one of us, pneumonia was made tolerable by the fact that it was kitten-season, and the day was punctuated by periods of wild activity as the three kittens chased each other over and under the bed, while between times we all slept companionably, the kittens curled in the crook of human knees. If the child is to be in bed for long, it is worth making a special effort to introduce and maintain this source of interest; for instance, it might be possible to set up a bird table just outside the window, or at least to hang a net of peanuts there to attract small birds. A young budgie is rewarding for a patient who has the time to teach it to talk. Fish in a tank, especially if it is lighted, are pretty to watch; more adventurous, perhaps, are terrapin, lizards and snakes. Even worms and stick-insects can amuse someone who has time to watch them and get to know them, and in our family we have unwillingly learned to love ants, through long exposure to a fondly tended colony of them. Plants, too, can help to amuse the long-term patient. The old favourites, beans in blotting-paper-lined jars, cress on flannel and carrot-tops in saucers never seem to pall, but in summer try more dramatic fast growers – morning glories climb the window frame almost as you watch!

Getting Better

The move from passive to more active occupations may be slow, and parents will be particularly helpful to the child if they are able to spend a good deal of time with him and so keep a finger on his psychological pulse, as it were, and be ready with extra encouragement and stimulating ideas at the right moment. Most of the activities we have talked about will be more attractive to the child if the parent is ready to join in, and this is a good opportunity not just to read and sing to the child, but to share old skills and try out new ones. When did you last play cat's cradle with a length of string, or tie some of the more complicated nautical knots? Did you ever get round to making a crystal garden, or a peepshow out of a shoebox? If the child is very young, how many of the traditional lap games and finger plays have you tried out with him? How many different shadow animals can you make on the wall by the positioning of your hands?[4] Have you ever played at guessing feelies (everyday objects felt through a cloth bag) or smellies (enclose smells such as spices, essences, toiletries, in folded rag)? If you have ever felt envious of the crafts that children nowadays learn in primary school, this might be the very excuse you need to try them.

Parents' participation allows the child gradually to be drawn further and further into independence, at whatever rate suits his need. Most of the more active occupations we have talked about have the function not merely of amusing the child, but of allowing him to move back from the feeling of being someone for whom (and to whom) things have to be done, towards the feeling of being a person who does things himself – and if some of those things can be for other people, so much the better. So long as he does not feel he is being made a convenience of, let him begin to help cook tea for the returning family, do protective things for the baby, make little surprise presents for people. Surprises can include jokes – and an excellent present for a convalescent child is a traditional vulgar joke or two from the 'magic' shop. Pencils with rubber points, bending spoons, the plastic blob of jam or worse, a floating lump of sugar – all these allow the child to 'have someone on', which puts him in a position of direction instead of helplessness. Similarly, one of our favourite puppets for a sick child is a small, fur finger-puppet mouse: cuddly and comforting at the passive stage of illness, its wary emergence from between the sheets can scare the caregiver most satisfactorily, and parallel the child's own emergence into a more positive period of recovery.

June Jolly, who completes this chapter with some observations from American paediatric centres, entitles her section

How to be in Hospital
without being Really Frightened[5]

When you're five, going to school clutching Mummy's hand is a big adventure – certainly not one that you would be expected or allowed to undertake on your own. Imagine how it would feel to land up in a large, strange and bright 'hall', sitting on an enormously high silver metal bed and seeing nothing but people dressed in white, all with unfamiliar faces. Probably much of the language would sound strange, someone would be crying and even mealtimes would come round when you were least expecting them. Add to this that you may be feeling unwell, or are made so by the things that are done to you. Quite quickly a series of events can build up that make a hospital experience for a young child very frightening indeed. There are, of course, some robust souls who never take a look backwards when they go to school for the first time, who are intrepid adventurers before they are four years old, but there are many more who do not seek such experiences willingly. It is for these children that staff in hospitals must be concerned.

Throughout North America much time, money and resources are spent annually on preventive measures to ensure that the child in hospital encounters a life-style that enables him to cope with these bewildering experiences in the only way he knows – through play. Play is the process through which a young child comes to terms with his feelings, and through which he is able to express all the anxieties and questions that adults are able to verbalize. Contact with home and the importance of knowing it is still there is experienced through domestic scenes, 'cooking pastry', washing up or even bathing the dolls, and telephoning, ironing and pushing the pram as at home. Necessary as it is to supply materials and facilities for such 'home' play, it is equally important to provide the wherewithal for the child to experience and handle situations that she finds in hospital. Games of doctor and nurse, with uniforms, stethoscopes and bandages, are well known in British children's wards. That they should be augmented with syringes, medicine glasses, masks, gloves and 'operations' is more rare.

Just to play may not, however, be enough. Some sensitive adult to guide and counsel the child at the right moment may make the experience more meaningful, and avoid any misapprehensions that the child has. Doll play is both fun and therapeutic. There are as many variations as there are schemes and personnel to run them.

Foremost in the care of the very young child, of course, is the continuing presence of the family, and parents in particular. Where some form of family continuity can be maintained, the child is less likely to feel lost and threatened. Even so, there are many things that will happen in hospital that the best family cannot prepare him for. He will need to be able to play through the sequence over and over again, repeating incidents in order to come to terms with them. They can then be absorbed into his fund of growing experiences and become positive means for his development and independence. We should be able to go further than Florence Nightingale's admonition 'To do no harm' and aim to provide an environment in which the child actually benefits from his stay in hospital. The American paediatrician, Dr Berry Brazelton, puts it this way:

I have very strong feelings that a child can learn some pretty positive things from experience in hospital and from an operation if it is handled in the right manner. A great deal of what a child learns about himself comes in stressful situations, and if a hospitalization teaches him that he can cope with pain, being in a strange and frightening place away from home, that he can manage for himself at times, that doctors and nurses want to help even though they hurt him, it can help him gather confidence in himself and in other people and this will be a positive experience in learning to master his world.

Preparation for Hospital

In some centres of progressive paediatric care in the USA a great deal of forethought and care goes into preparing children for hospital. Some arrange what they term 'pre-admission parties' to which the child and his family are invited. These are held regularly at fortnightly intervals and are staffed by volunteers from the play worker staff and nursing and medical personnel. The particular party I joined in Boston at the Children's Medical Centre was a very lively affair. About twenty children and their families had gathered in response to a written invitation, confirmed by a follow-up telephone call. There was a real party atmosphere with biscuits and squash, and balloons with large lettering advertising the hospital.

The scene was set for a sketch. Two cots and other hospital paraphernalia were at the centre of the stage. A narrator holding an outsize book, and dressed as the well-loved doll character, 'Raggedy Ann', was swinging gently in a rocking chair. She proceeded to take the children on a simple visual re-enactment of a typical admission to hospital. Student nurses dressed as a child, plus 'Mum and Dad', arrived on the scene. They were greeted by the 'hostess', and, having been undressed and put into the cot, the 'child' was examined by a 'doctor'. The 'nurse' subsequently took temperatures and blood pressure, and then brought a meal. Even the giving of bedpans was shown. As night drew on the 'parents' said good-bye and the 'child' was tucked down to sleep. This very simple demonstration held the children spellbound. After the 'show', refreshments were provided and the children were encouraged to dress up and handle various items of equipment. A doctor showed them how to look down his throat and hear his heart beat, while others had a great time swamped in theatre gowns, masks and gloves. Gradually the party split up and the children went home. It was obviously a therapeutic exercise for the parents as well as the children. The evident participation by the young nurses was heartening. On inquiry at ward level, I was assured that it was easy to pick out the children who had been to one of these parties, as they settled so much quicker, and with more confidence. Other hospitals have many variations on the theme, some using puppets and even home-produced films, but the purpose and results remain the same.

Children also receive individual preparation. Madeleine Patrillo, who has pioneered preparation by means of doll models, has a store of simple rag dolls, miniature drip sets, ECG leads, catheters, etc., which are attached to the dolls while explanations are given to the child as to why they are necessary, and what they are for. The children keep these dolls and often go over and over the 'treatments', pulling the tubes in and out and injecting the doll whilst making appropriate protestations. Miss Patrillo and Emma Plank (of Cleveland) make extensive use of simple outline drawings of the child's body, to explain what part of the body has been fixed or mended by the doctor.

The nurse would seem the most appropriate person to understand medical and nursing procedures and therefore should be the one to handle these explanations. I saw one particularly fascinating project at the James Whitcombe Riley Hospital where, in the Burns Unit, the sister gives each child admitted a doll. The child is given a pair of scissors and encouraged to cut out the 'skin' of the doll where it hurts. I was told that on all but one occasion the child has removed the exact area from the doll that approximates to the burned areas. On this one occasion the child cut out the whole of the back of the doll, much to sister's amazement as this was not the area affected. When asked why he did this, the child replied innocently, 'Cause this is where it hurts.' In this way the sister was able to discover that the child needed attention for his back, something completely undetected prior to this conversation. The child had never mentioned it to anybody. Following the cutting-out session, the child is allowed to take the doll with him whenever he has treatment, saline baths, etc. Should grafting be needed, gauze is sewn over the affected area. Before discharge the original 'skin' (which has been carefully preserved in a named envelope) is sewn back on by the child. The children almost invariably bring their dolls back to out-patient appointments or on subsequent admissions. Up to the present time the sister is the only member of staff using the dolls, but she is training other members of the ward team so that they can participate too. This was the most sophisticated use I saw made of these models, but it was impressive, and much valued by the children.

In several places where orthopaedics were practised I was shown dolls who were fitted with traction of various sorts, and where the child about to have a plaster-of-paris cast was busily putting a similar plaster on his doll. In this way he was really using his skills and involvement in play in learning about his own treatment. In cases where preparation is impossible (a frequent occurrence with the patient who comes in as an emergency), using the doll can be a very effective way to explain what has happened to their body whilst they were asleep. In one centre where wrist traction is being used to prevent contractures of the upper arm and thorax in extensive burns, the presence of a doll 'strung up' in a similar manner has helped the child to come to terms with the rather horrific realization that he has constraints through his wrists preventing him from moving freely. I was told of one such child who could not even bear to look at the doll for several days, but as he began to glance at the doll he was able to relax and eventually to look at his own hands.

At the Rainbow Babies' and Children's Hospital, Cleveland, the play organizer runs children's play interviews where he reckons to spend half to three quarters of an hour with an individual child. Through the play he helps the child to come to terms with any particular anxiety he may have during his hospitalization. This is obviously a psychotherapeutic exercise, and not one that untrained personnel would be expected or wise to undertake. There were a number of centres, however, where group sessions were held. The children were encouraged to play with any of the equipment laid out for them. Volunteer doctors or other staff became the patients. The children that I watched became quickly engrossed in their play, and the 'patients' received little sympathy and less mercy at the hands of their nurses or doctors. After about half an hour, when injections of enormous proportions had been put in tops of heads, faces and foreheads – never in the more conventional sites – the children lost the intensity of their play and started fooling around. The play before this had been serious and anything but foolish. Observation of such groups at work can be most revealing.

One does not need to have vast resources of money or space to make a child's hospital experience both bearable and a positive contribution to his development. One does need staff with imagination and the determination to meet the total needs of the children in their care. Staff do need to acquaint themselves with healthy child development and the means of communication a child has at his disposal. With a small group of volunteers to make rag dolls, tiny drips from discarded vials and so forth, a ward can have the same props that innovators like Madeleine Patrillo use for their projects. Perhaps most of all, one needs the sensitivity to appreciate and meet the child's needs of the moment. Listening to the child is probably the most important part a sensitive adult can play. It is clear that simply sitting by a child's bed, and deliberately working to create an atmosphere in which discussion is possible, will allow him to reveal a tremendous amount about his feelings and anxieties over his illness. The trouble is that so few people are willing to take time to do so.

Play as a concept has all the ambiguity of the very familiar. Like child-rearing, it is something in which everyone is an expert by virtue of close acquaintance. It has the significance of having made a contribution to every adult's growing-up, yet it is undervalued by children and adults alike in that both have the sense of moving on to more important or real matters, epitomized by the repeated pairing of the words 'just playing'.

Huizinga, whose study of play as a part of the culture pattern emphasized its universality, talks about the 'profoundly aesthetic quality' of play;[1] but its profoundly *personal* quality is equally significant. Our concept of play is rooted in our earliest memories, an essential element in the child each of us once was, who still, in a sense, inhabits the core of our being. Leslie Daiken describes the adult who momentarily participates in a child's play as 'salvaging his own childhood from under the crust of his later experience'.[2] Toys which one can remember having played with exert extraordinary evocative power precisely because of their capacity to symbolize in a very intimate way the childhood which is now almost inaccessible to us as adults; eavesdroppers in toy museums cannot fail to be struck by the special delight with which adults exclaim over these old friends, with far more emotion than the most exquisite miniatures inspire. In the same way, when we first imported whips and tops from the still traditional Midlands to our shop in Enfield (before the renewed fashion for traditional toys had got going), it was the adults, not children, who fell upon them: 'Look, look! A proper whip and top! *I* had one of those! Oh, just wait and I'll show you!' – and they would bear them away, marvelling at their cheapness, to see whether the ageing wrist had lost its cunning. Toys recognized from years past perhaps reawaken in us the passionate absorption of childhood which seems in retrospect somehow different in quality from adult preoccupations, however subjective such feelings may be.

The toy from an ancient civilization, which identifies children long dead with those of our own time, is as compelling in a different way. We may marvel at the richness and beauty with which ancient artists celebrated powerful men or sacred beliefs; but it is the bead rattle from Pompeii, the set of well-worn fivestones from ancient Egypt, or the stone ball used by a Scottish child three thousand years before Christ, which remind us of the continuity of childhood – indeed, the continuity of man – from one civilization to another, and move us by our very sense of the ordinariness of their former owners.

In this final chapter, then, we will take a lingering look at some of the toys which have a long history: those which must have a very fundamental potency, because they recur and persist, in different disguises to suit the time and the place, wherever toys have been made for children. Some of these toys we have already spent some time on: dolls, rattles and wheeled toys, for instance. But there are others which have been no more than briefly mentioned whose longevity alone demands a chapter to themselves. We will, however, scandalize these ancients by also allowing ourselves a glance at their opposites: craze-toys, ephemera and baubles.

Balls

Where better to start than with that most basic and perfect shape, the sphere or ball? The ball is almost a playmate in its own right, having in itself the capacity to engage play in the most positive way: held in the hand, it already begins to roll encouragingly towards the fingertips; dropped to the ground, it bounces, wavers and rolls on, inviting the child to follow. Is a round sea-polished beach-pebble so satisfying to hurl spinning into the sea just because of our long experience of smooth round balls? or would the child who had never seen a manufactured ball still search for the well-rounded stones that spin so cleanly from the fingers?

It seems odd to reflect that the bounceability of balls, a quality which we think of now as a major characteristic, and which we carefully test for when buying a ball, is something that for hundreds of years children had to do without. The bounciness that our own children expect had to await the use of rubber, as late as the mid-nineteenth century.[3]

Although rubber had been used for balls by the Aztecs, these were hard balls rather than bouncy ones. Children would, of course, from earliest meat-eating times, have had available the more balloon-like bladders from butchered animals, blown up and knotted for child and adult amusement. But round balls must for centuries have been used for different purposes according to the materials in which they were made; the stone and marble ones would have been intolerably dangerous to life and property if thrown, while the soft balls of skin, rush or rag would not have rolled well enough for anyone but a baby to find them satisfying.

Soft balls survive from ancient Egypt, made in papyrus fibre, or of rushes firmly plaited, knotted or merely twisted together, and these also appear in Egyptian wall-paintings dating from 1800 BC. Socrates illustrated an argument with a homely reference to a ball made from twelve pieces of soft vari-coloured leather, stitched together and stuffed; in such a ball, each of the twelve pieces is a pentagon, fitted together like patchwork, and these balls are still hand-produced for babies' use, usually in coloured felts, sometimes with an embroidered embellishment on each face: they are not very practical, in view of the licking and chewing that they are likely to receive from a baby, but they are extremely pretty. Leather, in various degrees of toughness, has been a traditional material for making balls for nearly two and a half thousand years, shaped into a sphere by both stitching and moulding, and enclosing inner stuffings of sawdust, feathers, hair, reed, straw and other fibres, or later used in the way familiar to us, as a protective exterior for an inner rubber bladder or core: Gwen White refers to the Elizabethan use of footballs made from leather with a sheep's bladder inside.[4] The morocco leather ball in Hans Andersen's story boasted proudly of having a cork body.

Plaited cane makes a very pleasant-to-handle light ball for throwing, and this material was used in ancient Greece and has persisted in Malaya for hundreds of years. There is a large one in the British Museum (8 inches diameter), and Gwen White refers to them as 'bouncing balls'; we have a modern one only three inches wide, which has a bell incorporated into the plait to make it suitable as a rattle, but it does not bounce very well. The gaps between the plaits make such a ball excellent for a baby to grip and to poke into, and the construction makes it a very slow ball in flight: the modern equivalent is the 'practice ball', a moulded plastic sphere with directional holes all over it, which you can buy in sports shops from golf-ball size upward. Perhaps the nearest modern successor to the papyrus ball is the pith ball still sold in craft shops; as children we used to peel reeds to make these little balls out of the almost weightless white pith, twisting and pressing it into shape, but nowadays they are made from a foamed plastic. They are not very good for throwing, except for the amusement of expending great energy to little purpose, but they are ideal for 'blow football'.

Almost any soft material can be (literally) pressed into service as something to throw; it is a natural action to screw up a piece of paper into a ball before throwing it into a waste-paper basket at a distance, and children soon learn to use paper as missiles in the classroom. Such a use has been formalized in some countries in the manufacture of play balls from pressed tissue-paper, decoratively coloured and bound; balls like this are still made in Japan, the multi-coloured paper showing through a string-and-tinsel net cover, but in this country they seem to be sold for decoration rather than play. Very similar ones in style, yet separated from them by more than two millennia, are the fabric balls enclosed in a network of painted reeds which have come down to us from ancient Egypt.

The advent of a sophisticated rubber technology in the nineteenth century transformed the ball as it transformed the wheel. However, although rubber continues to be very much used in balls made for 'serious' sports, as a material for ordinary 'toy' balls it seems to have had its day, and to have been superseded by various plastic compounds. It is still possible to find sorbo sponge-rubber balls, which have a very superior weight and bounce and a long life, and are much valued by older children who need a good firm bouncer for wall-and-pavement games; and vinyl rubber is often used for babies' textured balls. But the hollow rubber balls that we knew as children (some of which, let us admit, were disappointing in action, or went sticky if left too long in the sun) have all but disappeared. The brightly stencilled hollow balls in all sizes which have taken their place bounce moderately well, and are very good for young children; unfortunately they seem, like people, to become either flabby or wizened with old age, which sets in after a year or so: they are not very likely to grace the toy museums of the future.

An interesting development in the seventies has been the 'powerball'; not unlike a squash ball, but faster still, this has been produced more as a ball to astonish and confound rather than for throwing and catching. Its bounceability is extreme enough to elude catching by all but the most skilful older child, and it is also apt to bounce off at a tangent in surprising directions. The material of which it is made is presumably under unusual internal tension, and is not entirely stable; occasionally a ball will break apart unexpectedly. Some of these balls are produced in glowing colours, but the prettiest are, like Victorian glass marbles, transparent with multicoloured swirls, each one different from the last; the sizes vary from less than an inch in diameter to about two and a half inches, and as a technological innovation they prove that, while balls are almost as old as childhood itself, their history is by no means yet completed.

Bowls, Marbles and Fivestones

Games involving rolling rather than throwing probably evolved out of the nature of the pebbles that were the first play balls; once a rolling game exists, bounceability is a disadvantage in the balls used for it. Hard balls made for rolling have been better able to survive through time than soft ones, and many of them are very beautiful. Stone balls with a carved design have been found in Scotland, believed to be about 4000 years old, and other plain stone and alabaster balls found in Britain date from the Roman occupation. Hardwood has long been used to make balls for rolling, or 'bowls', and for balls intended to be hit along the ground with a bat or mallet; such games can be traced, through pictures and literature from many parts of the world, over two thousand years, and polo is much older still. The game of pele-mele, paille-maille, pell-mell or pall-mall, mentioned by Pepys and earlier, used mallets and a boxwood ball rather smaller than a croquet ball, which was apparently lofted into the air through a ring. At the time of writing, a handsome hardwood 'table croquet' set, with wooden balls and mallets, can be bought for well under two pounds; it closely resembles an Edwardian version, but was made in the People's Republic of China. Gwen White writes that 'beautiful balls of coloured porcelain were made for rolling along the galleries of the stately homes of England in Early Jacobean times', and these were sometimes called 'carpet bowls'; porcelain balls were also used in ancient Egypt and in Greece and Rome.

Balls for rolling must, of course, include marbles: those small ball-shaped objects which seem to differ from balls as such mainly in that, for almost any marble-playing purpose, it is necessary to have several of them. Marbles have been produced in such beautiful materials that they might have been mistaken for jewellery if only they had had holes through them. Jasper, agate, porcelain, decorated glass and marble itself have been used, dating from four thousand years before Christ right up to the present day, when decorative glass marbles (though not of the quality of the last century) are still being made. In the British Museum there is a very fine set of mottled marbles, mitre-shaped ninepins, and three long bricks that form an arch to go with them, from pre-dynastic Egypt: they are in grey and white marble, and came from a child's grave.[5]

Marbles seem to be among the most evocative toys of all, perhaps

because for so many children they have represented a currency more precious than mere money. Many adults still carry in their deeper memory an unshakable knowledge of how many commoneys cost a glassie and the exchange rate for a blood alley. The ha'pence of the marble currency were dull-coloured baked clay balls; ball-bearings ('steelies') have been used; glass marbles were prized according to the beauty of their colour or twisted internal patterns, and alleys, made of marble or alabaster, or blood alleys, with reddish flecks or streaks, were always highly valued. Readers of Mark Twain may remember that one of Tom Sawyer's bargains over the painting of the board fence was finally struck on the tempting offer of 'I'll give you a marble – I'll give you a white alley!' Victorian marbles now command the high prices of the antique trade, even though often the delicate twist-within-twist of their coloured tracery is seen only dimly through a surface worn with much use. Modern marbles, which were very difficult to obtain in any variety during the post-war years until the late seventies, are now coming back into fashion; they lack the symmetry of the older designs, but are still objects of beauty. Some contain a single rather solid twist of colour, or two colours combined; some have a tangle of coloured filaments; others again come in single glowing colours. Children still choose their marbles with great care, looking for the odd fleck or bubble that marks each out as different from the others; our own children knew each of their marbles by name and endowed them with personalities and rules of behaviour. Along with the possession of marbles goes the necessity for a marble-bag – traditionally a small cloth bag with a drawstring made by one's mother, small enough to be stuffed into the pocket, but big enough to take the winnings one hoped for. How many rags-to-riches capitalists were first motivated by the joy of a bagful of marbles?

Before leaving the rolling and throwing games, we should perhaps remember fivestones, though they are not usually spherical in shape. These too have been preserved from antiquity, sometimes in the form of five smooth knucklebones; we know from the dedicatory poems with which Greek boys and girls offered up their toys to the gods on leaving childhood behind them, that knucklebones were among them. Basically the game demands five stones or knuckles which can all be contained at once in the hand and which will roll a little way but not too far; it involves throwing up and catching the stones both in the palm and on the back of the hand and that stones on the ground be picked up quickly while another is still in the air. Like other ancient and long-persisting games, the name by which it is known varies both through time but especially from one region to another; in the UK, as well as 'fivestones' and 'knucklebones', children call the pieces and game 'dibs', 'jacks', 'alleygobs' and 'snobs'.[6] They are sold in England (under the name of dibs) as ridged cubes of white china clay, and also (jacks) as three-dimensional, six-pronged round-ended crosses of steel; Lynn and John Wheeldon, two English potters, make them in porcelain and stoneware to the ridged cube shape and call them snobs, although they find themselves corrected to all the other names by people who see their work at exhibitions.

Rolling and throwing play encompasses every degree of complexity. For the baby, as we have seen, just to push a ball from her and crawl after it is exciting enough, especially if the ball is an inflatable one, larger than herself; for the older child, solitary ball games range from the physical challenge of 'How high can I throw – how low can I catch?', to the constraints of the wall-ball games in which the challenge is to repeat a chain of bouncing movements, sometimes with complications of under-the-leg, turn-around and so on, without a mistake, often to a chanted rhyme of the kind collected by the Opies; and the sophistication can increase almost infinitely, either by bringing in competition as in tennis, or teamwork as in basketball; or by adding to the simple ball some kind of target (cup-and-ball) or obstacle course (croquet or billiards) – or all of these at once. Some of the newest of the ball games are played on a video-screen with nothing but a ball of light to be manipulated by the player, and at this point the ball becomes merely a symbol. That it should be capable of such transformations through its history confirms the ball as the most fundamental and versatile of all toys.

Toys for Gazing at and Peering into

Most of the toys which invite gazing and peering have in them some quality of movement or changeability which attracts and holds the eye. The toys we have in mind are either mechanical, when the mechanism is set in motion and the child thenceforth watches and wonders at its ingenuity; or they are optical, in that the whole experience is one of a new organization of visual perceptions, perhaps an illusion, made possible by the construction of the toy. Sometimes the two are combined, as in some tops, where the toy is set in motion by the 'pumping' of an Archimedean screw and, once spinning, allows the forming and re-forming of bands of optical colour which are produced by the mixing of colours in rapid motion and do not exist when the top is at rest. In a sense these are passive toys, in that all that is demanded of the child is that they should be activated by winding, shaking or whatever releases their power; yet we would not use the term in a derogatory way, since to be fascinated can be called an activity of the spirit, whether or not the intelligence is engaged.

Automata

Although mechanical toys have a long history, they do not belong to the history of childhood until comparatively recently when, with the industrial revolution, man's mastery over and enthusiasm for all things mechanical spilled over into children's playthings. Mechanical toys and automata were known in ancient Egypt, Greece and India, but were produced either by inventors as experiments in scientific principles (the toys developed by Hero of Alexandria about 150 years before Christ are notable examples) or were made for the amusement of wealthy adults; only royal children were likely to be given such treasures, and there are indeed records of richly devised performing toys in the royal nurseries of England and France, many of which must have been presented as diplomatic gifts mainly in compliment to the fortunate child's parents. Hans Andersen described a classic among adult mechanical toys in his story of the Emperor's nightingale, where the real bird was supplanted in the Emperor's favour by one which 'was made of silver and gold and studded with sapphires, diamonds and rubies. When you wound it up, it could sing one of the songs the real nightingale sang; and while it performed, its little silver tail would go up and down.' Other mechanical toys for adults have pandered to other tastes in their owners, like the life-size man-eating tiger in London's Victoria and Albert Museum, toy of Tippu, Sultan of Mysore in 1790, in which the dying victim feebly struggles while an internal mechanical organ simulates his groans.

 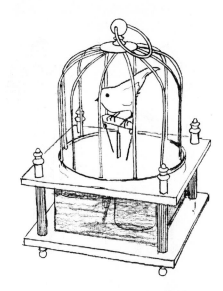

Musical toys with a clockwork movement became more available towards the end of the eighteenth century, mainly manufactured in Switzerland; but it was not until the mid-nineteenth century that cheap tin clockwork toys were produced in large numbers for the nursery market, and the use of flexible rubber soon extended the possibilities of such mechanisms. Nuremburg, for centuries the centre of the traditional wooden toy industry, and producer of automata since the seventeenth century, became a major source of these toys, with the manufacturers of France, America, Japan and England following hard behind. Clockwork creatures in enormous variety filled the toyshops, and many have survived; the London Museum has a caseful of cheap tin automata of the nineteenth and early twentieth centuries, among them a father mouse with a baby mouse in his raised arms that could have been the original of the hero of Russell Hoban's strange story for children, *The Mouse and his Child*, which relates the troubles of down-and-out clockwork toys once their nursery life is past. Unlike dolls, the special fascination of clockwork toys is not that, when you look at them, they look back, for few of them meet the onlooker's gaze; it is their simulation of an independent life that attracts, even though they are compelled to lie torpid until the child turns the key.

Now that old clockwork toys are collector's pieces, there are several books which do better justice to their history and variety than we can here; but it is worth making one or two observations about automata generally. Early in this book we suggested that babies and children are particularly fascinated by movement which is not fully predictable, so that mobiles, 'wobbly balls' and flames share with people's faces a life of their own which is not entirely under the child's control. The automata which are most 'alive' also have this built-in quality of unpredictability. Some of them include an eccentric wheel or weighted flywheel which causes the creature to check or spin and move off in a different direction, and these toys (usually ladybirds, beetles or mice) are still going strong today. Other such toys are not motivated by clockwork at all. The sand-operated toy, for instance, is a closed box with one or more jointed acrobats mounted on an axle on the front surface, and the axle connects to a finned sandwheel inside the box; a reservoir is filled with sand by turning the box sideways a couple of times, and its gradual release on to the wheel activates the acrobats in intermittent and unpredictable ways. This Victorian toy is once more available in England, hand-made in small numbers by the Suffolk toy maker and designer, Ronald Fuller. Toys with a similar quality combine clockwork with some other mechanism; we have a juggler mounted on a case containing a musical movement: when the key is turned and the music starts, this floppy-legged person is merely jiggled on the pin that holds him, but in doing so his hands strike with varying force on a ball mounted on a fine swivelling wire, which means that the ball is sometimes thrown from hand to hand and sometimes merely bounced on one hand, and it is this simple uncertainty of action which gives the toy its vivacity. This is a toy extraordinarily Victorian in conception; still more interesting, then, that it is made in plastic (by Reuge of Switzerland), bought in Cambridge in 1977 (see p. 243).

We must also not forget the traditional toys which are activated merely by the pull of a weight or a string or by the force of gravity. One of the more familiar ones, perhaps, is the Russian 'pecking hens' toy, in which the wooden hens are mounted on a board, each with a string running from the hen to a central pendulum beneath, which is swung in a circle to make the hens peck in quick succession: there are many versions of this basic idea still being exported from Russia. Jumping jacks are hanging personages whose jointed arms and legs spring up in response to a central pull-string; again, a beautifully carved Russian bear is a particularly fine example, and the Russians also make a carved owl whose wings spread wide when something is hung on a central hook (instead of a string). Another toy that has persisted for more than a century is the acrobat hanging from his hands from cords joining the top ends of an H-shaped structure; squeeze the bottom ends and he somersaults, or even stands on his hands in the best balanced versions. Another acrobat tumbles down a ladder on which he is slotted; a woodpecker pecks his way jerkily down a wire tree as he rocks on the vibrating stem. People and animals can be made with pivoted legs in such a way that they will walk down a sloping surface; in recent times, a similar movement has been achieved by trapping a partly-exposed steel ball in the base of a plastic robot so that the rolling of the ball down the slope made the robot appear to walk (or rather, to glide in the manner expected of robots). A jointed mountaineer has climbed a 'rope' alternately taut and loose for several hundred years; he is still made in the East German co-operatives which are the heirs of the medieval toy guilds, and modern versions in plastic now climb beside him. Rocking clowns tumble between curved rails; tight-rope walkers balance swaying on a point, their stability achieved by weighted wires reaching below the centre of support; a 'vaulting horse' appears about to leap from the edge of a table, rocking dangerously on hind legs, but is balanced by the weight on the end of a wire that curves from his stomach to a point well behind and below them. A toy in this tradition, but in a modern idiom, is the 'slinky' or 'flexi', a flexible steel spring in flat wire which by a process of extension and retraction will 'walk' itself downstairs like a two-headed caterpillar.

Optical Toys

Although children must always have seized upon the pieces of coloured glass that came their way in order to peer at a world transformed, toys devised especially to provide such visual experiences seem to have been rare until the nineteenth century. At this time the educational and scientific enthusiasms of the age were often epitomized in toys that combined wonder and instruction. For children who had yet to experience the cinema, let alone television, toys which gave the illusion of movement to pictures must have been particularly exciting. Such a toy was the Victorian 'zoetrope', a spinnable open cylinder on a stand, with slits in its sides through which to look at a series of drawings of a figure in progressive positions: as the cylinder was spun, successive glimpses made the figure appear to move. Spare bands of alternative figures were supplied, or, more instructive still, children could make their own. Similar moving-picture effects could, of course, be obtained with the minimum of equipment by making a 'flick-book', still a delight even to sophisticated modern children, in which the changing positions of, say, a running pin man are drawn on successive pages, which are then flicked through to produce the apparent movement.[7]

The kaleidoscope is an optical toy which, in its modern mass-produced commercial form, is seldom as beautiful as the old-fashioned version, but which has in fact also been developed in interesting ways. The original toy, rarely to be found today in shops, was made of three tapered strips of glass fitted together inside a black paper cover to form a darkened tapered tube; at the top, narrow end, a peephole was left, and at the base the cover-paper fell short on one side to create a window to admit light. Scraps of silver paper, tinsel, spangles and beads were enclosed in the tube and viewed through the peep-hole, when the reflections formed by the darkened glass would multiply the actual display by eight to form regular octagonal patterns in infinite variety according to how the contents settled after shaking. Modern commercial kaleidoscopes usually have the window at the end, rather than on the side; this means that the covering of the window must be somewhat opaque so as not to see straight through it, and normally 'frosted' plastic is used: the brightness of the pattern is thus considerably reduced. In addition, the use of tin rather than glass as reflector considerably diminishes the beauty of the display, and the contents, also, tend to be unimaginatively chosen.

A particularly interesting development of the kaleidoscope is the octoscope or decascope in which the contents are dispensed with and a clear lens inserted at the end of the tube, which the viewer does in fact look straight through: whatever he looks at is seen as a symmetrical eight- or ten-segmented circular pattern, that is, multiplied eight or ten times in mirror-image pairs. The pattern changes as the viewer trains the octoscope on different scenes, and the transformation of objects in the environment into elements of a pattern is extraordinarily visually compelling. Equally fascinating is a kaleidoscope whose base contains coloured oils; these do not mix, but merge with and enter each other, forming eddies of movement rather like cellular activity under a microscope, but once again multiplied by ten to create a regular yet dynamic pattern. A third kaleidoscope, marketed as the 'turn-a-scope', is especially ingenious and gives the most complex visual experience of all; the body has the traditional inward-facing reflective facets, but one looks on through the base at the perimeter of a transparent wheel mounted below it, containing loose vari-coloured fragments in compartments all round its circumference. The usual ten-sided pattern is seen, but there are two of them, one behind the other, being the far and near sides of the wheel. According to the direction in which the wheel is turned, one of these patterns will be seen to be centrifugal, the other centripetal. This incredible toy comes from Hong Kong; it is made entirely in plastic and cost 25 pence in 1977.

Spinning toys have long been valued for their optical interest. Tops appear and reappear in literature going back to Virgil and beyond, as a symbol of careless childhood joys, and it is likely that children would

soon learn to daub colours on the upper surface for the pleasure of
seeing them mix and change. Certainly by the nineteenth century the
top's visual possibilities were being exploited by manufacturers; the
Bethnal Green museum has a 'kaleidoscope top' (English, 1858) with
interchangeable colour discs and pattern discs, some supplied with the
top and some clearly home-made additions.* Gyroscopes were
produced in England as toys from the 1870s (one was awarded a medal
in a Moscow exhibition in 1872) and their design remains unchanged
over a hundred years later; but one would like to see a return of the
Gyrograph, a top produced in England in 1895, into which a pencil
could be inserted to form the spindle, thus drawing patterns as the top
was spun on a sheet of paper.

Most people will at some time have made a 'buzzer' or 'cut-water'
out of a button threaded and spun at the midpoint of a double string
alternately stretched and relaxed; it is treated as a familiar toy in a book
of indoor amusements of 1898.† Other optical effects are created by
toys that include discs or rings spinning in the other dimension. For
instance, a card disc with strings attached to opposite edges can have a
cage drawn on one face and a bird on the other, and the bird is caged by
the disc being twirled. A charming and simple optical toy, the 'goldfish
bowl', is illustrated in a richly inventive shilling booklet, *Toy Making
for Amateurs*, published in the nineteen twenties, and was obtainable
commercially as a cheap novelty in the sixties: a tin circle is threaded
through two holes in its perimeter on to a wire and the tin fish is
attached to the wire at the circle's centre; spinning the circle reveals
the illusion of a containing glass bowl.

Ride a Cock Horse

Children play at horses whether or not they have toy horses to play
with. Probably most of them are initiated into the idea of riding a horse
right back in babyhood, when the adult, carrying the toddler astride

---

* Bethnal Green also has a top dated 1800 by Jaques, a firm still making toys today,
which when spinning spawns eight baby tops one by one, all of them finally spinning
together.

† It is in fact much older. Eskimo and Japanese examples exist, and a buzzer made from
a William III coin was excavated from a British Army encampment on Staten Island.

back or shoulders, breaks into a trot and clicks his tongue in accompaniment, or encourages himself with a mock 'gee-up, horsie!' Allusions in literature to men playing with young children have many such examples going back to ancient Greece, and this must long have been a form of play which has allowed men contact with children without too much demeaning themselves. Knee-games, with the old rhymes that accompany them, confirm the delights of the 'horsie-ride'. The horse as an aid to man's mobility has a long history, and this is naturally reflected in the pullalong toys made for newly-mobile children to draw behind them, both in the form of horse-and-cart and in the horse on wheels, of which so many examples survive from ancient civilizations. Children can be seen playing at horse and rider (where one child *becomes* the horse) in Breughel's famous painting of children's games of 1560; they still do so today.

Playing at horses without a toy horse usually demands two children playing together; to become both horse and rider at once is difficult (although Velvet, in Enid Bagnold's *National Velvet*, managed it with the help of a paper cut-out horse in her hand, patting her own thigh with a switch as she cantered, and in bed at night driving her own feet with tape reins attached to her toes). Many children discover for themselves how to use a stick or sweeping-brush as a good-enough mount for solitary riding play. The urge towards a little more realism is seen in the hobby-horse, a horse's head on the end of a broomstick, sometimes with wheels at the base for easier riding. A hobby-horse was a member of Socrates' household, and they were played with in China in the first century AD. They seem to have been immensely popular through the Middle Ages, to judge by the frequency with which they appear in woodcuts and engravings of the time. A fifteenth-century print shows Christ as a child on a hobby-horse, and this toy was probably indeed an experience which subject and artist had in common. Nearer to our own times, Harrods catalogue for 1895 mentions hobby-horses while Gamages catalogue for 1913 offers them in two sizes (price 2s 9d and 3s 6d), as well as twenty-two other horse-riding toys (more if you count different sizes) and numerous pullalongs. Leslie Daiken wrote in 1963 that hobby-horses were 'no longer seen by the modern child', but we doubt whether they ever entirely disappeared; the Opies, collecting street games through the nineteen sixties, report two children in Weybridge whose three hobby-horses were home-made each from an old sock, stuffed, with eyes, ears and bridles sewn on and attached to a stick, and one of the authors had just such a horse in the forties. Recently hobby-horses have returned to favour and are fairly easily obtainable from the better toyshops; some are made with stuffed fabric heads by individual craft people, but firms such as David Lethbridge Design and Woodpecker make wooden ones on a larger scale, and larger rocking-horse manufacturers (Pegasus) have begun to produce hobby-horses in a luxurious quality similar to their rocking versions.

We should perhaps mention another version of the hobby-horse, in which the horse's body is simulated by an oval frame surrounding the child's body and suspended from the shoulders: the head and neck rear up from one end of the ellipse and the tail hangs from the other, while between the two a fabric cover imitates the caparisoned body of a medieval charger. This hobby-horse has persisted through time in various versions of morris dancing. James MacKay, in his book on *Nursery Antiques*, reserves the term *hobby-horse* for this version, and calls the simpler kind *cock-horses*. He describes the caparisoned horse as popular in the sixteenth and seventeenth centuries, but says that it 'had virtually died out by the nineteenth century'; however, it appears in the 1913 Gamages catalogue as the 'Old time hobby horse', costing 6s 6d and advertised as 'sure to be favoured with the little riders' approval'. Gwen White illustrates a very similar-shaped horse to be held between the legs, a 'lantern-horse' from China of the same period.

More substantial horses for riding astride or behind came into their own in the nineteenth century, as mechanical toys became commoner and cheaper. The horse on wheels which is simply a large version of the pullalong has never been very versatile as a riding animal, because a willing adult or sibling was necessary to provide the power. With the mechanical age, however, the horse motif could be incorporated in tricycles and scooters. A horse tricycle (with the improvement of rubber-clad wheels if desired) was advertised in Harrods catalogue for 1895 at between 27s 6d and fifty shillings according to size. Ernest Shepard, illustrator of the Christopher Robin books, describes a similar toy in his autobiography: he is referring to the year 1887, his seventh birthday:

... I always thought there must have been some direct divine influence working on my behalf to guide Aunt Alicia on this occasion, leading her away from the more useful gifts; and that the Angel Gabriel, disguised as the shopwalker in Mr. James Shoolbred's store, had led her to Septimus where he stood, with eyes dilated and distended nostrils, pawing the air with his two forelegs as though yearning to discard his three wooden wheels. It was some days before I mastered him, but after that I would carry him down the front steps and pedal along the Terrace, 'clank, clank', to the end and back again, my little legs spinning round till Septimus and I stopped for lack of breath, or the face of Lizzie, the cook, appeared at the area steps to say that dinner was ready. Tethered to a lamp-post, Septimus would then await his master's pleasure.[8]

By 1913, mobile riding horses offered in Gamages catalogue include tricycle horses from 10s 9d (starter size with iron wheels) to 52s 6d (with gig seat, chain-driven wheels, lamp, horn and two independently galloping horses!), stool horses on castors, two different wheeled horses on springs which allowed the rider to 'impart a natural trotting motion', and a 'gee swing' (a large horse on ropes to swing forward and back), as well as rocking horses and chair rockers with horses' heads.

It is the rocking horse, however, which competes with the dolls' house for the status of family heirloom; less demanding of attention than the dolls' house (though usually more greedy of space), it is probably a more generally coveted toy. One of the earliest wooden rocking horses to have survived came from the royal nurseries of Charles I, dated about 1628; it is fairly typical of most rocking horses of the seventeenth century, in that the body of the horse is merely suggested by the head and neck, while the rockers make up the greater part of the toy, being almost semicircular in form and of solid wood. A similar horse of the same century is in the London Museum; larger and more solid still, it has seats for two children and is furnished with wooden footrests and a holster for a wooden pistol. One of two seventeenth-century horses that have survived are carved more naturalistically, legs and all: they stand on platforms which in turn stand on rockers. In the eighteenth century, rockers lost their solidity and the legs of the horse became an important feature, held in the extended position familiar to us now and fastened directly to the rockers; the platform shrank and became merely a strengthening device. Meanwhile the horses themselves became both more detailed in form and more spirited in character. Rockers continued in the bow shape through two centuries, extended well beyond the hooves at each end for safety; then, as now, a rather large nursery was needed to accommodate the horse's size. It was not until 1880 that the rocking horse swinging on iron hoops from an immobile stand was patented by Dunkleys of London, and in the same year an American company in Ohio acquired the British patent, since when this design has remained the standard: it allows an exciting and convincing ride with a maximum of safety, and therefore has the enormous design advantage of pleasing parents and children alike.

During the twenty years after the 1939 war, new rocking horses were difficult to obtain, though one or two craftsmen continued to make a few. The popular market came to be served by painted metal horses hung on springs from a frame and too small to be used by children over six, while those who still remembered the old wooden rocking horses were likely to be able to buy a Victorian or Edwardian relic at a reasonable price; our own two, bought in 1951 and 1967, cost us five and ten pounds respectively. The nostalgic seventies, however, turned the old rocking horses into antiques for which prices well over a hundred pounds were normal. Meanwhile, new technology was translating old designs: the two rocking horse designs most sold in England today are a wooden horse padded and covered with a convincing 'ponyskin' hide of acrylic fabric (Pegasus, Equestris), and another which looks very like the dappled mounts that we regard as more traditional, but is in fact strongly moulded in fibreglass (Haddon Rockers); both are saddled and bridled in leather and vinyl. Both safety stands and the more old-fashioned bow rockers are once again available, still in the traditional material of painted or varnished wood. These horses are enjoying something of a boom, despite the fact that they are nearly as expensive to buy as their antique ancestors. From time to time other versions appear: a rearing horse was shown at the 1977 toy trade fair in England, on a system of springs, and for some children the only experience of a riding horse will be the rather rigid mechanical action of coin-in-slot rides at the entrances to some multiple stores such as Woolworths. The basic concept of the horse on rockers has, however, withstood the passage of four centuries and the coming of motor cars and spacecraft; it is not likely to be lost to the nursery now.

Baubles and Ephemera

What makes a toy ephemeral? That depends on how we choose to define the word, for toys can be enjoyed for a while and then pass into oblivion for quite different reasons. Some toys are amusing when first encountered but have no staying power because they are too contrived to catch at the child's imagination or to fulfil any need in him. Others are ephemeral as an essential quality in themselves; they were never intended to be permanent, and one almost feels that their survival for very long could be an embarrassment, for they are toys of the moment: party toys, fairground toys, decorative trifles. Others again are permanent members of the toy family, but come briefly into intensive use as a fashion, perhaps in a special guise or played with in a special manner.

We cannot know as much as we would like about the 'trifles' of the past, because by their nature they are unlikely to have survived, being cheaply produced in flimsy materials and usually recognized as transient by their owners, however much they may have been delighted

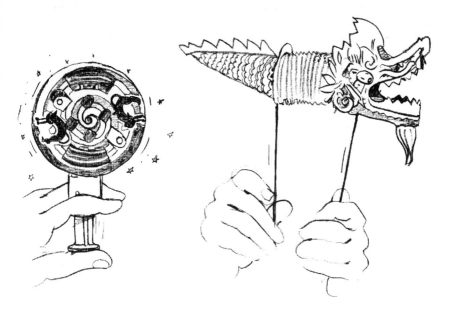

in at the time. How we should love to have now in our collection the tiny domestic and landscape scenes, made in card and matchstick wood and set up in a matchbox, on which one of us at the age of seven regularly spent her Saturday penny! Whatever happened to the paper bird with a spun-glass tail, the inch-long penknife with the Lord's prayer written on the handle, the tiny duck with a lump of camphor under his tail to make him swim? We only have to look around us now to become aware of the toys which our own children will think of lovingly, and how difficult it would in fact be to keep them in good condition for posterity, especially if they had once been played with. A prime example of an ephemeral toy, and also one of the most delightful, is sold at Nottingham Goose Fair every October: it is a pale green transparent balloon filled with hydrogen, and from the top of its inner surface, as it bobs in the air, hangs a 'goldfish' on a thread; long may we have a child by the hand as an excuse to buy one! Another Goose Fair toy is a paper bird hanging from a stick, with tail feathers of wood shavings; as the bird is swung round one's head, the tail revolves with a loud twittering sound. Other fragile paper toys are those dragons, birds and so on which arrive folded tightly and open out into shapes of honey-combed tissue-paper, snakes on sticks with plaster heads and wriggly bodies in that same versatile honeycomb, the rolled-up blow-out paper tubes with a feather on the tip with which children astonish each other at parties, hot-air balloons, and windmills or whirligigs. A little more durable are straw insects and chenille birds and animals from China, maize dolls from Czechoslovakia and pressed cotton dolls from Russia. Some toys are consumed by the very act of playing with them: Japanese paper flowers, tight-rolled like lozenges and packed in seashells, which blossom and grow when dropped in a glass of water; an explosive charge in a screw of paper to be thrown against a wall or pressed between the fingers while looking studiously in the opposite direction; the sparkler and spark-gun, which work by the scrape of a flint on steel and have only a short life.

Some long-lived toys have traditionally been played with only at certain seasons of the year, and are in that sense alone ephemeral: tops in the early spring, skipping ropes to follow them, marbles at the beginning of the school year and of course conkers as they ripen and fall. But urban children pay far less heed to the 'proper' season than they did even twenty years ago. Instead, a particular manner of using a toy is suddenly taken up, to be dropped again as suddenly, maybe not to reappear for years. For a brief time in the sixties, 'Chinese skipping' was the rage: the child tied one end of the rope loosely around one ankle and, by skipping from one foot to the other, moving the roped ankle in circular motion the while, got the weighted end flying in a sweep around her – the challenge being to leap the rope with the unfettered foot as it came round. Hoops, which had for years been rarely seen except in schools, returned with a vengeance (literally – witness a large number of parental slipped discs) as hula hoops, to be kept spinning horizontally around the body by the gyration of the pelvis. The production of hoops in plastic made such a use possible – the iron hoops of earlier days could hardly have been played with so – but this does not explain why hula hoops disappeared as precipitately as they had arrived, not to be found in ordinary shops until years later. Back in 1939 there was a craze for Hi-li, a small rubber ball attached to a wooden bat by elastic; and earlier still the yo-yo, a toy known for centuries, inspired a similar transient obsession.

Much of this book has naturally been concerned with the toys which persist through time; in so far as children continue to be childlike, their needs and interests are timeless. Toys which persist are those which satisfy the child's wish to grow in skill and in power, which feed his imagination, absorb his emotion and seize his curiosity, and which purely and simply amuse him, surprise him and make him laugh. None of these qualities is less valid than the others. We should in particular be sorry if reading a book like this had the effect of making adults over-conscious of function, and perhaps afraid to give children ephemeral toys. We said earlier that our most appreciated present to a three-year-old was a carrier-bag full of hats; other exceptionally successful gifts have been a bag of horrors (rubber worms, slugs, spiders, and the like) for a four-year-old, and a boxful of jokes (false teeth, hinged spoon, rubber pencil and so on) for a five-year-old. Some children would prefer an object which has never seen the inside of a toyshop at all. Perhaps in choosing a toy we need to shift our focus; to ask not 'which toy?' but 'what would this particular child enjoy doing, and what will meet that end?' What we have tried to do in this book is merely to consider possibilities.

Notes

All books are published in England unless otherwise stated.

2. People as Playthings: lap and cradle play

1. Ambrose, J. A. (ed.), *Stimulation in Early Infancy*, Academic Press, 1969.
2. Sandhu, J. S. and Hendriks-Jansen, H., 'Special School Environments for Handicapped Children', report of the Built Environment Research Group, Polytechnic of Central London (mimeo), 1974.
3. Winnicott, D. W., *The Child and the Family*, Tavistock, 1957.
4. Newson, J., 'An Intersubjective Approach to the Systematic Description of Mother-infant Interaction', in Schaffer, H. R. (ed.), *Infant Interaction*, Academic Press, 1977.
5. Newson, J., 'Towards a Theory of Infant Understanding', in Bullowa, M. (ed.), *Before Speech*, Cambridge University Press, Cambridge, 1978. See also John and Elizabeth Newson, 'On the Social Origins of Symbolic Functioning', in Varma, V. P. and Williams, P. (eds), *Piaget, Psychology and Education*, Hodder and Stoughton, 1976.
6. Trevarthen, C., 'Early Attempts at Speech'; this is one of a number of interesting and not-too-technical articles in Lewin, R., *Child Alive*, Temple Smith, 1975.
7. For instance, by Susan Pawlby and Olwen Jones, both working in the Nottingham Child Development Research Unit. Some of their work is described in Pawlby, S., 'Imitative Interaction', and in Jones, O. H. M., 'Mother–child Communication with Pre-linguistic Down's Syndrome and Normal Infants'; both published in Schaffer, op. cit.
8. The Opies comment that 'rhymes which accompany infant amusements are probably among the oldest verses there are'. There are many references to peep-bo games in sixteenth- and seventeenth-century literature, and the Opies mention one in a manuscript of 1364. Simply touching different parts of the baby's body or face is a feature of some rhymes such as 'Here sits the Lord Mayor, here sit his men'; others involve poking, finger-walking, tickling or knee-jogging, or a combination of these, usually moving from gentle to exciting. One of the writers was jogged by her grandfather to this version of a rhyme which appears in different forms:

> This is the way the ladies ride,
> Niminy, niminy, niminy, niminy [daintily];
> This is the way the farmer rides,
> *Oom*buluh, *oom*buluh, *oom*buluh, *oom*buluh [ponderously];
> This is the way the tradesman rides,
> T'trot, t'trot, t'trot, t'trot [brisk];
> And this is the way the gentlemen ride [expectant pause]:
> A-GALLOP, a-GALLOP, a-GALLOP, a-GALLOP!

– to which we added when our own children inherited this play:

> OVER a five-barred gate and DOWN into a ditch!

– which addition possibly came from the 'Listen with Mother' programme or possibly from a nursery rhyme book. Thus are modern children's lap rhymes a mixture of family inheritance and versions formalized by the media.
Opie, I. and P. (eds), *The Oxford Dictionary of Nursery Rhymes*, Oxford University Press, 1951. A book that specializes in lap rhymes and finger play is *This Little Puffin* by E. Matterson, Penguin Books, 1969.

9. Gregory, S. (then Susan Treble), 'The Development of Shape Perception in Young Children', doctoral thesis, University of Nottingham, 1972.
10. Gray, H. 'Learning to Take an Object from the Mother', in Lock, Andrew (ed.), *Action, Gesture and Symbol: the Emergence of Language*, Academic Press, 1978.

3. Toys For the First Two Years: a developmental progression

1. Haskell, A. and Lewis, M., *Infantilia: the Archeology of the Nursery*, Dobson, 1971.
2. From a test known as the 'Psyche Cattell', after the name of its deviser. Cattell, P., *The Measurement of Intelligence in Infants and Young Children*, Psychological Corporation, New York, 1940.
3. *Gamages Christmas Bazaar, 1913*, (facsimile reprint), David and Charles, Newton Abbot, 1974.
4. White, G., *Antique Toys and Their Background*, Batsford, 1971. Patrick Rylands won a Duke of Edinburgh award for elegant design in 1970.
5. Pawlby, S., in Schaffer, H. R. (ed.), *Infant Interaction*, Academic Press, 1977.

4. Some Timeless Toys and Play Equipment

1. Stallibrass, A., *The Self-Respecting Child*, Thames and Hudson, 1974.
2. Manning, K. and Sharp, A., *Structuring Play in the Early Years at School* (Schools Council project), Ward Lock Educational, 1977.
3. Newson, J. and E., *Seven Years Old in the Home Environment*, Allen and Unwin, 1976, and Penguin Books, 1978.
4. The Opies give a great variety of such rhymes in their *Lore and Language of Schoolchildren*. Many persist from generation to generation, incorporating variations according to topical interests. The mother of one of us taught us the following ball-bouncing chant from her own childhood in Berkshire (known by the Opies for that date and currently):

> One, two, three a-lairy
> My ball's down the airey*
> Don't forget to give it to Mary
> Or to Charlie Chaplin.

*airey means 'area' – the sunken yard outside the basement of a terraced house, reached by steps from street level.

A variation on this rhyme was collected by the Opies in Edinburgh in 1940 and in Kirkcaldy in 1952, still as a ball-bouncer:

> One, two, three a-leary
> I saw Wallace Beery
> Sitting on his bumbaleerie
> Kissing Shirley Temple.

The following skipping rhyme collected in 1957 in Swansea includes both a film idol and actions for the skipper; it is very similar to another used both recently and in the thirties, featuring Charlie Chaplin, who seems to be the most persistent of folk heroes:

> Hi Roy Rogers!
> How about a date?
> Meet me at the corner
> At half past eight.
> I can do the rumba
> I can do the splits
> I can do the turn-arounds
> I can do the kicks.

5. Such uses are not so far from our own times and societies. Carl Fox's beautifully illustrated book includes a chilling photograph of two three-inch cotton voodoo dolls found in a small coffin-shaped box on Coney Island beach in the 1960s. They were wrapped in paper torn from a

notebook on which was scrawled six names, and were pierced in head, arms and body with long needles. Fox, C., *The Doll*, Abrams, New York, 1973.

6. For instance Max von Boehn, *Dolls*, Dover, New York, 1972 (originally published in German in 1929).
7. White, G., *European and American Dolls*, Batsford, 1966.
8. Newson, J. and E., *Four Years Old in an Urban Community*, Allen and Unwin, 1968, and Penguin Books, 1970.
9. Pakenham, E., *Points for Parents*, Weidenfeld and Nicolson, 1954.
10. Three of Morgenthaler's dolls of the fifties are illustrated in Bachmann's *Dolls the Wide World Over*, Harrap, 1973.
11. An interesting discussion of this aspect of the toy (with an introduction by D. W. Winnicott) will be found in Olive Stevenson's 'The First Treasured Possession', in *The Psychoanalytic Study of the Child*, Vol. IX, Imago, 1954.
12. Bel Mooney, article in the *Guardian*, 8.1.76.

5. Props for Fantasy

1. Newson, J. and E., *Seven Years Old in the Home Environment*, Allen and Unwin, 1976, and Penguin Books, 1978.
2. Vygotsky, L. S., 'Play and Its Role in the Mental Development of the Child', a lecture originally given in 1933; in Bruner, J. S., Jolly, A., and Sylva, K., *Play – Its Role in Development and Evolution*, Penguin Books, 1976.
3. Hostler, P., 'Play with a purpose', in Blishen, E., (ed.), *The World of Children*, Paul Hamlyn, 1966.
4. Newson, J. and E., *Four Years Old in an Urban Community*, chapter 7, 'Shared and private worlds', Allen and Unwin, 1968 and Penguin Books, 1970.
5. Ibid. chapter 12, 'Who told thee that thou wast naked?'
6. Newson, J. and E., *Seven Years Old in the Home Environment*, chapter 5, 'The constraints of reality', op. cit.
7. *Open Stage Kits*, devised by Janet Simpson and Guy Chapman.

6. Miniature Worlds

1. Axline, V., *Dibs: In Search of Self*, Penguin Books, 1971.
2. Some examples of particular interest can be found in the following: Bowyer,

R., *The Lowenfeld World Technique*, Pergamon 1970; Isaacs, S., *Social Development in Young Children*, Routledge and Kegan Paul, 1933 (but still unsurpassed); Moustakas, C., *Children in Play Therapy*, 2nd edn, Ballantine, 1976; Tanner, J. and Inhelder, B., *Discussions on Child Development*, vol. III, chapter by E. Erikson, Tavistock, 1956.

3. Some discussion of the development of sex differences in children's play preferences can be found in J. and E. Newson, *Seven Years Old in the Home Environment*, Allen and Unwin, 1976, pp. 143–8, and Penguin Books, 1978, pp. 155–60. A further discussion appears in J. and E. Newson, D. Richardson and J. Scaife, 'Perspectives in Sex-Role Stereotyping', in J. Chetwynd and O. Hartnett, *The Sex Role System*, Routledge and Kegan Paul, 1978.

4. The developmental stages of children's drawings of people are summarized by us in Lorna Selfe's *Nadia: a Case of Exceptional Drawing Ability in an Autistic Child*, Academic Press, 1977; and an illustrated audiotape, *The Innocent Eye* (Elizabeth Newson), can be hired from the Medical Recording Service Foundation.

5. Ken Edey, managing director, has been quoted in a toy trade journal as saying that Sindy is a phenomenon that he will never understand. 'Last year we sold more than half a million Sindy dolls and I cannot imagine where they all go. We expect to sell between six and seven hundred thousand this year, and yet there are only 350,000 girls born in the UK each year.' *British Toys and Hobbies*, 26.7.1977.

7. Play and Playthings for the Handicapped Child

1. The responsive kaleidoscope was shown in the exhibition *Playthings for the Handicapped Child* organized jointly at the Royal College of Art, London, in 1971 by the RCA Industrial Design (Engineering) Research Unit and University of Nottingham Child Development Research Unit. The use of a projection kaleidoscope with an autistic child (together with details of how to make it) is reported in Jellis, Trevor and Grainger, Sam, 'The back projection of kaleidoscopic patterns as a technique for eliciting verbalizations in an autistic child', *British Journal of Disorders of Communication*, *8*, 1972, pp. 157–62.

2. Sandhu, J. S., and Hendriks-Jansen, H., *Environmental design for Handicapped Children*, Saxon House, Farnborough, 1976.

3. Kay Mogford: 'The communication of young severely handicapped children: a preliminary to assessment and remediation', internally

circulated paper, Child Development Research Unit, University of Nottingham.

4. An example of this kind of assessment is described in Elizabeth Newson's 'Parents as a resource in diagnosis and assessment', in Woodford, P. and Oppé, T. (eds), *The Early Management of Handicapping Disorders*, IRMMH/Elsevier, N. Holland, 1976.

8. Using Toys for Developmental Assessment

1. A full description of the workings of this clinic, which involves parents as full members of the clinic team, will be found in Elizabeth Newson's 'Parents as a resource in diagnosis and Assessment', in T. Oppé and P. Woodford (eds). *The Early Management of Handicapping Disorders*, IRMMH/Elsevier, N. Holland, 1976.

2. Wood, H., 'The Development of Children from Birth to Six Years of Age: a Collection of Eighteen Developmental Tests', mimeo, obtainable CDRU, University of Nottingham, £1.50.

3. Woodward, M., 'The Assessment of Cognitive Processes: Piaget's Approach', in Mittler, P. (ed.), *Psychological Assessment of Mental and Physical Handicaps*, Methuen, 1970.

4. Lunzer, E. A., 'Studies in the Development of Play Behaviour in Young Children Between the Ages of Two and Six', unpublished doctoral thesis, University of Birmingham, 1955. Also, see his 'Intellectual Development in the Play of Young Children', *Educational Review*, II, 205–17, 1959.

5. The repertoires are obtainable with full notes, on receipt of a large stamped addressed envelope, from the Child Development Research Unit, University of Nottingham.

9. Using Toys and Play Remedially

1. A pamphlet which describes these toys, 'Hear and Say: Toys for Children with Hearing, Speech and Language Difficulties', Susan Knowles and Kay Mogford, is published by the Toy Libraries Association (see note 2).

2. Joan Head and Kay Mogford started the first professionally-run toy library in England at the University of Nottingham Child Development Research Unit in 1970, as part of a research project on play resources for handicapped children and their families, supported by the Nuffield Foundation and by Action Research for the Crippled Child. Joan Head's study of the toy library movement is available from this Research Unit on

request. Further information, and advice on setting up a toy library, can be obtained from the Toy Libraries Association in the UK, Seabrook House, Wyllyotts Manor, Darkes Lane, Potters Bar, Herts.

3. Two books which give practical guidance on play for severely handicapped children are Nancie Finnie's *Handling the Young Cerebral Palsied Child at Home.* 2nd edn, Heinemann, 1974; and Peggy Freeman's *Understanding the Deaf/Blind Child*, Heinemann, 1970, a rich source of ideas for working with *any* handicapped child.

10. Toys and Play for the Sick Child

1. Harvey, S. and Hales-Tooke, A., *Play in Hospital*, Faber, 1971.
   Noble, E., *Play and the Sick Child*, Faber, 1967.
   Plank, E., *Working with Children in Hospital*, Western Reserve University, 1962, and Tavistock, 1964.
2. Newson, J. and E., *Four Years Old in an Urban Community*, Allen and Unwin, 1968, and Penguin Books, 1970; *Seven Years Old in the Home Environment*, Allen and Unwin, 1976, and Penguin Books, 1978.
3. *Body Tricks*, Gribble and McPhee, Penguin Books, 1976.
4. Useful texts for these activities are:
   Haddon, K., *String Games for Beginners*, John Adams, Wargrave, Berks., 1978; Fry, E. C., *The Shell Book of Knots and Ropework*, David and Charles, Newton Abbot, 1977; Matterson, E., *This Little Puffin ...; Finger Plays and Nursery Games*, Penguin Books, 1969; Bursill, H., *Handshadows*, reprint of 1859 original, Dover, New York, 1967.
5. We are indebted to the *Nursing Times* for permission to re-publish this extract.

11. Toys Through Time and Space

1. Huizinga, J., *Homo Ludens*, Routledge and Kegan Paul, 1949.
2. Daiken, L., *Children's Toys Throughout the Ages*, Spring Books, 1963.
3. A. A. Milne's new light on King John's private life and motivation,

> 'And oh! Father Christmas, if you love me at all,
> Bring me a big, red indiarubber ball!'

turns out, alas, to be an anachronism. From Milne's *Now We are Six*, Methuen, 1927.
4. White, G., *Antique Toys and Their Background*, Batsford, 1971.

5. A good photograph of these toys will be found in Robert Culff's *The World of Toys*, Hamlyn, London, 1969. An excellent illustrated account of marbles generally is *The Great American Marble Book*, by Fred Feretti (Workman Publ. Co., New York, 1973). Buttons have also been used similarly to marbles, stored on a string, with a parallel system of currency values.

6. A game called Sgreaga is described as having been played with five stones on the island of Arran; the rules, originally given in Gaelic, are quoted by Leslie Daiken in his *Children's Games Throughout the Year* (Batsford, 1949), and sound very like the game of alleygobs which we played as children in the nineteen forties. A parallel to the range of names given to the same game in different regions is the series of 'release words' which momentarily grant immunity from being caught. The Opies have documented the following truce terms for the UK: *Snakes, keppies, barley, keys, skinch, croggie, kings, blobs, trucie, screase, nicks, fainites, fains, cruce, cree, scruce, exes, peril, bars, barsy, scribs, crosses, scrames* and *screens,* and others, as well as the private school *pax;* these to be used in games of tig, tugger, tib, touchy, catchy, touch, he, it, tip, kip, catchers, hits and dobby. Maps of the incidence of these terms, region by region, are given in their books *The Lore and Language of Schoolchildren* (Oxford University Press, 1959) and *Children's Games in Street and Playground* (Oxford University Press, 1969).

7. Clear instructions for making zoetropes, kaleidoscopes, balancing toys, crystal gardens and many other delights will be found in Carson Ritchie's *Making Scientific Toys* (Lutterworth Press, 1978), which draws on both Victorian ingenuity and modern technology.

8. Ernest Shepard, *Drawn from Memory*, Methuen, 1957, and Penguin Books, 1975.

List of Suppliers

Readers who are interested in specific toys mentioned in this book can make inquiries at the address nearest to them. Remember, though, that often an equally good version of the toy will be produced by another, perhaps little-known, manufacturer: this list is merely a short guide to a few outstanding producers of toys.

Manufacturer	U.K.	U.S.A.	Canada	Australasia	Reference pages:
Beck	All inquiries: Beck Toys, Brook House, St James St, Narberth, Dyfed.				62
Brio Scanditoy	Brio U.K. Ltd, Belton Rd West, Loughborough, Leics.	Brio Scanditoy Corp, 6531 North Sidney Place, Milwaukee, Wisconsin 53209.	Brian, Hulst and Woton Ltd, 127 Portland St, Toronto, Ont. M5V 2N4.	Modern Teaching Aids Pty, P.O. Box 608, Brookvale, N.S.W. 2100	54, 133

Manufacturer	U.K.	U.S.A.	Canada	Australasia	Reference pages:
Crowdys Wood Products	All inquiries: Crowdys Wood Products Ltd, The Old Bakery, Clanfield, Oxford.				57, 60
Chad Valley	Chad Valley Co. Ltd, 234 Bradford St, Birmingham B12 OPP.	not available	not available	John Sands (Pty) Ltd, P.O. Box 164, Herbert & Frederick St, Artarmon, N.S.W. 2064.	68
E.S.A.	All inquiries: E.S.A. Creative Learning Ltd, Pinnacles, Harlow, Essex.				74, 168
Escor Toys	Escor Toys Ltd, Grovely Rd, Christchurch, Dorset.	Childcraft Education Corp., 20 Kilmer Rd, Edison, N.J. 08817 Ruth Glasser Inc., 1107 Broadway, New York, NY 10010.	Louise Kool & Sons Ltd, 13 Sunrise Ave, Toronto, Ont. M4A 1B6.	Hop-Scotch, Melbourne and Sidney.	51-2, 60-2, 65, 68, 120, 165, 168, 174, 197-8, 201-2

	UK	USA	Other	Pages
Fisher Price	Fisher Price Toys Ltd, Scottish Life House, 29 St Katherine St, Northampton.	Fisher Price Toys, East Aurora, Erie County, NY 14052.	Fisher Price Toys, 98 Rutherford Rd, South Brampton, Ont. L6W 3J5.	Consolidated Merchandise, 124 Exhibition St, Melbourne.	50, 52, 60, 62, 120, 131, 201
Fischer-technik	Artur Fischer (U.K.) Ltd, 25 Newtown Rd, Marlow, Bucks.				135–7, 203
Galt Toys	Galt Toys, Brookfield Road, Cheadle, Cheshire. (head office)	Galt Toys, Northbrook Court, Northbrook, Chicago, Ill. (and many other outlets – inquire)	Louise Kool & Sons Ltd, 130 Sunrise Ave, Toronto, M4A 1B6. (and many others – inquire)	A. R. Whitelaw & Co. Pty Ltd, 51a Russell St, Melbourne 3000. (and many others – inquire)	53, 66, 126, 168, 174, 204, 210
Haddon	All inquiries: Haddon Rockers Ltd, Station Rd Industrial Estate, Wallingford, Oxfordshire.				252
Huntercraft	All inquiries: Huntercraft, Stalbridge, Dorset.				79

Manufacturer	U.K.	U.S.A.	Canada	Australasia	Reference pages:
Kiddicraft	Hestair Kiddicraft Ltd, Godstone Rd, Kenley, Surrey.	F. A. O. Schwartz, 745 Fifth Avenue, New York, N.Y. 10022.	Sopamco Inc., 449 Rue St Vincent, Granby, Quebec J2G 4A3.	Kenbrite Corp. of Australia Pty Ltd, 1–3 Power St, South Melbourne, Victoria 3205.	47, 63
Kouvalias	Agents: Dean's Childsplay Toys, Pontypool, Gwent. (for Kouvalias, 3 Klisthenous St, Athens, Greece.)	Reeves, 1107 Broadway, New York, N.Y. 10010.	Irwin, 43 Havana Ave, Toronto.	Atgemis, 247 King St, Newtown 2042.	62–3
Lego	British Lego Ltd, Wrexham, N. Wales.	Lego Systems Inc., 555 Taylor Rd, Enfield, Connecticut 06082.	Samsonite of Canada Ltd, 753 Ontario Street, Stratford, Ont.	British Lego Ltd, P.O. Box 281, North Ryde 2113, N.S.W.	65, 132, 135–7, 203
George Luck	All inquiries: George Luck, 12 Gastons Lane, Martock, Somerset.				204

Matchbox	Lesney Products Co. Ltd, Lee Conservancy Road, London E9 5PA.				62–3, 84, 120, 131, 132, 133
Meccano	Meccano Ltd, Binns Road, Liverpool L13 1DA.	AVA International Inc., P.O. Box 7611, Waco, Texas 76710.	Parker Brothers, P.O. Box 600, Concord, Ont.	Liberty Trading Pty Ltd, 38 Marshall St, Surry Hills, N.S.W. 2010.	135–7, 203
Merrythought	All inquiries: Merrythought Ltd, Dale End, Ironbridge, Telford, Shropshire.		A. C. Lambe, 117 Donegan Ave, Pointe Claire, Quebec.		118, 225
Mothercare	Mothercare, Cherry Tree Rd, Watford, Herts.	Mothercare Stores, 150 Lackawanna Ave, Parsipanny, New Jersey 07054.	As U.K.	As U.K.	47, 52, 59, 60, 63, 174, 178f.
Orchard Toys	Orchard Toys Ltd, Main Street, Keyworth, Notts.	As U.K.	As U.K.	A. R. Whitelaw & Co. Pty, 51A Russell St, Melbourne, Victoria 3000.	80

Manufacturer	U.K.	U.S.A.	Canada	Australasia	Reference Pages
Pegasus	All inquiries: Pegasus Toys Ltd, Springfield House, Second Ave, Crewe, Cheshire.				250, 252
Rovex (Pedigree)	Pedigree Dolls and Toys Ltd, Market Way, Canterbury.	Louis Marx & Co. Inc., 633 Hope St, Stamford, Conn. 06904.	Marx Toys, 98 Rutherford Rd, Brampton, Ont.	Lidrana Pty Ltd, 70 Clarendon St, Melbourne 3205.	47, 52, 94, 138–9, 174, 178f.
Vera Small	All inquiries: Vera Small, 6 Shepherd's Bush Road, London w6				95
Tonka	Tonka Ltd, Fishponds Rd, Wokingham, Berks.	Tonka Toys, Division Head-quarters, P.O. Box 1188, Spring Park, Minnesota 55386.	Tonka Corp. Canada Ltd, 7630 Airport Road, Mississauga, Ont.	Tonka Corp. Pty Ltd, P.O. Box 157, West Ryde, N.S.W. 2114.	79
Trendon (Sasha)	Trendon Ltd, Stockport, Cheshire.	International Playthings Inc., 151 Forest St, Montclair, New Jersey 07042.	Pierre Belvedere Inc., 105 East St Paul East, Montreal.	Kangaroo Trading Pty Ltd, Box 7005, GPO Sydney 2001.	90, 93, 94

Tridias (Honeychurch houses)	All inquiries: Tridias, 8 Saville Row, Bath BA1 2QP.			129, 131
Tupperware	Tupperware Co., Tupperware House, 43 Upper Grosvenor St, London W1V OBE.	Tupperware Home Parties, P.O. Box 2353, Orlando, Florida 32802o.	Tupperware Canada, Suite 201, 1111 Finch Ave West, Downsview, Ontario M3J 2E5.	Tupperware Australia, Trak Centre, 445 Toorak Rd, Toorak, Victoria 3142.	66
Willis (and Nicol)	Willis Toys Ltd, Elsenham, Bishop's Stortford, Herts.	Ruth Glasser, Inc., 1107 Broadway, Suite 1410, New York, N.Y. 10010.	Steppe Enterprises Ltd, 243 Lilac St, Winnipeg, Manitoba.	Judios Pty Ltd, Box M15, Sydney Mail Exchange, N.S.W. 2012.	60, 204
Woodpecker	All inquiries: Woodpecker Toys Ltd, Burvill St, Lynton, North Devon.			57, 62, 126, 250

Further Reading

References given in the chapter notes are not all re-listed here, but are recommended.

Books on Play

ALLEN OF HURTWOOD, LADY, *Planning for Play*, Thames & Hudson, 1968

BENGTSSON, A., *Adventure Playgrounds*, Crosby Lockwood, 1972

BLURTON JONES, N., *Ethological Studies of Child Behaviour*, Cambridge University Press, 1972

BOWYER, RUTH, *The Lowenfeld World Technique*, Pergamon, 1970

BRUNER, J., JOLLY, A. and SYLVA, K. (eds), *Play: Its Role in Development and Evolution*, Penguin, 1976

CARR, JANET, *I'm Handicapped – Teach Me*, Penguin, 1979

CUNNINGHAM, C., *Handling Your Handicapped Baby*, Souvenir Press, 1978

DICKINSON, S. (ed.), *Mother's Help*, Collins, 1972

FRAIBERG, SELMA, *The Magic Years*, Methuen, 1968

GARVEY, CATHERINE, *Play*, Fontana/Open Books, 1977

HERRON, R., and SUTTON SMITH, B., *Child's Play*, Wiley, New York, 1971

HOSTLER, PHYLLIS, *The Child's World*, Penguin, 1959

JEFFREE, D., MCCONKEY, R., and HEWSON, S., *Let Me Play*, Souvenir Press, 1976

LAMBERT, J. and PEARSON, J., *Adventure Playgrounds*, Penguin, 1974

LEAR, ROMA, *Play Helps: Toys and Activities for Handicapped Children*, Heinemann, 1977

LINDSAY, ZAIDEE, *Art and the Handicapped Child*, Studio Vista, 1972

MARZOLLO, JEAN, and LLOYD, JANICE, *Learning through Play*, Penguin, 1977

MATTERSON, E. M., *Play with a Purpose for Under-Sevens*, Penguin, 1965

MATTHEWS, G. and J., 'Apparatus, Toys and Games' (booklet), from *Early Mathematical Experiences* (Schools Council Project), Addison-Wesley, 1978

MILLAR, SUSANNA, *Psychology of Play*, Penguin, 1968

OPIE, I. and P., *Children's Games in Street and Playground*, Oxford University Press, 1969

PIAGET, J., *Play, Dreams and Imitation in Childhood*, Heinemann, 1951; new edition, Routledge, 1972

PINES, MAYA, *Revolution in Learning: the Years from Birth to Five*, Allen Lane, 1969

SHERIDAN, MARY, *Spontaneous Play in Early Childhood*, National Foundation for Educational Research, 1977

SINGER, J. L., *Child's World of Make-Believe: Experimental Studies of Imaginative Play*, Academic Press, New York and London, 1973

STEVENS, M., *Educational and Social Needs of Children with Severe Handicap*, Edward Arnold, 1976

TIZARD, B. and HARVEY, D. (eds), *The Biology of Play*, Heinemann, 1976

WARD, COLIN, *The Child in the City*, Architectural Press, 1978

WINN, M. and PORCHER, M. A., *The Playgroup Book*, Fontana, 1971

WINNICOTT, D. W., *Playing and Reality*, Penguin, 1974

Books on Toys

CADBURY, BETTY, *Playthings Past*, David and Charles, 1976

CULF, ROBERT, *The World of Toys*, Hamlyn, 1969

DAIKEN, LESLIE, *World of Toys*, Lambarde Press, 1963

DAIKEN, LESLIE, *Children's Toys throughout the Ages*, Spring Books, 1963

HASKELL, A., and LEWIS, M., *Infantilia: the Archeology of the Nursery*, Dennis Dobson, 1971

HILLIER, MARY, *Automata and Mechanical Toys*, Jupiter Books, 1976

MACKAY, JAMES, *Nursery Antiques*, Ward Lock, 1976

PRESSLAND, DAVID, *The Art of the Tin Toy*, New Cavendish Books, London, and Crown, New York, 1976

WHITE, GWEN, *Marks and Labels*, Batsford, 1975

Books on Dolls and Dolls' Houses

BACHMANN, M., and HANSMANN, C., *Dolls the Wide World Over*, Harrap, 1973

BAKER, ROGER, *Dolls and Dolls' Houses*, Orbis Books, 1973

VON BOEHN, M., *Dolls*, first published 1929; Dover Books, New York, 1972

COLEMAN, DOROTHY, ELIZABETH and EVELYN, *The Collector's Encyclopaedia of Dolls*, Hale, 1968

DESMONDE, KAY, *Dolls*, Octopus Books, 1974

FLICK, PAULINE and JACKSON, VALERIE, *Dolls' Houses: Furniture and Decoration*, Blond & Briggs, 1974

FOX, CARL, *The Doll*, H. N. Abrams, New York, 1973

JOHNSON, AUDREY, *How to Make Dolls' Houses*, Bell, 1957

JOHNSON, AUDREY, *How to Repair and Dress Old Dolls*, Bell, 1967

JOHNSON, AUDREY, *Dressing Dolls*, Bell, 1969

JOHNSON, AUDREY, *Furnishing Dolls' Houses*, Bell, 1972

KING, C. E., *Dolls and Dolls' Houses*, Hamlyn, 1977

WHITE, GWEN, *European and American Dolls*, Batsford, 1966

WITZIG, H., and KUHN, G. E., *Making Dolls*, Sterling, New York, 1969

WORRELL, E. A., *The Dollhouse Book*, Van Nostrand Reinhold, New York, 1964

Index